PERGAMON INTERNA
of Science, Technology, Engin
The 1000-volume original paperba
industrial training and the
Publisher: Robert

Casework in Context
A BASIS FOR PRACTICE

THE PERGAMON TEXTBOOK.
INSPECTION COPY SERVICE

An inspection copy of any book published in the Pergamon International Library will gladly be sent to academic staff without obligation for their consideration for course adoption or recommendation. Copies may be retained for a period of 60 days from receipt and returned if not suitable. When a particular title is adopted or recommended for adoption for class use and the recommendation results in a sale of 12 or more copies, the inspection copy may be retained with our compliments. The Publishers will be pleased to receive suggestions for revised editions and new titles to be published in this important International Library.

SOCIAL WORK SERIES

Editor: JEAN P NURSTEN

Other Titles in the Series

Casework in Context

A BASIS FOR PRACTICE

BY

D. E. F. TILBURY

Principal Lecturer in Social Work,
Sunderland Polytechnic

PERGAMON PRESS

Oxford · New York · Toronto · Sydney
Paris · Frankfurt

U.K.	Pergamon Press Ltd., Headington Hill Hall, Oxford OX3 0BW, England
U.S.A.	Pergamon Press Inc., Maxwell House, Fairview Park, Elmsford, New York 10523, U.S.A.
CANADA	Pergamon of Canada Ltd., 75, The East Mall, Toronto, Ontario, Canada
AUSTRALIA	Pergamon Press (Aust.) Pty. Ltd., 19a Boundary Street, Rushcutters Bay, N.S.W. 2011, Australia
FRANCE	Pergamon Press SARL, 24 rue des Ecoles, 75240 Paris, Cedex 05, France
WEST GERMANY	Pergamon Press GmbH, 6242 Kronberg-Taunus, Pferdstrasse 1, Frankfurt-am-Main, West Germany

First edition 1977

Library of Congress Cataloging in Publication Data

Tilbury, D   E   F
Casework in context.

(Social work series)
1. Social case work. I. Title.
HV43.T47   1977   361.3   76-57674
ISBN 0-08-019744-2 (Hardcover)
ISBN 0-08-019743-4 (Flexicover)

Printed in Great Britain by A. Wheaton & Co., Exeter

Contents

Introduction

To write a book on social casework (by which I mean a text which focuses on work with individuals and families) at this point in time, may seem distinctly old-fashioned, given the modern trend to break away from methodological models and embrace all social work practice in new conceptualisations. New concepts, however, still have to be operationalised and turned into good practice and my experience both as a fieldworker and a teacher of social work convinces me that insofar as work with individuals and families is concerned, nothing in the 'new' invalidates the 'old'. I feel I have no need to justify the existence of social casework. This is not to say that attacks on casework have not been justified as well. If for nothing else, I am glad such attacks have destroyed the claim casework made at one stage—quite speciously—to be the panacea for all social ills. We have come to recognise its limitations; but within these limits it remains the most effective way of working. Detractors of casework, in their turn, have not been guiltless of specious claims of their own; but hopefully we are now reaching the point when we can recognise the validity of a variety of theories and methods of practice in appropriate situations.

What has changed dramatically in the last few years is the context in which casework is practised and perhaps a new book on social casework is justified now to put practice into this new context. Not only have new concepts about social work emerged, but a re-emergent radicalism has forced us to question the social processes and the social purposes of social work. In Britain, especially, sweeping organisational changes have obliged us to look again at what we mean by generic practice and re-examine relations between practice and the organisations within which it is set. In this book I have tried to relate these changes in social work thinking, organisation and practice to what is now needed in my view for students' education in social work.

This text, then, examines the societal, ethical, organisational and developmental context of practice; and discusses what is common ground to all practice with individuals and families in direct and indirect ways of working. It acknowledges the limitations of this way of working, but insists on the validity of this work within those limitations, since other ways of working will not meet all needs adequately either. The book does not attempt to deal with particular areas of specialisation either by setting or client group, or particularised functions such as adoption or fostering; though the illustrations used are drawn from a range of areas of practice. Other texts about such specialised work need to be used in addition and some suggestions about further reading are made at the end of Chapter III.

I said earlier 'education in social work' deliberately, since although this is a text on casework, I have tried to highlight all through those elements of principle, practice and setting which are germane to all methods of practice. Any subsequent (or antecedent) teaching about other separate methods of practice, or a unitary approach (using this text to particularise subsequently), should therefore mesh in without undue difficulty. I have built teaching on group, community and residential work (to students whose main area of practice was casework) on the foundation of this casework course.

The material for this book is the product of several years teaching on two year, full time, non-graduate social work courses leading to the Certificate of Qualification in Social Work and in some ways reflects my dis-satisfaction with existing casework texts. I have found that while many were excellent in examining practice face-to-face with clients (material I have tried to retain), too little related to those areas of practice outside the interview situation. My field experience convinced me that what I did away from direct contact with clients could be as material to the success or otherwise of what I was trying to achieve as that which transpired in the direct contact itself. I make no excuse, therefore, for the substantial part of this book which examines some of such areas of practice.

I originally distributed much of the material which appears in this text to students in the form of handouts before our meetings. Inevitably, since the material largely substituted for lectures, it was mainly concerned with information and opinion, and tended to be theoretical. In revising it for publication I have tried to clothe dry theory with rather more warmth and humanity by using brief case illustrations. But I would still suggest this is a text which needs to be discussed, not just read, for students to see just how the theory applies and assists practice in live, human situations. Typically, this realisation came in the interchanges between teacher and student, and student and student in discussions, seminars and tutorials as we endeavoured to relate ideas to the actual problems, people and settings we experienced in the field. It is for this reason that at the end of each chapter I have suggested areas for discussion based on my own experience of students' reception of my material—something other texts have not attempted.

With the practicalities of the students' situation in mind, I have also deliberately kept references to a minimum and discussed only a limited number of sources for further reading.

This book owes a tremendous amount to my clients (who forgave me much), my colleagues' patience and experience (especially the late Joan Hatfield, my mentor at Leeds Polytechnic, who encouraged me to think of publication), and not least to my students who have taught me so much over the years. Acknowledgment, too, must go to all those other writers on social work: so much of their work has become part of me that I have since forgotten that it really belongs to someone else. If I have used material without acknowledging its source I hope the originators will bring this to my notice so that I may properly attribute it to them in any future editions. Needless to say, any faults in this book are my own: others taught me, but I have not always learned.

Finally, I must express my gratitude to my wife, who has not only contributed through her experience to the material in this book and endured me during its preparation; but she has also read, criticised and helped me to revise the text.

PART I
The Context of Casework

CHAPTER I

Social Work and Society

Social work is concerned with psycho-social mal-functioning: with problems in the area of interaction between the individual (whether an individual person, family, group or community) and their environment—physical (including their own bodies), material (resources of all kinds) and social (whether at family, group or community level). This focus on the interactional sphere distinguishes social work from analysis on the one hand, where the focus is on the individual as such; and from a host of other individuals, organisations and institutions directly and indirectly concerned with aspects of the environment on the other—doctors, public health inspectors, trade unions, conservationists, educators, housing departments, social security, planning, political parties, etc. etc. Interaction is the nub of our professional expertise.

Psycho-social problems arise, very broadly, from the impact of 'sick' people on their environment; or the impact of a 'sick' environment on people—the 'sickness' (again, very broadly) being psychological (emotional or developmental), physical, material or social—or a combination of these elements. Social work, therefore, works with the 'well' (i.e. where there is an absence of 'sickness') as much as the 'sick'. Diagrammatically, the situation looks like this:

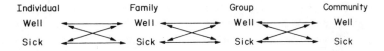

The interactional impact route can travel through any combination of the above, in either direction; for example, a well individual may belong to a well family, set in a well group, but that group is set

in a sick society. A well society may have an interactional impact
on a sick group, but that group contain well families and well individuals.

In reality, it is not quite as simple as this, of course, since, as
I have already suggested, the 'sickness' may have differing bases and
it is very unlikely that any one element is either all sick or all well.
An otherwise well individual may be physically sick in that say, he
suffers from crippling arthritis. His family may be well, but since
the physically sick person is the breadwinner, the family may become
materially sick through loss of income. The group may be otherwise
well, but psychologically sick in that for reasons of its internal functioning it cannot tolerate a physically handicapped member/family
and therefore it excludes them, adding a degree of social 'sickness'
via isolation to that individual/family. The group is set in a society,
however, that would like to assist the physically handicapped and
their families, but physically has no cure for arthritis, may be materially 'sick' and have little in the way of resources to help; or may
be socially 'sick' in the sense that it has not yet found the administrative means to channel help to the physically handicapped, nor the
educational means to influence group attitudes to break down the
social isolation 'sickness' of certain physically handicapped indivi-
duals/families.

Social work has now developed a range of methods of intervention
to try to deal with this range of derivations of psycho-social problems: with individuals and families (casework) with families and
groups (groupwork) and at the community level (community work);
and for those who, whether for psychological, physical, material or
social reasons, are unable to function in society as it is, residential
care as an environment specially created for them has been developed. This is not to suggest, of course, that social work attempts
this task of psycho-social problems solving on its own: given the
range of reasons for mal-functioning obviously it works in conjunction with a whole range of individuals, groups, disciplines, organisations and institutions also concerned; but contributing its special
expertise. Nor does the interventive repertoire I have mentioned com-
prise the totality of social work activity, since some would consider
these primary functions, but requiring support from a range of

secondary activities such as social work research, social work education, and social planning.

Again, however, there are complications, in that the 'sickness' and 'wellness' that social work tries to deal with are often personally and socially defined, not absolute concepts. The definitions variously given may or may not coincide. Someone suffering from say, appendicitis would very usually see himself as physically 'sick'—though not always: he may attribute his pains to possession by devils or sins he has committed. The 'sick' definition would also usually be accepted by his family, his group and the community and he would be treated accordingly. But his complaint may be of 'low back pain'. He would see himself as physically sick, but his family, other groups and the community could define him as a malingerer—i.e. shift his sickness into the psychological or social category which could elicit very different responses from them and very different treatment—and not at all in line with the expectations of someone defining themselves as physically sick. An individual suffering from say, a paranoid delusional system might however, consider himself well and those who disagreed with him or told him he was sick could then be defined as sick themselves by him. A 'Black September' member would probably consider himself a well individual belonging to a well group; perhaps considering those who disagreed with him (whether family, groups or communities) as sick. Others might consider him and his group sick (or him well but his group sick). Even if they shared the Black September view that society was sick, they might still regard the aims and/or methods of the Black September group as sick.

In other words we are here in the middle of the whole question of values. Values are by no means constant: even a brief historical glance will demonstrate how they have shifted over time, especially in societies undergoing rapid technological and social change. Nor have social work values remained constant: over the years they have shifted from roots in Christian morality, through social reform, and a period of clinical neutrality to a new re-appraisal which struggles to combine a recovered concern for social reform with a professionalism which tries to retain clinical skills even if clinical neutrality is now seen as an untenable position.

Simplistically, the basic tenets of social work may be stated as:

(1) The intrinsic worth of the individual, irrespective of class, creed, colour, age, sex, intelligence, physical or moral state. Perhaps as a derivative of this tenet comes the second:

(2) The democratic rights of the individual; which might be re-stated as his legitimated needs. Unless accorded these rights, the individual cannot fulfil the concomitant of rights—obligations; which in turn has implications for the rights of others.

Rights are sometimes grouped into basic rights (to food, shelter, clothing, etc.) which remain inviolate; and secondary or conditional rights which may be withdrawn in varying degrees—usually depending on individual capacity and behaviour. We do not expect someone with a reduced capacity (such as a child) to fulfil the total range of adult obligations, but the withdrawal of obligations, meant as a protection, often involves the withdrawal of certain rights (for example, a small child's right to decide where he shall live); though his dependent position may mean devising other rights to protect him from abuse (for example, if he is battered by his parents to get him into a 'place of safety'). 'Criminal' behaviour (so defined after a 'due process' which protects against the arbitrary designation of behaviour as criminal) may also involve the loss of the right to decide where to live, if the punishment is imprisonment; while the 'insane' (again when determined as such by due process) may also lose this right by compulsory admission to a psychiatric hospital for treatment.

Given that basic rights exist, the categorisation of conditional rights varies, but they may be grouped as:

(1) Respect for the individual's opinions. In democratic societies this respect is accorded in the 'one man, one vote' ideal with no one opinion being accorded more weight in the ballot box than another. I realise that the ideal is subject to a range of distortions for a variety of reasons; and I also realise that voting is typically found in political spheres at election times. Elections are not confined to politics; but effective means of reflecting opinion have yet to be devised in many institutions even in 'democratic' countries. Industry, housing, planning, education, etc. tend to have only limited ways

of engaging opinion as yet; and such limitations may account for a good deal of the current unrest even in politically democratic countries.

Respect for opinion implies, however:

(i) Access to information on which to base an opinion—which has implications for education, the media and a host of other institutions and organisations from Local Authority planning departments to industrial wage negotiations.
(ii) The right to express an opinion and to try to influence others' opinions—which has implications for the right to free speech, free assembly, access to the media—and even picketing.
(iii) A sufficient degree of social tolerance—by the majority of minorities and vice versa; together with institutionally accepted ways of allowing minority opinion to become the majority.

(2) The opportunity to fulfil potential. Basically this means securing the development opportunities for the individual all through life—including later life and old age. Development is not just a matter of childhood and youth, though obviously what happens in early life is a crucial matter for the whole of it. Access to role is vital (see below) but some pre-determined roles can constrict development—for example, at 65 a man is consigned to the 'old age' role and his potential development in many ways—such as employment—choked off. The woman's role in society generally may inhibit potentiality development for many women—and the same may be said of men, too. Development of potential must rest on a base of secure family life, employment, health services, housing, income, recreation (whether sporting, artistic, interest-based, or just plain social), an ongoing access to educational opportunity; and a society which is tolerant of individualism and sees that its institutional arrangements allow of it.

(3) The opportunity for role fulfilment. Role fulfilment again rests on basic provisions such as health, housing, income, education, recreation and family life (or an adequate substitute). It is not just a matter though, of access to the typical roles of parent, employee, neighbour, but the quality of life within such roles. Access to a role that is oppressive to fulfil is hardly fulfilment. It is also a matter

of access to a range of roles. A man with the potential for a senior position is hardly likely to feel fulfilled by a job on a production line—even if both are described as employment roles. Even if his potential limits him to a 'production line' job, the choice of production line may be of great significance for his fulfilment. Roles, too, have varying degrees of influence, some of which are, in many people's view, unfairly skewed at present. It is usually more influential to be a managing director than a mechanic; but both are dependent on the same employer, with the mechanic a good deal more vulnerable perhaps. Access to certain roles such as councillor or magistrate which are typically influential but not tied to the economic sphere, are virtually disbarred to many people who might welcome the opportunity of filling them and be very good in them, for economic reasons. They cannot get time off work, or if they can, they cannot afford the costs involved. A sufficient spread of role fulfilment (and I acknowledge that access to some roles will remain numerically limited) would pre-suppose an open and egalitarian society—and one that made provision to see that it was.

It is out of such basic tenets that some of the principles of social work have come. From the worth of the individual have come individualisation, acceptance and confidentiality; and from democratic rights, client self-determination, non-judgmentalism and purposive expression of feelings.

Yet these tenets present difficulties. Worth is a noble concept, but how do we translate it in say, economic terms? How do we measure the worth of the individual in terms of the wages we pay him, or the pension? How, in the health sphere (given that resources are inevitably limited), do we decide between a kidney machine for the one or a cervical smear screening programme for the many? Or determine between developing health services as compared with education?

Democratic rights cannot be absolute either. It may be one thing to hold an opinion; another to express it (for example, slander, incitement); yet another to act upon it. The 'insane' believing he was Napoleon, the 'criminal' believing he had a right to other people's property; the revolutionary believing the only way to change society is to smash it first; the jealous believing they had a right to keep their spouse housebound; the 'dropout' believing the world owed him a living; the parent, believing that the only way to bring up children is to beat them into obedience—if these people acted on their opinions, most people would not tolerate it and would seek to remedy matters in various ways. We are in a situation, in effect, of one person's right to act on their opinion impinging detrimentally on another's rights; and being obliged to make a decision as to whose rights should supervene. The way decisions are arrived at, who makes them, and with what consequences are of crucial importance. We have set up a wide range of institutions, courts, administrative tribunals, arbitrators, and professionals (including social workers) which or whom we trust (via procedures or training) to come to informed, impartial (i.e. un-arbitrary) decisions with (as far as possible) predictable and/or trusted consequences. In other words to exercise judgment—which is a function of professionals as well as courts or quasi-courts. As a safeguard we build in appeal systems—though there is rarely an appeal from a professional opinion except a second opinion.

There are many social judgment systems, of course, which do not have any safeguards: gossip, ostracism, many forms of denigration (of which stigma is only one) are applied. They may be ill-formed and arbitrary; and there may be little chance of appeal. They can be very damaging. When clients are involved, perhaps here is a task for the social worker concerned for social justice, since justice is not just a matter of the formal machinery of justice.

Again, not all potentials would be generally seen as valid to fulfil. Skills as a pickpocket are not likely to be encouraged, since once more we are in a situation of clash of rights.

Role fulfilment has similar difficulties. While a sex role involving lesbianism may be tolerated, it is not likely to be a subject for evening classes to learn how to do it. Again, in economic terms, it may be very hard to reconcile individual role fulfilment with over all demands for a workforce containing certain numbers with certain skills.

In other words, virtually no values are absolute, but relative, and set in a social context. The very nature of social work, with its psycho-social focus, involves an area of endemic tension, and decision making about priorities. The tensions are made even more acute because social work values are not necessarily shared by other sections of society, or they may be accorded different priorities or different interpretations in specific situations. It would be extremely hard for the social worker to act independently of social values even if he wanted to. His client will have his own ideas, anyway; both he and the social worker will be acting in a social milieu which they cannot ignore; but more significantly, the social worker is not independent. In fact he is caught up in what has now become a social institution in itself. Social work is a social institution, which produces all sorts of complexities.

As Geoffrey Pearson suggests, 'However we choose to characterise the welfare professions...the growth of their power is a significant *societal* shift'[1] (Author's italics). By an institution I mean a sociologically identifiable, socially acceptable way of arranging significant social activities involving values, attitudes and norms of behaviour, together with elements of organisation, and persisting over time. This definition is my own, but arrived at as a conglomerate of the many and varied definitions of an institution which appear in the standard sociological texts. By this definition, I feel that social work qualifies as an institution. As I have indicated, it is certainly concerned with values, attitudes and norms; it has elements of organisation (British Association of Social Workers, the Central Council for Education and Training in Social Work, etc.) and though its emergence as an institution is comparatively recent, it certainly looks like persisting over time. That social work is acceptable is evidenced by the multitude of reports that call for more of us and the way social workers are being asked to extend their sphere of operation. The social activity of social work is a method of dealing with a certain range of social problems, while its significance—given society's on-going, if fluctuating, pre-occupation with issues such as deviance—is undeniable, even if as an institution, social work remains rather small.

Even now, the great bulk of psycho-social needs are, of course, met with a sufficient degree of satisfaction by the ordinary social institutions—especially the family, which is still the cornerstone of the social fabric. If it were not so, social work would be overwhelmed and it is salutary for social workers to acknowledge, now and again, that for most people, most of the time, they are dispensable. For the rest we are frequently additional props in situations where the main weight is still taken by others; only for the few does the main weight fall on us. I realise that for the individual social worker it may not feel like this at the end of the day, whether they have a limited number of 'main' weights (as in residential care or fostering) or a larger number of 'propping' operations (as in fieldwork); while the weight of exercising professional judgment rests on all of us.

Social work as an institution has emerged from the processes of industrialisation and its concomitant, urbanisation.[2] This is not to suggest that elements of what we would now recognise as social work did not exist many centuries before, but they were typically carried out as adjuncts to the functions of other institutions, whether the extended family, the church, the aristocracy or voluntary associations. But the industrial revolution produced problems that were different in type, problems on a much larger scale than before, problems which became increasingly identifiable, threatening to society and of political as well as social significance. Clearly, existing institutional forms were not coping and many devices were used to buttress, supplement and substitute for existing forms (such as state health, social security, education and unemployment services, housing subsidies, etc.) or to assist their change towards more effective coping (the Married Woman's Property Act, Workmen's Compensation, Legal Aid, regional development policies, etc.).

Social work as we now understand it, in its institutional form, was late on the scene, for a number of reasons. It had to await the development of other disciplines such as psychology, sociology and administration, in which it is rooted. It had to await the development of its own theory, evolved from practice, and modified in a way which not only identified its particular area of competence but also made it transmissible. It had to wait until society felt that despite all that was provided in the way of services, problems still existed which this new thing, social work, might assist with; and finally it had to wait until society felt that, with the basic problems of sheer existence for the great majority largely resolved, part of the wealth created by industrialisation could be expended on the slightly less pressing problem of the quality of that existence. In other words, social work had to wait until an identifiable expertise and a felt need for it existed.

The first theoretical formulation of social work is often associated with the publication of Mary Richmond's book *Social Diagnosis* in 1917, though again, much of what is now identifiable as social work theory antedates this: the Charity Organisation Society, the many philanthropic and reformist agencies and individuals in the voluntary and statutory services and the early training courses all produced material; but nevertheless, it was Mary Richmond's writing which identified, codified and made transmissible the professional activity we now recognise. While the theory has developed enormously since, the initial focus remains: dealing with psycho-social problems.

Practitioners in social work became useful (and social work an established institution) when society recognised that social services were not reaching all those who needed them and for whom they were intended; when it acknowledged that some people when reached were not engaging with those services; when it became clear that when some became engaged they became 'grit in the system' to everyone's detriment; and that these 'blocks' were both practical and emotive in origin. This process was assisted by the widespread acceptance of psychological, sociological and social administrative findings. These findings had also led to the acknowledgement that people could suffer from emotional problems as such which were just as distressing to them as physical pain and were a matter of humanitarian concern. Some rudimentary services existed to meet them, but now social work could be added, in conjunction with these services or as a new service to meet such needs. This development was reinforced when it became accepted that some of those who suffered in this way subsequently came the way of other services (be these courts, mental hospitals, children's homes or the social security system) at a point where their difficulties were far more intractable. the basic concern for the quality of life and social work's involvement could be humane, preventive and arguably economic.

Some would see the re-organisation of local authority personal social services, following the Seebohm Report[3] as the final accolade of social work's becoming a social institution.

Within its area of expertise and as a social institution I feel that social work has three functions: social caring, social control and social change, and I think these functions would be broadly accepted by the three 'parties' to the social work institution: clients, social workers and society. But these functions are so closely interlinked as to be almost inseparable in practice: tension arising because of the differing views of the parties concerned as to which function social work activity serves in a particular set of circumstances and whether this function and activity is justifiable.

Social workers, for example, are asked by society to 'care' and much of our work is demonstrably this. We help to nurture the sick, the elderly and deprived children. But among those we are asked to care for are families in intolerable housing conditions (intolerable even by society's standards). Social workers would be much more likely to interpret this activity as a form of social control; as damping down dissent; and see true caring as demanding social change—views in which their clients would join them. Yet if social workers, wanting to change matters, refused to undertake this controlling activity so the dissent would boil over and so force profound remedial change, many of them would find it hard to reconcile this with their caring function in terms of the suffering clients would have to endure before what is inevitably a time consuming remedy could be implemented. Even the orthodox caring of the traditional casework can be viewed as a force for social change. If we succeed in giving clients the skills and confidence required to deal with certain problems (which clients and society as well as ourselves would welcome) we cannot control how they subsequently use these skills. It could be to ends which society did not envisage and about which it felt very uncomfortable.

Again, society asks social work to assist in controlling deviance in many forms. Many social workers regard this function as abhorrent—and rightly so when so many controls are experienced as oppressive by our clients. We seek social change of such controls as our way of expressing our social caring function. But no society exists (or can conceivably exist) without norms of behaviour and by implication, therefore, some form of sanctions to reinforce them. So it becomes not a question of controls as such but what sort of controls, directed to what ends, and how they are applied. Even in our own society, with all its need for change, a good many controls are there to protect its members from physical assault, theft, exploitation and many other forms of damage and if social workers are caring people we cannot *not* care for those who suffer as a result of our clients' actions (especially the helpless, such as children) and so occasionally we have to invoke controls because we care, even if our clients would hardly see this as an expression of our caring for them. There are controls, too, which we can invoke to protect our clients and if we did not, our clients would rightly see us as not caring. Few social workers would hesitate either, as an expression of caring, to invoke controls to prevent suicide or murder[4] or even to prevent their clients landing themselves in situations where more coercive controls than their own would be applied—say prison instead of a probation order. Our real agony arises when we realise the situation calls for more control than we possess yet the controls we are contemplating invoking may be quite destructive as we see them.

Our basic tool anyway, is to 'care' people back within norms, which may share the objectives of more coercive measures even though it may be a much more acceptable method of doing so to the client. We will sometimes, too, have clients who ask us to care by assisting their own efforts to control—for example, those who suffer from phobias, obsessions, compulsions, temper outbursts, etc.— using control as a way of bringing about social changes, really, they want to see in themselves. Occasionally, of course, elements in society will carp about our caring forms of control and see them as unfair to the norm-abiding majority and we shall be forced into the position of defending them by demonstrating their effectiveness[5] and/or economy: not a position we like nor a position many of our clients would find acceptable on our part, either.

Society asks social workers to promote social changes, too. Some of the changes we are asked to promote are very thinly disguised measures of control in that we are asked to change 'abnormal' criminals, the mentally disordered and problem families into 'normal' citizens. Understandably social workers and clients react and see change as something society needs rather than clients, in terms of attitudes, tolerance or resource reallocation. But society does care, too, and because it does seek change for individuals, groups and communities, uses social workers in a way which both they and their clients would welcome. It is true that in the past even this sort of caring has had more than a smack of control about it in that we swept people into out-of-sight, out-of-mind institutions; but with the development of community care and the gradual reform of institutional life, our expression of caring is now much more in line with what social workers and clients would wish—towards enabling people to live as 'normal' a life as possible. To live outside the 'normative', even if this means embracing obligations which are difficult to achieve, is often intolerable and humiliating. The physically handicapped would be a case in point. They wish to respond to the usual controls of the work ethic, marriage and family life and we are right to assist this. Imperfect as it may be, the opportunity for satisfaction is probably greater within society than outside it, controls and all. Other examples of the sort of caring change society wants to see in which social workers are willingly involved would be Education Priority Areas, community development projects, and the increasing employment of community workers in Social Services Departments. Of course, social workers will need to go on pressing for change. Our society contains too many injustices for us to be quiescent or complacent. Society may not like some of the changes we press for, whichever reformist style we use. Even those changes which now seem generally acceptable, such as the community care programme, will still be resisted by some—perhaps the majority when it comes to paying for them or according them the priority in resource distribution we would wish to see. Some social workers, from a political base, would go further and argue that without a radical restructuring of society, our priorities will never be achieved. The resistance to this sort of argument is likely to be fierce, especially from established institutions—of which social work itself may now be one.

While many of the changes we press for will be shared by clients it behoves us to be careful that we are not using them in a way they would certainly not agree with in order to further our own ends of aggrandisement and control, and I hope the radicals will keep a watch on us in this respect. Nor should we assume either, that we know what changes clients want before we ask them about it. This may put us in a dilemma, for while we may feel (and society, perhaps, too) that it is intolerable that elderly people should live in 'back-to-backs' with outside lavatories, the old people themselves may see nothing wrong with it since that is what they are used to and feel at home with. Deprivation is relative.[6] Nor must we be trapped into a situation of 'my client right or wrong'. Clients are almost as likely to be wrong-headed and self-centred as social workers or any other group, as most of us will know from aspects of our practice. It may be as much part of our function to bring change in terms of a little more understanding, tolerance and sympathy for others into clients' activities as it is for us to bring similar qualities into society's—controlling as this may seem to the client. Not all that some clients demand of us is either possible or reasonable, especially when they ask that husbands, wives, children, parents or neighbours would unconditionally adapt their behaviour and needs to suit theirs. Again, we know from experience that the changes some clients initially ask for are not always the answers to what is really troubling them: they do at times 'present' problems with varying degrees of consciousness, and despite Barbara Wootton's strictures[7], we know that we would not really be caring for our clients if we always took the changes they asked for at face value. On the other hand, it is equally uncaring to dismiss the changes a client seeks as of no account since 'we know best', whether our 'knowledge' is derived from a doctrinaire Freudianism which sees all symptomatology in terms of the unconscious, or a doctrinaire political philosophy which sees all symptomatology as a product of the defective working of the environment. This would be both uncaring and controlling in the client's view.

Social work is not alone in being in a state of tension since most other institutions are—education, law, politics, the church and even the family. Social work may be in an especially acute position, though, partly because of its acknowledged responsibility to each of the parties concerned with its processes,[8] and partly because of its area of competence: tension between the individual and society is endemic and at best, probably, is a matter of balance. While not suggesting that some existing tensions cannot be eased, to ask for social work to be tension free is to ask for the impossible. Not only impossible, but perhaps also immature—if coping with tension is a sign of maturity. How we cope with ours will be an indicator of our own maturity.

As an institution we are inevitably part of the interaction with other institutions. It is true that, like other institutions, social work has an organic life of its own, fed not only by values but by knowledge and skill; but this is influenced by the processes of other institutions while we contribute to theirs. The fact that, for example, social work's ethical stance has moved through morality, reform, professionalism and back to reform again has not happened by accident but in part has been a reflection of other social trends. Together with other bodies and institutions, social work has contributed to developments in social policy and provision in the areas of social security, penology, preventive intervention to support family life, within education and health services and made some contribution to the gradual acceptance of the idea of 'consumer participation' in a wide range of spheres.

It can claim two particular contributions from its development of professional expertise, I feel:

(1) the impact of stress on the individual;
(2) the impact and use of relationship in contacts between 'professionals' and clientele.

These contributions are now being taken up by a wide range of groups—doctors, nurses, social security officials, health visitors, Marriage Guidance counsellors, Citizens Advice Bureau staff, personnel departments and many others where a 'social work' element comes into their job. The fact that it contributes now to others' professional development is perhaps a factor which indicates social work has now professionally 'come of age'.

Institutionalising social work has involved one other significant factor for social work: it has meant the development of social work agencies, or the employment of social workers by other agencies or institutions. We have become caught up in organisational systems which have values and processes of their own, with a profound effect on social work practice—especially as in this country the agencies are predominantly governmental. Social work tends to operate, therefore, within an 'establishment' value system, and within processes which are geared to lay accountability which produces many tensions for professional practice. To a degree, we have become bureaucratised. I do not want to develop this theme a great deal here as I elaborate on it in the later chapters on professionalism and administration.

But to summarise, the social worker is inevitably part of a network of personal and social processes at five identifiable levels:

Personally he will have an individualism of his own which will shape his values, his views and his practice in relation to the other levels. These may help or hinder his work in terms of how he feels about his clients, his professional identity, his agency or society generally. Awareness of his own feelings is crucial to his practice. He will be engaged with

Clients who are individuals, too, with views of their own caught up in processes which are peculiar to them. The way they feel about their inter-action with the other levels (including the social worker) may again, help or hinder. Worker and client will be engaged with an

Agency with (as I have suggested) values and processes of its own. Client and/or worker may or may not feel comfortable in their inter-action with it. The worker will additionally be involved with a

Profession which he may well find supportive and yet his identification with it may create tensions in other spheres—within his agency or within society. Worker, client, agency and profession are in their various ways, the products of, and interacting with

Society with all its complexity of processes and mixture of values. For social work practice the key questions always are:

(1) What right have I as a social worker to intervene? That right may be given by the client (if he asks for intervention), by the profession, by the agency or by society.

(2) Having intervened, what right have I to try to influence matters in a certain direction? Again, the right may be given by client, profession, agency or society. The according of rights by any one of these groups may, however, be profoundly influenced by the perceived knowledge and skill of social work (be those percep-

tions realistic, under- or over-estimations). But as we have seen, the issue of rights is no simple one.

All of this makes social work a tough job, which by its very nature is never going to be easy in that answers are rarely clear cut. The social worker will always be called upon to exercise his judgment and to do so in an area in which conflict and tension are endemic. All one can say is (in President Truman's epic phraseology) that if you don't like the heat, get out of the kitchen. The satisfaction is that if you can stand the heat and manage to cook up something that can satisfy the varied hungers of some people, one can sit down to one's own meal with a degree of content—even if one is still aware of the hunger that goes unmet and awaits your tomorrow.

References

1. Geoffrey Pearson, 'Social work as the privatised solution of public ills': *British Journal of Social Work*, Summer 1973.
2. *The inalienable element in social work*: discussion paper no. 3, British Association of Social Workers, 1973.
3. Report of the Committee on Local Authority and Allied Personal Social Services, Cmnd 3703, H.M.S.O., 1968.
4. *Confidentiality in Social Work*: discussion paper no. 1, British Association of Social Workers, 1971.
5. T. C. Puckett, 'Can social treatment be effective?': *Social Work Today* (14.6.73).
6. W. G. Runciman, *Relative Deprivation and Social Justice*: (Routledge & Kegan Paul), 1966.
7. Barbara Wootton, *Social Science & Social Pathology*: (George Allen & Unwin), 1959.
8. *A code of ethics for social work*: discussion paper no. 2, British Association of Social Workers, 1972.

Further Reading

A 'must' for students is Brian J. Heraud's *Sociology and Social Work* (Pergamon) and I would also suggest Peter Leonard's *Sociology in Social Work* (Routledge & Kegan Paul). While it focuses on the American experience, *Industrial Society and Social Welfare* by Harold L. Wilensky and Charles N. Lebeaux (Free Press) traces the interlocking development of technological society and welfare provision; while in *Regulating the Poor*, Frances Fox Piven and Richard A. Cloward take an angry look at the way welfare provision buttresses the existing social structure. Robert Pinker in *Social Theory and Social Policy* (Heinemann) examines the connections and disconnections between these two spheres. *Social and Moral Theory in Casework* by Ray-

mond Plant (Routledge & Kegan Paul) looks at ethical issues, while casework princi-
ples are explored by F. P. Biestek in *The Casework Relationship* (George Allen &
Unwin). A number of relevant articles are gathered together in *Social Work and Social
Values*, edited by Eileen Younghusband (George Allen & Unwin), while the title of
Ray Lees's book *Politics and Social Work* (Routledge & Kegan Paul) speaks for itself.
Paul Halmos's books *The Faith of the Counsellors* and *The Personal Service Society*
(both published by Constable) also have much to say that is pertinent.

   Among the articles I would recommend are 'The case for radical casework' by
Nicholas Bond (*Social Work Today*, 29.7.71), 'The challenge of primary prevention'
by Peter Leonard (*Social Work Today*, 3.6.71), 'Consensus or conflict?' by Carole
R. Smith (*Social Work Today*, 13.12.72) and 'Social conflict: implications for social
work' by Ben Knott (*British Journal of Social Work*, Winter, 1972). An astringent
case illustration is discussed in 'Professionals in the firing line' by Richard Bryant
(*British Journal of Social Work*, Summer, 1973).

Discussion

   I have deliberately put a chapter on social work and society at
the beginning of this book since the issues it raises permeate the
whole of social work teaching and practice. Whatever aspect of practice one is examining, somewhere along the way ethical and social
issues emerge.

   Whether one starts a social work course by looking at these issues
is another matter. I have typically done so, but it has its disadvantages. To begin with, the material is inevitably fairly abstract and
sophisticated. Not all students can cope initially with this level of
abstraction, feel bewildered and threatened and the situation is made
worse for them if they are not equipped with some basic sociological
knowledge—and few of them are at the beginning of a non-graduate
course, at any rate. Also the material may seem almost totally irrelevant to the day-to-day practice at the 'grass roots' level which has
been their usual pre-course experience. It tends to jar upon their
initial mental set towards the course, which, as a generalisation, they
see as equipping them to carry out more effectively the job they
have already been doing. When I first came into social work teaching
I was almost shocked by the ignorance of the average student about
what went on in the upper reaches of their own departments, let
alone in the wider fields of administration and politics. Over the
years students have noticeably come to courses not only with a better
basic education but also with a greater political awareness, so the

problems of abstraction, sophistication and relevance have become less acute even though they still remain.

There is always the occasional student who uses abstract ethical and political discussion, whether he knows anything about the matter or not, as an intellectual defence. The rest of the group becomes increasingly irritated.

But many students will welcome the chance to look at issues that have been troubling them, if only half consciously, and which they have not really had the chance to ventilate before amid the press of busy-ness. Seminar work, based on a case study, can knit some of the abstractions into a specific situation and so assist those students who question the relevance of this material.

But if this material is used at the beginning of the course, it may be wise not to expect too much of students in discussion and to reassure them that if they do not fully grasp it at this stage, it is quite all right. The issues will constantly recur, providing new opportunities for learning; and it could be fruitful to go back to it again quite specifically say, at the end of the first year and/or at the end of a course, when it should make more sense. Students will have knowledge from other disciplines by then and a good deal more experience, to integrate it and identify its fundamental relevance.

Obviously, in discussion there is going to be some tension between those students who basically have a consensus model of society and those with a conflict model; and since both views are often closely linked to personality factors and identity, there could be some strong feeling flying around. Issues around authority, responsibility, accountability and social justice are bound to emerge. The student who sees social work (and themselves) as nurturing may begin to question whether they are not after all just social controllers; while the student who sees social work as concerned with social change may start to realise that some of what he is saying is as authoritarian as the utterances of the establishment.

In other words, discussion should start to loosen students up, both at the intellectual and feeling levels in a way which could augur well for their subsequent learning and development as social work practitioners. This may be the justification (despite the disadvantages and discomforts) for using the material right at the beginning.

CHAPTER II

The Development of Social
Work Conceptualisation

The development of social work conceptualisation—that is the development of theory—has taken time to emerge. In addition to the reasons for this delay mentioned in the previous chapter, there have been perhaps, two other factors involved:

(1) The complexity of motivations around social work development; among them, genuine concern (for individuals, groups or communities); the fear of unrest or revolution, crime and deviance (a control motivation); economic concerns (from bringing the handicapped into productive employment at times of labour shortage, to the prevention, by early intervention, of later, more costly remedies); democratic motivations (for the redress of power imbalances, participation, consultation, etc.); and motivations around developing potential (often centred about educational or recreational activity or health care).

Some of these complex motivations have been seen in the past (and are today) as incompatible (for example fear of unrest compared with redress of power imbalances), leading to tensions not only between social workers but between some social workers and influential sections of society, and between some social workers and some of their clients—the sort of complexities around caring, control and change that we looked at in the last chapter.

(2) Perhaps as a reflection of the range of motivations, social work has begun in a wide range of different places in society, typically using different methods; and over time, these have had a range of different experiences and developments, again making a unification more difficult to achieve. Some of the problems are evidenced in

the following brief review of the history and development of social work (analysed by method).

CASEWORK

Casework has been practised in a rudimentary form from St. Vincent de Paul to Octavia Hill, with its more modern origins in the Charity Organisation Society, and the development of training courses at the London School of Economics and elsewhere at the turn of the century. Its real launch is frequently dated from 1917 with the publication of Mary Richmond's book, *Social Diagnosis.*[1] Although it may be true to say that casework originated in Britain, its development took place in America, possibly as a reflection of that country's more individualised society with its 'frontier' traditions. Here, although the 1909 Poor Law Commission majority report had largely backed the C.O.S. individualised approach, the collectivised approach and the development of social services (rather than social work) advocated by the Webbs, was implemented.

According to its critics, its individualised focus led casework away from social concerns and reform into the realms of therapy, laid it wide open to its takeover by Freudian psychoanalytic concepts from the 20's to the 30's, sent it chasing after professionalism on a basically medical model, involved its concentration on an articulate, motivated, mainly neurotic and middleclass clientele (who could use the therapeutic techniques) to the detriment of its concern for the underprivileged, and led to an elitist, divisive development in that to become a recognised, qualified social worker in the United States meant being a graduate with a two-year Master's degree. Just what is an acceptable professional worker and whether a social worker's association should be inclusive of all practitioners or exclusively of the trained, are issues which are still with us—even complicated by the decision of the Central Council for Education and Training in Social Work to implement two types of training.

The negative trends mentioned above were exacerbated, it is said, in the 30's with the transfer of income maintenance responsibility during the depression to the American New Deal organisations. The voluntary agencies and the professional workers (who stayed with them) were left to focus on family casework, involving psychological problems, and the use of therapeutic methods.

The defenders of casework would suggest that it would have been impossible to develop theory or practice if the individual focus had been lost in generalised reform activity. Without this development much would have been lost:

(a) By individuals in need (and not all problems are structural) who were offered a high standard of service;
(b) By other spheres who have utilised what casework developed (including reformers);
(c) The growth in terms of numbers of workers and influence of social work as a whole would have been seriously inhibited. There would have been no local authority Social Services departments, for example, without the development of professional practice.

Casework itself began in a wide range of agencies, each developing skills in specialised settings (general and psychiatric hospitals, probation, child and family welfare agencies, etc.). By 1929, the experiences culled from these disparate settings had been sufficiently worked out for the common ground of casework activity to be identified and the American Association of Social Workers subscribed to the genericism of casework and encouraged generic courses. This genericism at times appeared rather thin as controversy raged between the functionalist, diagnostic and problem-solving schools, and varied emphases were advocated—ego orientated casework, aggressive casework, etc.

Casework did not stand still in this country after 1909; training for Probation and Medical social work was introduced, but it was not until 1929 that we started to develop courses on the American model with the setting up of the Psychiatric Social Work course at the London School of Economics under the impetus of the Child Guidance movement. Training for the various settings remained separate in this country though, until the coming of generic courses in the 50's—though the generic approach was in use before this.

American casework theory has, however, needed some modification for application in this country, since the circumstances of casework's development here has differed. Casework has been a more marginal activity (professionally speaking) not really arriving in a primary setting (as opposed to the secondary settings of Probation, Psychiatric and Medical Social Worker) until the setting-up of the Children's Departments in 1948, and barely developing in the Health and Welfare fields until the 'Younghusband' courses were established in the early 60's. More significantly though casework was developed here in the statutory rather than the voluntary agencies as in the United States. This meant a number of differences:

(1) British social workers have had to deal with 'all comers'. We have had to deal with reluctant clients as well as the motivated, and to wrestle with problems of authority consistently. We could not argue (as some American theorists did in the 30's and 40's) that any degree of coercion was incompatible with casework. I would suggest that British social work contributed greatly to the development of ideas around the use of authority in casework now accepted as valid.

(2) Being statutory has involved us in providing a universally available service with all that entails in terms of caseload pressure, management, priorities, etc.—and the necessity to fill posts whether staff were trained or untrained (a rather mixed blessing as regards training development here).

(3) The statutory involvement has meant, though, that casework in Britain is associated with the poor and the deviant. It has little acceptance among the middle class—with the possible exception of Child Guidance work and some Medical social work. This association of stigma handicaps access to many problems and inhibits preventive work—even among the poor.

(4) British social work has typically been more involved with bureaucratic processes. This is not quite so true of child guidance clinic, hospital, or probation work, where the ethos has been more that of an agglomerate of professionals among which social work gradually established itself. Children's Departments were caught up in the local government structure but were late enough on the scene to have a more professionalised identity from the beginning, supported as they were by an influential group at the Home Office. It was the former Welfare Departments that were the most

professionally disadvantaged. The Departments themselves were the rump of the old Poor Law system that was broken up in 1948, but as such were basically an adminstrative service. Professional practice had to fight its way into these departments and then up their hierarchies. Although the new Social Service Departments are technically professional in that Directors and senior staff are expected to be qualified social workers, the Departments are administratively complex and the tensions between administrative and professional practice which British social work has long had to live with, still persist.

Whether modified or not for their applicability here, the British debt to American experience is, however, both profound and ongoing. While social work thinking and writing has grown enormously in recent years, we still cannot match either the volume or the originality of American work, rooted in their highly developed agencies, innovatory practice, and scholarly University Schools of Social Work. The number of occasions in this book I refer to American authors is a reflection of this indebtedness.

The war period contributed little to the development of casework: problems were national rather than individual and, interestingly, the incidence of 'individual' problems, despite all the stress and upheaval, seems to have diminished. (The problems of child evacuees is the possible exception and gave a fillip to child care and the post 1948 developments.) Immediate post-war developments, such as economic prosperity and the coming of the Welfare State, made some question whether social work was necessary at all; but caseworkers, at least, found an additional role for themselves in individualising generalised social services and assisting clients to find, engage with, and benefit from the complex new organisations.

The 're-discovery' of poverty in the early 60's (with economic recession) plus the emergence of racial problems (following immigration here, but endemic in the United States) led to a revised concern among caseworkers with issues of reform: while revolutionary movements in many parts of the world (Algeria, Cuba, South America, China) have developed a radical politicised element, critical of, but significantly influencing, casework ideology and practice throughout North America and Western Europe.

GROUPWORK

Groupwork again, has been practised for ages, but with varying ideologies behind it—self-help, service to others, as a form of democratic action, recreational, or with the ideas of personal development and enrichment. It was not until the early 20's though, that the study of group processes began in scattered specific situations; and it was not until the 30's that general theories of group processes emerged. The American Association for the study of Groupwork was founded in 1936, but its base remained undefined (lodged in education, recreation, democracy, etc.). The war gave a tremendous impetus, especially in the United States, to the study of group processes, stimulated by a horrified fascination with the emergence and methods used by Nazism, a concern for Army efficiency (T. groups emerged in officer selection, for example); the shortage of psychiatrists to deal with war service neuroses led to developments of group therapy methods; while later, the effects of imprisonment, concentration camps and brain-washing techniques added to the dimensions of knowledge of the effects of group processes and their use.

The American Association of Groupworkers (as it had become) determined in 1946 that groupwork belonged to social work and joined the A.A.S.W. for three reasons:

(1) Groupwork involved the conscious use of relationship to achieve community (i.e. social) ends.
(2) It arose out of the human need for self-respect and belonging (concerns of social work).
(3) Its aims were those of social work: on an individual basis, to assess and assist the integration of inner and outer needs, and on a social basis, to help change the environment where this was unhelpful.

This amalgamation and the reasons for it, therefore, established the genericism of, at any rate, casework and groupwork in the United States.

Groupwork, although practised in this country for as long as the United States, remains the most under-developed of the social work methodologies here. There are, perhaps, two reasons for this:

(i) With the possible exception of the Youth Service (and even this has now styled itself the Youth and Community Service with all this implies in terms of the primacy of method), we have typically regarded groupwork as a method of practice to be used by social work staff already in post, rather than employing group-workers as such, as has happened in America. The same goes for hospitals staff (with rare exceptions, such as the Henderson Hospital). While this practice may have certain advantages (as well as economy), it has I feel, crippled the development here of groupwork practice, theoretical development and training.

(ii) Since we use groupwork as a method rather than employ group-workers, we are still arguing here whether groupwork really belongs to social work or not. Youth work's identity is still split between education (and Local Education Authorities still sponsor it predominantly) and social work; while group therapy is still allied to medicine, often.

However, the development of Intermediate Treatment and a renewed concern for day care provision have provided a new stimulus for interest in social groupwork.

COMMUNITY WORK

Again, community work has a long history and a wide range of ideologies and practical focii. There would seem to be at least four streams:

(1) *Social planning stream* Ideas of community were behind the development of new towns: New Lanark, Saltaire, Bournville, Welwyn Garden City, the post-war New Town and expanded town programmes (now employing social development staff). But this stream has also concerned itself with the old as well as the new. The 'community' dimension was implicit in many of the 19th century reform movements in the areas of public health, housing and delinquency; and has re-emerged in 20th century planning concern (Gen-

eral Improvement areas, housing action areas, etc.) and in attempts at reform (Education Priority areas, Community Development Projects, are examples).

(2) *Community development stream* This began possibly in Britain's Imperial heyday in attempts to equip colonial administrators with some community work skills, even though these were geared (in critics' eyes) to objectives of economic exploitation. The tradition of community work training for under-developed countries has persisted here and has been utilised for training indigenous workers by these countries themselves. Ideas and experience developed for rural, agricultural and under-developed situations have in recent years found a new application in advanced, industrial, urban communities, both old and new.

(3) *Community organisation stream* Originating with the C.O.S. ideas of co-ordinating local voluntary effort (though now with a promotional/developmental rather than a preventing waste/discouraging indigence motivation) this stream has been taken over by the Community Chest movement in the United States and the Councils of Social Service movement here.

(4) *Community action stream* In broad terms, this stream seeks to assist the disadvantaged—in these days not just the 'usual' poor, handicapped or weak, but the more powerful, affected by pollution, airport and motorway developments and consumers generally. The focus of this wide range of groups may be specific and local, or wide and national. Their tactics may range from self-help, a group offering a service to others, to pressure activity ranging from information, education, practical assistance, lobbying, to confrontation activity (road blocks, strikes, etc.). The ideology of such movements may range from concern, paternalism, reformism or revolution: their base of operations range from a specific locality, a voluntary organisation, client groups, educational, recreational, or religious organisations or political parties.

Given these variety of streams, let alone the disparities within streams, it is understandable that there is little agreement about what community work is; or whether its base is administration, education, politics or social work. Social workers like to think it is social work, but I suspect few community workers would see it this way.

The development of community work has also had to wait the evolvement of sociological and political theory; while the impetus for its development (at any rate from the 30's) has emerged from a plethora of sources—the depression years in the United States and here; New Town 'blues'; the 'discovery' of 'twilight areas' in the big cities; the rediscovery of poverty and the identification of its multiple causation; the recognition of the failure of coordination of specifically based remedial programmes (health, housing employment, etc.); the remoteness of large-scale bureaucratic organisations (commercial or state) which ride over the individual; together with a new, worldwide concern for minorities, the under-privileged and the oppressed.

RESIDENTIAL CARE

Again, this method has been used for many years though the original motivations have often been punitive (prisons), merely custodial (mental hospitals) or a religiously-based 'rescuing' of the 'damned'. The method has been exploited as a convenient way of getting rid of social problems, administratively 'tidy', even economic (economies of scale); as a 'dustbin' for those with whom other methods had 'failed'; or, more genuinely, as the only way we had of dealing with some problems until new treatments and new methods were available with the coming of new knowledge.

Residential institutions have been under heavy fire all through: the poor hated the workhouses; the 19th century prison reformers attacked a vicious system; while during the 50's and 60's we had a whole spate of 'literature of dysfunction': the Curtis Report[2] on children's homes, Barton[3] on institutionalisation, Goffman[4] on mental hospitals, Townsend[5] on old people's homes, the Morrisses[6] on Pentonville, etc. We have come to recognise that large institutions at least are uneconomic compared with community care and quite unable to cope with a wide spectrum of problems. 'Omnibus' institutions like the Poor Law workhouses have been diversified into general, subnormality and mental hospitals, old people's homes, etc.—a process still continuing with special provision for alcoholics, ex-prisoners and other groups. Large institutions also engender atypical social processes (become deviant, in effect) which means that the

people who leave them are ill-equipped to deal with normal society:
i.e. they create problems which then have to be solved in their turn.
Institutions, too, are frequently bitterly hard on individuals: dehumanising, categorising, stigmatising and processing. Residents are at
the mercy of staff and we have had to invent inspectorial systems
to protect residents from abuse—though how inadequate these systems still are has been underlined by recent scandals.

What institutions can achieve positively has been demonstrated
by a long series of pioneers: Tuke, Maxwell Jones, Aichorn, Bettel-
heim, Homer Lane, David Wills—and their ideas and methods have
gradually won acceptance, even if a variable application.

The disparagement of residential care has rubbed off on the status,
remuneration, recruitment and training of residential staff and crippled the development of a theory of residential work. While theory
has been developed in respect of child care and is on the way with
regard to the chronic sick, there is little in prospect with regard
to old people's homes, and virtually nothing that endeavours to
embrace them all. Generic courses (embracing the Williams Report[7]
concept of a profession of residential care) are now emerging which
may throw up the conceptualisations needed; but I feel it is significant that in those concepts which try to bridge social work methods
only fieldwork methods are typically considered. Residential work
is largely ignored—though I suppose it could be argued that residential work is not a separate method, but a combination of the other
three (a view I do not share).

We are beginning to recognise the positive elements in residential
care, acknowledging that it is a task that calls for at least as much
skill as fieldwork, and setting about remedying the status, remuneration, conditions of work and training of residential staff.

The emergence of Certificate of Qualification in Social Work
courses in which both field and residential training figure is an acknowledgement of this.

There were, however, increasing misgivings among social workers
about the developing preoccupation with methodologies, on three
grounds:

(1) That a tendency existed to 'bend' social problems to fit the meth-
odology of the practitioner involved. This, to say the least, was putting

the cart before the horse. It meant that some clients were excluded from help because they could not utilise the method, while others, though getting some help, were not being assisted really effectively.

(2) That the methodologies were becoming increasingly isolated from each other, splintering what it was felt ought to be one profession, and denying to themselves the potentially enriching contributions of knowledge and skill being built up in other methods.

(3) The experience of social work practice, whatever the 'official' methodological skill of the worker, underlined his involvement with each method at least to some degree. Psycho-social problems, while they might have a particular emphasis in terms of causation at the individual, family, group or community level, or require a methodological emphasis in terms of solution, were in the final analysis, indivisible.

In 1955 the American National Association of Social Workers set about the attempt to find basically, the common ground which existed between the fieldwork methods and their various settings. The N.A.S.W. report identified five elements in this 'common base':

(1) Values—the worth and dignity of the individual, and his rights in democratic society to execute choice and fulfil his potential.

(2) Purpose—to enhance individual and societal functioning and well-being;

(3) Sanction—the authority of society (usually vested in agencies but also accorded to the profession) to engage in practice to achieve its purposes; this sanction also being accorded, or at least accepted, by clientele;

(4) Method—based on assessment, to establish ends to be attained by identifiable means, carried through stages, with the use of the professional self of the worker;

(5) Knowledge—derived from the social sciences, principally psychology, sociology and social administration.

This 'common base' approach was carried further by such writers as Ruth Smalley[8] and Harriett Bartlett[9], though each with a particular viewpoint. Ruth Smalley identifies five principles of generic practice:

(i) Diagnosis, which is developed during the giving of service, involving the clientele in the process of establishing it. It is constantly revised, but is brought out at appropriate points by the worker for the clientele to use, consider and share in. Into this process the worker will put his knowledge, understanding, his assessment of client capacity and his clients' objectives. Out of it in discussion with his clients, will emerge the goals of the intervention.

(ii) A conscious use of time phases. Each intervention will have a beginning involving clarification and partialisation; a middle of hard work and an ending involving separation.

(iii) An agency function which gives the work focus and direction for a productive engagement as well as ensuring accountability for the work undertaken.

(iv) A conscious form derived from function which gives the work a shape along the dimensions of time, place, policy and procedures.

(v) A conscious use of relationship to foster the engagement of client and worker in a purposeful way.

Harriett Bartlett identifies social work's central focus as social functioning—people coping with life situations. Social workers become involved when there is an imbalance between people's coping efforts and the demands of the social environment. This imbalance can arise for many reasons: coping resources may be limited or the demands excessive. Social work's primary orientation and primary concern is for the people involved in these situations. Others primary concern may be the medical, technological, administrative or many other facets of them. It is from the primary concern for people that social work's values stem (individual worth, etc.) and our concern for people in life situations will determine the body of knowledge we require to practise. From values we derive our attitudes to people (respect, acceptance) and from knowledge we derive our understanding. We bring both to bear in our interventive repertoire—working with individuals, groups, communities and organisations either directly or in collaborative action with others. This common base approach is applicable whether we are directly involved with clients or at one remove in social work education, administration, research or social planning.

Other attempts to find a common base have revolved around the social work role—or rather nexus of roles. Whatever our method or setting, there are common elements in this nexus. We are all at times:

Educators—resource people for information, advice and opinion, whether for clients or others. Education is not just a matter of facts and opinions, however; it may well involve getting into the open the feelings and attitudes which often influence the selection of 'significant' facts, the interpretation of facts, or underly opinions. Stigma, for example, is often a matter of attitude rather than fact.

Family substitutes—social workers may be in a quasi-parental position with those in a permanent or temporary dependant position; or clients may use us in a quasi-sibling or even quasi-child way.

Enabler—with some support or practical help from us, clients may be able to tackle their difficulties themselves; or they may need assistance from us with personal, social or practical difficulties which are inhibiting their access to other services or groups they need.

Intermediary or interpreter—where communication has broken down for whatever reason (for example, an inability to express or an inability to comprehend) to work towards establishing effective communication whether this is between parent/child, husband/wife, client/official, home/school, patient/doctor, gang/neighbourhood, black/white —or even between members of the same helping team.

Advocate—which may involve not only putting someone's case for them, but doing so with a sufficient degree of power (however organised) to redress the power imbalances often present and operating to the disadvantage of the power-less—whether that powerlessness stems from being inarticulate or an insufficiency of political 'clout'.

Representative of authority—whether that authority rests on a social, legal, professional, agency or relationship basis.

Resource providers and allocators—the resources concerned may be held by the community at large, or by specific organisations (even individuals). They may not be resources we can command but if we intervene on behalf of clients we are to that extent influencing allocation, to a degree accepting an allocation function and accepting the responsibility and accountability that go with it. If the resources are within our command in the sense that our agency controls them, we will in part be providers and certainly allocators in that we will be involved in a priority determining process (given that resources are typically finite). As social workers are resources of a kind in themselves, we cannot escape the responsibility and accountability of how we provide and allocate ourselves in our work. Part of our responsibility as resource providers and allocators is to complain constructively if we establish that resources needed are short or priorities are inappropriate. We shall not always get our way; but we are being irresponsible if our case goes by default.

Team-member—implying an understanding of the functions of others and an understanding of our own function so we can communicate this to others. They cannot understand our function if we cannot or do not tell them. Effective teamwork involves a sharing to determine where the priorities in a situation lie, allocating responsibilities in the light of them, and adapting the tasks of the team members to most effectively meet the salient needs within whatever constraints exist. As situations and needs change over time, so the work of the team will need constant revision and adaptation—as well as the composition of that team.

Co-ordinator—involving seeing that the team is complete in terms of the problems presented, that plans drawn up in the light of priorities are implemented and continually assessed and re-assessed.

Individualiser—assessing individual situations and on the basis of identified needs/difficulties/capacities selecting that combination of resources/services required in this instance. Our task will be to assist clients to identify and engage with services/resources—or sometimes, to develop their own. We may also be called upon to represent individuals to those services, groups or organisations where they seem to have difficulty in responding to the needs of the individual.

Therapist—where the worker arranges and is involved[e] in healing encounters typically directed to intra or inter-personal difficulties involving face to face meetings, relationships and feelings.

Employee—carrying out an effective, responsible job for the agency with the expectation that we shall be provided with appropriate working conditions in terms of pay, hours and facilities.

Reformer—taking our place whether as employees, professionals or people, in politics, pressure groups, professional groups, trade unions; within our agencies, with other agencies, or within our personal circle; to try to bring about those changes than concern us.

More recent attempts to unify social work conceptualisation have had a rather different basis—that of systems theory. This predicates that the individual is in himself a 'system', engaging with other individuals in face-to-face relations which then constitute systems in themselves—relations with a spouse, a nuclear family, an extended family, with groups in the immediate neighbourhood, at work, at school, at leisure, etc. These face to face systems are themselves part of wider systems—the school, the factory, the town, with links into trade unions, commercial enterprises, local government, and elsewhere. Even these systems are enmeshed in still wider systems—national government, capitalism, etc. themselves reflecting still more profound systems such as stratification and the distribution of power.

In this sense, systems theory is a tool of diagnosis—a means of identifying the system or systems which are creating the difficulties. But it is also a guide for determining where the intervention needs to be put and suggests the most appropriate form or forms of that intervention.

Pincus and Minaham[10] carry this analysis into social work practice itself, identifying four types of system in the process:

(1) The change-agent system—that is, the social worker and his agency. The agency is included since almost all workers are employed in agencies.

(2) The client system—the person, family, group, organisation or community which engages the services of the change-agent system, 'contracts' with it and expects to benefit from its services.

(3) The target system—the person, family, group, organisation or community (or some part or combination of them) towards which the change-agent system directs his efforts (directly or indirectly) in order to benefit the client system.

(4) The action system—which is composed of all those people and processes the change-agent system works through to influence the target system. The action system may already be extant and operating; or it may involve bringing together existing systems already operating but in an unco-ordinated way; or it may involve the change-agent system creating a new action system altogether.

These systems are not necessarily discrete entities, however. The change-agent system can become the target system if difficulties are being created for the client system within the worker/agency itself. The client system can become wholly or in part the target system if, similarly, the difficulties lie wholly or in part within that system. The client system may well become part of the action system if they are engaged in activity bearing upon the target system. And so on.

Pincus and Minaham also identify a 'common ground' intervention process—the phases of planned change through time. They suggest five phases:

(1) The recognition of the problem and the engagement of the change-agent and client systems;
(2) The identification of the systems (client, target, change-agent and action) related to the problem and establishing the contract with the client system;
(3) The formation of the action system;
(4) The operation of the action system;
(5) The evaluation, termination or transformation of the action system.

These phases are again, not discrete, but overlapping.

They also approach the analysis of social work in a similar 'common ground' way, suggesting skills may be categorised in three ways:

(1) Data collection. This may involve questioning (verbal, written in the form of questionnaires, etc., or involve projective tests, role play, etc.); observations; or using existing written material—records, minutes of meetings, budgets, census statistics, and so on.

Data may be collected in structured ways such as questionnaires or involve unstructured methods such as open-ended interviews. What data is needed will depend on the problem, but the collection techniques used and the speed with which data needs to be assembled will also have a bearing.

(2) Data analysis. Two elements are involved here: making sense of the data, which is not only a matter of theoretical knowledge but also an ability to connect that theory with an actual situation; and making decisions based on that data. Decision making has many complexities. The worker needs to be aware of himself, his function, the context in which he works, the analytic models he is using, who is involved in the processes, the acceptability and effects of decisions, how sure he can be about his decisions, the risks involved and the time available to him to come to a decision. All these elements will influence his decision-taking.

(3) Interventive skills. While these are not analysed in detail, they are broadly grouped as indirect means of influence, which mainly focusses on work with the action system and highlights the planning aspects of the social work task; and direct means of influence, which focusses on the worker's face to face relationships within the systems, and highlights the interactional skills of the worker.

Pincus and Minaham go on to examine the implications of their conceptual framework in terms of working with dyads (the typical one-to-one of casework), small groups (within which they subsume the family) and organisations and larger social systems.

Howard Goldstein[11] also bases his approach on systems theory but suggests that what he terms social learning is a prerequisite to the changes that are inevitably involved in problem-solving. This applies whether individuals, families, groups, organisations or communities are concerned in change. Change in any of these will depend on the capacity of people to learn new facts, attitudes and ways of behaving—their capacity for social learning, in effect. Social learning is involved whether the change is initiated by social action or individual therapy; and he sees this concern for social learning as the unifying factor in social work and the focus of its professional identity.

Goldstein identifies six stages of problem solving:

(1) Need of difficulty felt or observed;
(2) Formulating, locating and defining the need or difficulty;
(3) Surveying the information required around the need/difficulty;
(4) Formulating possible solutions;
(5) Appraising the consequences of possible solutions;
(6) Testing, accepting and internalising the solution.

He suggests that the social learning processes which go with these stages are:

(1) Arousing and focussing attention and concern;
(2) Organising and evaluating the problem and planning further action;
(3) Searching for and acquiring new information and perceptions;
(4) Experimenting with alternative means, behaviours and consequences;
(5) Rehearsing for action; verifying solutions and gains;
(6) Acting, evaluating, incorporating the gains and (if necessary) reformulating the problem.

The social work contribution at each stage becomes:

(1) Assisting the identification of the problem, using guidance, raising motivation, evaluating, informing, defining;
(2) Assisting the evaluation of the problem; helping to formulate plans, contributing to the assessment of capabilities and resources; promoting motivation, assisting role clarification and evolving commitment;
(3) Stimulating an awareness of the salient practical, psychological, social and transactional factors;
(4) Enhancing problem-solving efforts through sustaining, testing, evaluating, guiding and motivating;
(5) Assisting the reality testing by providing opportunities for this; evaluating them, reinforcing and confirming the social learning experienced through them;
(6) Assisting the reinforcement of the social learning through validating the capabilities of those involved, assisting the analysis and

implications of the outcomes of the process and planning for the termination of the process.

Goldstein, on the basis of this model, suggests there are three phases of social work practice involved: the induction phase (incorporating stages 1 and 2 of the problem solving, learning and social work processes); the core phase (incorporating stages 3, 4 and 5); and the ending phase (stage 6). He analyses these three phases in a 'common ground' way suggesting that all through there is a close inter-relationship between the aims and actions of the social work practitioner. Each phase has its characteristics and involves what Goldstein terms strategies, identified as study and evaluation, intention and intervention, and appraisal. He recognises and explores, however, some of the differences in practice in these strategies when the worker is dealing with individuals, families, groups, organisations and communities.

Goldstein eventually builds us a three dimensional model of social work practice: the dimensions being targets, phases and strategies. Each dimension is divided into three: targets into individuals, families/groups, organisations/communities; phases into induction, core and ending; strategies into study and evaluation, intention and intervention, and appraisal. In diagrammatic form he emerges with a cube of twenty-seven component 'bricks'.

Not all those who use a systems approach as their basis end up by unifying social work, however. In the process they throw up some of the difficulties of the unitary approach, particularly those around the knowledge base, skill base, and orientation.

Whittaker[12], for example, makes a distinction between micro-systems, in which every member of the system is involved in face-to-face relations with all other members (for example, families and small groups); and macro-systems where, at best, only a small number of those within the system know and inter-act with each other. Social work practice within micro-systems (i.e. work with individuals, families and small groups) will involve the practitioner in inter-personal helping with the members of the system in efforts to help that micro-system function. With macro-systems (neighbourhoods, organisations, communities or societies) the worker will be engaged in some

face-to-face relationships but these will be with only some of those
involved (representatives or key figures) though the focus will remain
on helping all those within the system even though for a variety
of reasons—many of them practical—the bulk of the system members
may never be directly involved with the work or the worker. Whittaker feels there are sufficient distinctions between working with mic-
ro- and macro-systems in terms of knowledge, objectives and strategies used, to treat them separately even if they remain complementary
and with certain areas of overlap. For example, he sees the 'micro-
systems' worker intervening in formal and informal structures and
the community, but essentially on behalf of the micro-systems he
is trying to assist, not with the objective of trying to change macro-
systems *per se.*

Whittaker sees the worker in this 'micro' social treatment process
as using means of direct counselling, crisis intervention and advocacy
on behalf of his clients; contrasting these with the macro-workers'
means of community organisation, social action, lobbying, canvass-
ing, co-ordinating and community analysis.

Given his micro-focus and the roles of treatment agent, advocate/
ombudsman, teacher/counsellor and broker which emerge from it,
Whittaker suggests there are four substantive areas of knowledge
involved in micro-working: psychoanalytic theory, social learning
theory, systems theory and humanistic-existential approaches. These
contrast with the knowledge base of macro-system interventions
drawn from sociology, economics, political science and industrial
relations. Whittaker examines micro-systems theories in terms of
their major assumptions, the view of man they imply, their major
tenets, their implications for social treatment and their limitations.
Each theoretical system, he suggests tends to shape the worker's view
of the client and so imposes a value 'set' on the total helping relationship. Rather than the dubious unity of a particular theory, Whittaker
sees the unifying framework as the problem solving process, which
he suggests has a beginning, covering intake, assessment, determination of goals, the formation of a treatment plan and the establishing
of a working agreement; an intermediate stage, covering the sustaining of the social treatment; and an ending, containing evaluation,
termination and after-care. He goes on to examine these eight ele-

ments in the three phases in terms of the objectives, worker activities, client perspectives and resources involved.

Whittaker explores indirect intervention (with formal and informal structures and the community) with particular reference to power —its bases and locus. He suggests that the worker has different types of power—reward, coercive, legitimated, referent and expert—which may be used in interventions on the client systems' behalf in the family, peer group, organisation or community systems. The worker typically uses these different types of power within his roles of advocate/ombudsman and broker.

Whittaker acknowledges that in direct work, which form of social treatment is used (individual, family or small group) and the particular type of each form (since there are many, of which he gives examples) will require careful choice in relation to the client's difficulties. He sets up a very useful range of basic questions to be asked to guide this choice.

Middleman and Goldberg[13] bring micro and macro-working together, but at the price of eschewing any social work concern with what might broadly be termed therapy. They argue that individual ills are much more a matter of the pathology of structures than of individuals; and they see the purpose of social work intervention as to change these pathological surrounding structures. With this remit, however, social work can begin with either individuals, with the focus on services delivery; or with structures, with the focus on social planning. They draw up a very interesting quadrant, placing these 'extremes' of practice in diagonally opposite quarters. The links between these extremes are placed in the remaining quarters: in one is work for the individual through others like him with similar problems; in the other is work with others (that is, non-sufferers) but on behalf of the sufferer(s). The argument is that whether starting at the individual or the structural level, work with groups of sufferers and work with non-sufferers is involved. In these areas the micro and macro meet and overlap.

The authors focus on the micro level of intervention and outline four basic principles: that the worker is accountable to his clients; that he follows the demands of the client task (usually into work with fellow-sufferers and non-sufferers); that he maximises the poten-

tial supports in the clients' environment (usually by modifying existing structures or creating new, since structural change will persist
and continue to assist clients after the worker has withdrawn); and
that he proceeds from an assumption of least contest (i.e. that he
uses only that degree of force necessary since the over-use of force
will produce counter-forces and be counter-productive).

From these principles four roles emerge: advocate, mediator,
broker and conferee (that is, someone with whom the client confers).
The authors discuss with great acumen the content of these roles
and the circumstances of their use.

This is not to suggest that Middleman and Goldberg eschew the
feeling element in situations. They discuss it in connection with roles
in a way which would be 'common ground' with many a therapeutically oriented social worker; and their concern for feeling emerges
even more clearly when they discuss social work skills. They categor-
ise skill under six headings:

(1) Stage setting—including the significance of positioning, engaging, and providing a congenial medium for communication (which
may be the traditional interview);

(2) Attending;

(3) Engaging feelings—reaching for, waiting for and 'getting with'
them; reporting on them; reaching for a feeling link with the client;

(4) Engaging information—reaching for it from clients and partialising it as well as giving it; examining alternative courses of action
and possible consequences; connecting discrete events; re-casting
problems and summarising;

(5) Managing interaction—checking on inferences; providing feedback; re-directing messages; amplifying subtle messages; toning down
strong messages; talking in the idiom of the other;

(6) Managing obstacles—referring back to the contract to re-establish focus; pointing out obstacles; challenging taboos; confronting
people with contradictory reality.

Much of this analysis would be common ground, too, with therapeutic social work: establishing the climate for communication and
reaching for information and feelings, for example; while providing
feedback, re-directing messages and amplifying subtle messages are
skills which would be used in say, reflective consideration of

dynamics in therapeutic work. Common to all practice would be their interesting chapter on the organisational context of practice which examines the way the 'metawork' (i.e. the work generated by the contact with the client or involvement with agency administration) may bog practitioners down in quite inordinate preoccupations with diagnosis, recording and supervision.

But I feel that they would again appear divisive in their discussion of the social science base of practice. While there may be much in their suggesting that theorists (whether psychological, sociological or political) tend to be culture and personality bound, and that theories should be selected in terms of their usefulness in practice; they also suggest that theories should be selected for their philosophical compatibility. As their philosophical basis is structural, they accept those theories which illuminate social influences on behaviour but reject those which locate pathology/deviance within the individual, including psychoanalysis. There are many practitioners who would be unhappy to make such a distinction and who might also find the academic ethics of it questionable.

Though he values the systems approach, Siporin[14] develops Bartlett's 'common base' approach; seeing social work as a part of a range of welfare provisions, with a particular concern for social functioning. This focus involves ideological issues as well as knowledge. Knowledge is both applied science ('factual' material derived from other disciplines or social work theory) and applied art (skills in differential assessment, the exercise of judgment, the use of relationship, a concern for experience, and the creative use of the social worker's self). Ideology gives rise to ethical practice principles; knowledge to technical practice principles. Both are inseparably enmeshed in the basic helping task. The task may be carried through in a range of ways with a variety of approaches (analytic, behavioural, ecological, etc.); but there is a common ground in the methods, processes and roles used and in the stages concerned. All social workers are, in this sense, generalists; all are concerned with 'private troubles' and 'public issues'; and with the multifactoral causation of social dysfunctioning.

Social work practice involves communication and decision-making; and requires skills in analysing data and interacting with others. All social work takes place in situations where their meaning is defined both by the participants and other people; it takes place in an ecological habitat; and involves a client (individual or group) and a worker who belongs to a profession as well as an agency.

The common stages are *engagement*: deciding there is a problem social work can help resolve, exploring it to understand it, the people involved and the context of it. *Intake* explores possible solutions, what resources are needed on what terms and conditions, allocating tasks and roles, and inducting to those roles (including the client role). The *contract* spells out the objectives, means, roles and tasks by which the problem is to be tackled, providing the 'base line' for both intervention and evaluation. *Assessment* involves a study of the problem(s), person(s) and situation in an integrated formulation which concludes with a recommended plan taking into account the resources available and needed. Assessment is a joint client/worker product calling for reason and judgment as well as a constructive working relationship. *Planning* is a learning process in itself: considering alternatives, making predictions. Plans are directed to goals— vital for sustaining motivation and focus. Goals are typically multi-target, multi-level, may involve a range of strategies from collaboration to confrontation. To achieve them may require a developing and changing intervention system.

Intervention is the implementation of the plan. It involves the worker's use of authority; and his skills to develop client(s) resources, to intervene, to summon up welfare resources (or create them), to refer, and keep the intervention system going. *Evaluation* (monitoring) is on-going. In this, records are crucial. At the end of an intervention, evaluation reinforces for the client and teaches for the worker. Evaluation is based on the contract objectives. Endings need planning since the separation may not be easy for client or worker. Evaluation is not just an internal matter: social work itself is being evaluated by others for effectiveness and efficiency.

I have considered it worthwhile to examine these unitary approaches to social work thinking in some detail, since they have enormous implications for social work practice, social work agencies and social work teaching. The unitary approaches are not new in that, in a way, they have been implicit in practice certainly since Mary Richmond's day. But they have crystallised much that was vague and ill-formed. My own field experience certainly validates them for me (if only in retrospect). Although 'officially' a caseworker in the mental health field, in practice I was involved with individuals, families, groups, residential establishments, a wide range of community groups and a host of organisations of one sort and another, involving officials, professionals and elected representatives; and I found myself with a bewildering array of different 'hats'.

But if unitary approaches help to make sense of experience, they do not in themselves resolve all the problems. They create as many as they solve. I would like to look at three in particular: professional judgment, partialisation and organisation; and in order to clarify the issues involved I would like to set up a hypothetical (and rather facetious) example. Given that social work's focus is psycho-social difficulty typically involving aspects of role, the role of football player may be blocked in a variety of ways. The block may occur at different levels—individual/family, group or community; and for differing reasons, which may be grouped as psychological (covering emotional disturbance, ego deficiency or cognitive development), social educational, and resource. Using these dimensions, and citing examples of reasons, this sort of scheme emerges:

| Level | Block | | |
	Psychological	Social educational	Resource
Individual/ family	Agoraphobia. Temper, fouling, sent off, barred	Does not know rules of game	Only one leg. No money for football kit
Group	Internal dissension over captaincy— team falls apart. Team so dislikes losing, wreck opponents' pavilion, barred	No member knows how to act as secretary or treasurer for team	Only 10 players. No money to hire pitch
Community	Soccer players stigmatised. Open victimisation	No one locally knows how to run a league	No land for pitches. No money to acquire land available

Simplistically, thinking in methodological terms, one could consider applying casework at the individual/family level, group and community work at the group and community levels. Residential work as a method could be considered when the problems were psychological but the relationships required to deal with the difficulties were not possible to develop in the extant situation. (Since it would be impossible to take a whole community into residence, the method would be limited to key community figures, perhaps.) At the social educational level, the residential method could come in where the knowledge required was highly specialised and to convey it with a degree of economic viability would mean taking the people to the knowledge source rather than the other way round. Courses for league secretaries, for example, might be residential. In resource problems, one could think of situations where the particular resources required were either so esoteric or so expensive that again, provision could only become viable by taking the people to the resources. (This would hardly apply to football, but would be true in say, the medical sphere with regard to intensive care units.)

But matters are typically not simplistic. There may be difficulties at more than one level, requiring a concurrent use of methods. With a difficulty at one level dealt with, one might then come up against difficulties at another, requiring a sequential use of methods. There may be a need to move from one method to another in order to complete a healing process. For example, progress made within a one-to-one relationship might need to be transferred out to a group situation before it could be said that the difficulties have been sufficiently resolved. There may be a need to assess a client's capacity to use a method before settling for this mode of intervention. The problem may be individual but the intensity of the one-to-one relationship may be too threatening and so suggest a group approach initially where the client might feel less threatened by what he may experience as a rather more diffuse focus, a more oblique approach to his difficulties he could tolerate until he was ready for the more intense work.

To assist a client to use his capacity at one level he may need support at another. An individual may need help to face a group situation, or an individual or group need help to face a community situation. We may need to use one method, at least supportively, since other methods take time to work—for example, support at the individual, family or group level since what is basically a community level problem may take years to resolve.

The method selection will be a matter of the client's choice as well as the worker's. There may be occasions where this choice may be inappropriate: for example through activity at the community level an individual may be trying to work out personal problems. It would then be up to the community worker (say) either to attempt intervention at the individual level, or secure the acceptable (to the client) intervention of say, a caseworker.

Even if it is not a question of personal problem but merely personality, the significance of individual characteristics is a dimension of situations all workers must be aware of; in effect, demonstrating the common ground of diagnostic knowledge required within methodologies.

(A) Professional Judgment

While a unitary approach provides an evaluative framework it does not remove the need for professional judgment. Unitary theories will not, of themselves, provide the professional with a value base; they will not pre-determine whom he regards as his client (i.e. whose interests he tries to promote); they will not pre-determine his role in the situation (advocate, mediator, therapist, etc.) nor will they pre-determine the ends to which he works. The worker will still have the responsibility for assessing the situation (influenced as this will be by the foregoing) in terms of the nature and locus of the difficulty, identifying the resources needed and those available, determining how he is to intervene, what needs to be tackled in terms of saliency and what needs to be tackled first in terms of urgency and accessibility —i.e. where the priorities lie. I acknowledge he will not be the only one assessing the situation: his clients and many other individuals and groups (including his own agency) will be doing the same. He will need to take their assessments into account; but others' assessments will not absolve him from the professional responsibility to assess and exercise his own judgment.

In determining the mode of intervention, I feel it is important that the particular strengths of each method should be identified. Though not suggesting that the strengths are exclusive to that method, I would see them as:

(1) CASEWORK (WITH INDIVIDUALS)

(i) The opportunity to provide a measured relationship, especially in respect of acceptance and confidentiality. This would seem to suggest that casework may be of particular value where there are personal problems around self-worth and guilt.

(ii) The opportunity to provide a quasi-parental relationship containing elements of nurture (including provision) protection and guidance. Here the problem would be one of dependency on its various manifestations: and not just too much (i.e. an over-dependence on others) but also too little (basically a denial of inter-dependency in relationships). Good nurture could involve not only material and emotional support, or the allowing of dependency as a stage in a maturing process leading to greater independence; but also the encouragement of potential and the provision of opportunities for its development, since social work is not merely concerned with pathology. Protection, too, might not just involve sheltering the vulnerable, but also protection (for example through the use of authority) from the consequences of impulsive action, whether action is a matter of few or stretched internal controls or *lack* of guilt. Guidance may be a particular function of work involving developmental or experiential crisis—whether stemming from tensions generated by inner conflict, inter-personal relationships or external factors.

Clearly, the sort of quasi-parental relationship offered will need to be caring, understanding and sometimes firm—particularly where clients have already experienced parenting that was rejecting, dogmatically authoritarian or vascillating; and especially where what we are attempting is to resolve the difficulties generated by previous poor parenting by a new and more positive experience of good parenting.

Work with individuals can be pursued in either field or residential settings. In instances of intensive or extensive difficulty, work in a residential setting would probably be the setting of choice. Individual work in a field setting probably infers that the client has sufficient 'going for him' (including the worker's help) to sustain a viable place in the community.

(2) FAMILY GROUP WORK

This would be the method of choice in those family situations where the difficulties stem not so much from the 'pathology' of an individual family member, but from a 'pathological' interaction between members of the family. This can be the case even where the symptomology of the pathological interaction is being carried by one member of the family.

(3) GROUPWORK

This has four particular strengths:

(i) A potential richness of activity-based experience, providing opportunities for creativity, development and compensation in situations where people are denied or starved of them.

(ii) A more total situation, akin to 'real-life' situations, providing opportunities for not only more comprehensive diagnosis but also for more immediate feedback and analysis of events and their origins. A group situation might, therefore, be of value where dysfunctional defences are extensively used.

(iii) It provides an association with peers. This may be of particular value where there are certain types of difficulty around authority—i.e. where the authority of the peer group is more acceptable than that of authority of figures. Peer association may also be of help where isolation is a factor and the support of others 'in the same boat' is of particular potential. The peer situation also provides the opportunity for giving to others with all the value of this in terms of self-esteem and the need to be needed.

(iv) It offers a diversity of relationships, especially as regards role, intimacy/distance and choice of personnel. Groupwork would have much to offer, then when role-diversity is denied elsewhere or where a range of roles need to be rehearsed for transfer out elsewhere. Intimacy/distance can give the group member some choice of what is comfortable for him as a sort of 'launchpad' into the sort of relationships which he finds less easy; while the diversity of personnel gives him more chance of finding another person or subgroup with whom he finds himself in sympathy.

Groupwork, too, can be practised in a community or residential setting.

(4) COMMUNITY WORK

The strength of community work is in circumstances which call for collective action on a commonly felt and identified difficulty (whether the commonality arises from a difficulty of the group or the difficulty of another group about which there is a shared concern) giving more hope of success through the pooled resources (whether of thinking, feeling, acting, influence or material) than individual actors would ever achieve.

(5) RESIDENTIAL WORK

This provides the opportunity to create a designed environment in human and/or material terms to meet need or provide opportunity. There are endemic tensions of scale in terms of what is economically viable and the needs to be met or opportunities to be provided (and we have discovered to our cost that some residential provision is far too large in scale); but there is an inevitable upward limit to scale which precludes the use of residential work as the means of resolving a range of community problems—other than through key figures or small groups as I have earlier suggested. As a method it may well be at its best in dealing with certain individual or small group problems (the intensive or extensive)—or specially selected larger groups.

Residential situations may well have some characteristics of family, group or community and call for modes of work appropriate to these as well as provide for work with individuals.

(B) Partialisation

In looking at professional judgment we have seen some of the elements of partialisation at work—saliency, urgency and accessibility. But however valid the unitary approach may be, the implications of it in terms of the knowledge and skills required take it beyond the possibility of the entirety being practised by any individual worker—quite apart from any limitations derived from individual interests or aptitudes; or such practical limitations as the length of training which would be required for it. Nor do the protagonists of the unitary approach suggest that it is more than a framework out of which subsequent specialisation (that is, partialisation) springs. The framework of subsequent specialisation is still a matter of debate: method, field, client group, agency or patch (area) are among the bases suggested.

Social Services Departments here, after an uncertain excursion into genericism, seem to be developing specialisms again, but with no clear overall trend. A number have differentiated between short and long term work; but examples of specialisation by method, client group, field or setting (for example hospital based social work) still exist widely. Probation (at least in England and Wales) has a delineated field and is extending its range of methods but at the same time seems to be seeing some degree of specialisation in particular appointments—for example court liaison officers, community service officers, etc. It is also having to grapple with issues raised by settings: for example how specialised is work within prisons, Borstals, detention centres and after care hostels.

(C) Organisation

Even if the unitary approach were within the compass of the individual in terms of knowledge and skill, I still feel it would throw up enormous problems in terms of how that individual worker organised himself, allocated his time, determined his priorities, etc. The sheer practicalities would oblige him to revert to partialisation in some form, I feel sure.

Similar problems would also confront the agency. Such an enormous brief, with the ensuing issues of organisation, administration, recruitment, deployment, priorities, funding, communication, and co-ordination would be overwhelming. The exciting thing about Social Services Departments is that they have the potentiality to implement the unitary social work approach; but they have already thrown up the organisational problems and endemic tensions involved (quite apart from the question of resources) and have, in effect, partialised their brief in some form (for example gone no further than their statutory obligations).

I would like to try to bring together what I have been saying in the latter part of this chapter through the use of a hypothetical case illustration.

Bill Watson is aged 48 and a West Indian by origin though he emigrated to this country twenty-five years ago. He was referred to a social worker after a rather half-hearted suicide attempt, having been quite depressed for some time. Bill attributed his depression to frustration. He had never achieved what he felt he was capable of. All his working life he had been a semi-skilled labourer, never getting any further. He was bored with his job, but more importantly he felt his lack of fulfilment was steadily eroding his self-esteem and he had become increasingly guilty about not being able to provide more adequately for his family. He desperately wanted job advancement.

Using the earlier framework, some of the possible causes for his frustrated ambitions, singly or in combination, might look as shown in table on p. 54.

In practice, of course, the social worker would gather further information which would very probably close off some of these options; but keeping all the options open for the moment, there are a number of possible ways of intervening. He could work with Bill individually to try to restore his self-confidence; get him on to a training course; try to improve his capacity—or help him to come to terms with his lack of it and/or find other compensating outlets for him. He might work with Bill and his wife to try to ameliorate the dominance difficulty, however this arose.

It might be possible to intervene with the work group to try to clear the blocks to Bill's acceptability as foreman and so enable his employer to appoint him to the vacancy; or to bring to the work-

| Level | Block | | |
	Psychological	Social educational	Resource
Individual/ family	Endemic lack of self-confidence. Dominant wife: too threatened by his promotion to allow of it	Has not the knowledge/training required for promotion	Does not have the capacity for promotion (but does not recognise this)
Group	Foreman post vacant but work group torn over Bill's acceptability, so employer has not appointed yet	Agreed working practices mean a chargehand vacancy should exist—but Bill and workgroup unaware of this	Small employer (who acts as foreman himself) with no grading differentials viable for other employees
Community	Fierce group solidarity which sees foremen as capitalist lackeys. Colour prejudice	No courses for re-training available—need unidentified	Need for training for promotion recognised but no courses set up—lack of funds: or, courses available but no funds available locally to second local residents

group's notice through Bill the fact that they should have a charge-hand appointment and support them in their subsequent approaches to their employer over this. Since a social worker is not a qualified business consultant, it would hardly be possible for him to advise Bill's employer directly regarding the possible expansion of his business to allow of staffing differentials; but he could possibly discuss this with the employer and put him in contact with a consultant. Expansion may not be a feasibility, however, and the alternative might be, practically, to help Bill find another job with a larger employer where promotion opportunities existed.

Intervention at the community level might involve efforts to change attitudes: to help people to see that becoming a foreman does not necessarily change one's relationship with the economic system—foreman are not capitalists but still workers in terms of the class struggle; or to combat racialism. In community social educational terms it might mean uncovering the re-training need and getting the case for provision accepted and implemented by the appropriate authority. Or in resource terms, it might mean trying to get more resources altogether for the community so that the 'extra' could be spent on re-training facilities—or getting existing priorities changed so that resources were switched from less urgent areas to that of training—at the national or local level.

If more than one causation existed, simultaneous interventions would be required: or intervention might need to be sequential, since until say, the marital interaction 'cause' was worked through, there might be little point in trying to get Bill a job with a larger employer which involved promotion. Either his wife would see that he soon gave it up, or the marital tension would rise to the point where it became a major problem in itself. As things stand, that problem seems to be quiescent (a factor which might make it more difficult to work upon).

The worker's agency may see itself in the sphere of work with the individual and family, but not in the sphere of race relations. Thus the worker would have a remit to intervene with Bill or with Bill and his wife. If the problem were racialist, this would involve him in referring the matter elsewhere, though given that social attitudes in this sphere are hard to change and take time, the original worker might still have a brief, if only that of supporting Bill during this period and endeavouring to ameliorate his distress.

Whatever his agency remit, the worker himself may see his skill as in work with the individual or family and call in another worker to tackle the endemic racialism—whether that worker is employed by his own agency or another. To restore Bill's confidence (if this is the difficulty) could involve working with him as an individual to begin with, but he still might need a subsequent group experience to confirm the work carried out on an individual basis; or the worker may find that the work required on the marital interaction (if the problems lie here) could be done much more effectively in a group composed of couples with similar problems rather than on their own as a 'threesome'.

All through, the worker will be exercising his judgment, determining where the difficulties lie and how effectively to intervene; but bearing in mind his agency remit and his identification of his own capabilities. In effect, he will be partialising.

My choice in this book has been to partialise by method—casework—intervention with, and on behalf of individuals and families; recognising that this partialisation remains typical of many social work organisations, or the workers within them. For other methods and for work with particular client groups, I can only refer the student elsewhere. I think what I have written here about casework is generic in the sense that it cuts across the boundaries of agency, field and setting, to focus on what is common to all casework. I hope that I have established casework within the context of the unitary approach—in thought, if not always in language—and filled out the detail of work with individuals and families that a unitary text can never quite accomplish, to enable the practitioner to intervene effectively in this particular way—and identify where it is appropriate to do so.

References

1. Mary Richmond, *Social Diagnosis* (Russell Sage), 1917.
2. Report of the Care of Children Committee, C.M.N.D. 6922, 1946.
3. Russell Barton, *Institutional Neurosis* (John Wright), 1959.
4. Erving Goffman, *Asylums* (Pelican), 1968.
5. Peter Townsend, *The Last Refuge* (Routledge & Kegan Paul), 1962.
6. Terence and Pauline Morris, *Pentonville: a Sociological Study of an English Prison* (Routledge & Kegan Paul), 1963.
7. *Caring for People*: report of the Committee of Enquiry set up by the National Council of Social Service, Chairman Lady Williams C.B.E. (George Allen & Unwin), 1967.
8. Ruth E. Smalley, *Theory for Social Work Practice* (Columbia University Press), 1974.
9. Harriett Bartlett, *The Common Base of Social Work Practice* (National Association of Social Workers), 1970.
10. Allen Pincus and Anne Minaham, *Social Work Practice: Model and Method* (Peacock Publications), 1973.
11. Howard Goldstein, *Social Work Practice: a Unitary Approach* (University of South Carolina Press), 1973.
12. James K. Whittaker, *Social Treatment: an Approach to Interpersonal Helping* (Aldine), 1974.
13. Ruth R. Middleman and Gale Goldberg, *Social Service Delivery: a Structural Approach* (Columbia University Press), 1974.
14. Max Siporin, *Introduction to Social Work Practice* (Collier/Macmillan), 1975.

Further Reading

With a substantial list of books referred to above, most of which a student ought to read to familiarise himself with current social work thinking, it may well seem hard to suggest more—especially as some of the books referred to are quite solid reading. Some of the following suggestions, however, could represent some short cuts to an adequate understanding.

For the overview of social work development, there are *From Charity to Social Work in England and the United States* by Kathleen Woodroofe (University of Toronto Press) and *The Expansion of Social Work in Great Britain* by Phillip Seed (Routledge & Kegan Paul); but there are also excellent chapters on the history of social work in the books by Smalley, Bartlett and Goldstein referred to above; in Gisela Konopka's *Social Group Work: a Helping Process* (Prentice Hall); and in the opening chapters of *Problems and Issues in Social Casework* by Scott Briar and Henry Miller (Columbia University Press). Within the residential field part of Julius Carlebach's *Caring for Children in Trouble* (Routledge & Kegan Paul) is a review of developments in what used to be the approved schools system. For those students who would like to explore the varied approaches of the different schools of social casework *Theories of Social Casework* by Robert R. Roberts and Robert Nee (University of Chicago Press) is an excellent source.

For those students who would prefer the 'standard texts' route to comprehending the main social work methods, my suggestions would be:

For casework:
> Florence Hollis, *Social Casework: a Psychosocial Therapy* (Random House).
> Helen H. Pearlman, *Social Casework: a Problem-solving Process* (University of Chicago Press).
> Noel Timms, *Social Casework: Principles and Practice* (Routledge & Kegan Paul).

For groupwork:
> Gisela Konopka, op. cit.
> Helen Northen, *Social Work with Groups* (Columbia University Press).

For community work:
> George W. Goetschius, *Working with Community Groups* (Routledge & Kegan Paul).
> Murray G. Ross and B. W. Lappin, *Community Organisation Theory, Principles and Practice* (Harper).
> George F. Thomason, *The Professional Approach to Community Work* (Sands).
> T. R. and M. Batten, *The Non-Directive Approach in Group and Community Work* (Oxford University Press).

For residential care:
> Richard Balbernie, *Residential Work with Children* (Pergamon).
> Christopher Beedell, *Residential Life with Children* (Routledge & Kegan Paul).
> E. J. Miller and G. V. Gwynne, *A Life Apart* (Lippincott).

For short cuts, there is excellent material in:

For casework:
> Helen H. Perlman *et al.*, *Casework within Social Work* (Newcastle University).

For groupwork:
> Lorna Walker, *Groupwork with the Inarticulate* (F.S.U.).

For community work:
> E. Roche, 'Guide to Community Work in Seven Stages', *Social Work Today*, Feb. 1971.
> G. Popplestone, 'The ideology of professional community workers', *British Journal of Social Work*, April 1971.
> *Current Issues in Community Work*, Gulbenkian Foundation Community Work Group (Routledge & Kegan Paul).

For residential care:
> Marilyn J. Miller, 'Residential care', *Social Work Today*, 25.7.74.
> *Care in a Planned Environment* (H.M.S.O.).

There is barely as yet a short cut to grasping unitary approaches to social work other than through the texts themselves; but I would recommend Anne Vickery's article 'A systems approach to social work intervention—its uses for work with individuals and families' in the *British Journal of Social Work*, Winter 1974; Ron Baker's 'Toward generic social work practice—a review and some innovations' in *The British Journal of Social Work*, Summer, 1975; Though hardly a short cut, John Haines's book *Skills and Methods in Social Work* (Constable), is an excellent, straightforward introduction. 'Social work and system theory' by Anthony Forder in *The British Journal of Social Work*, Spring, 1976; and 'Some implications of an integrated model of social work for theory and practice' by Roger Evans in *The British Journal of Social Work*, Summer, 1976. Unified practice via the role concept is succinctly presented by Ron Baker in his article 'The multi-role practitioner in the generic orientation to social work practice' in *The British Journal of Social Work*, Autumn, 1976.

Discussion

Most students thoroughly enjoy examining the historical development of social work and the emerging ideas and concepts that have been thrown up. It seems to help establish a framework for them: with roots in the past; a sense of process which gives them a sense of direction for the future as well as a concept of what is now; a sense of relief as they recognise that the issues that trouble them have troubled and still trouble, the 'experts' in the profession; but discussion provides a place into which they can fit their practice and their professional identity.

Not that discussion is always easy-going: it presents challenges in respect of personality, ideology, capacity and experience. The sorts of difficulty which emerge may be grouped as:

(1) Comprehension. This may occur because of a student's limited ability to conceptualise anyway; or may be connected with a student's limited (even non-existent) pre-course experience—in other words, he is wrestling with abstracts which may have little tangible

meaning for him. The former will remain a problem at whatever stage in the course this area is tackled; the latter is more of a difficulty if the topic is tackled early on. Yet it is so basic to subsequent teaching and learning, it seems to demand early consideration. I typically tackle it early but try to reassure those students having difficulty with comprehension for experience reasons that it will 'gell' in time; reinforcing this process by:

(a) Constantly referring back to this material in subsequent teaching and
(b) Backing discussion with case studies (the Bill Wright case in Goldstein's book is an excellent example) or films such as 'Kes'.

(2) Application. A student may, in effect, be saying 'Yes, I understand; but the theory is so remote from the actuality of my experience that it is irrelevant. Please give me something I can use.' The response would be to take some of the student's own cases and tease out of them the implications in terms of unitary theories—in effect, to stretch the student's imaginative thinking—but at the same time to recognise the validity of his difficulty. Unitary approaches (language difficulties apart) are inevitably pitched at a high level of abstraction which needs some hard graft to turn into working practicalities. One of the risks with some students who enthuse about unitary approaches is that they will use them as vehicles for endless abstract talk to avoid actually doing anything with them.

(3) Ideology. Most students come on to a course with some sort of an image of social work and of themselves as practitioners. A unitary approach is likely to challenge that image to some degree, whether the image is conservative or radical. Unitary theories in themselves are neither one nor the other. I have heard Pincus and Minaham accused of conservatism and Middleman and Goldberg accused of radicalism when there is evidence enough in each text to support the opposite view. Unitary approaches, *per se*, do not resolve that tension. But they are approaches which stretch thinking and imagination and as such will oblige students, teachers and agencies to re-appraise their existing conceptions of practice and their self image as practitioners.

(4) Personality. This is sometimes hard to separate from ideology

since there are such close links between the two; but the particular aspect I have in mind here is the effect of unitary approaches on the student's feelings about his competence. The implications in terms of professional responsibility, knowledge, skill and organisation could be overwhelming and lead to despair. The logic of the unitary approach could be interpreted as taking on the whole world's burdens so ill-equipped in knowledge and skill as to be beyond the possibility of any success. It would seem to me vital to couple teaching about the conceptual validity of such approaches with a clear indication that expectations in terms of implementation in practice need to be partialised too—whether the expectations derive from students' expectations of themselves, their teachers' expectations of them (or what the students think these are), or their agencies' expectations of them (as students or as subsequent employees). We need to convince students that the expectations are manageable; that they can demonstrate their competence. To rob students of their feeling that they have competence is one of the surest ways of rendering them incompetent.

PART II

The Interview

CHAPTER III

Client Needs and the Worker's Response

The interview is the caseworker's basic tool. As a tool, though, it has certain limitations, mainly because it is primarily a verbal exchange (though from this exchange certain practical activities may ensue for caseworker and/or client) or it is via the verbal exchange that the relationship develops which becomes the medium of the problem-resolving process (even though this may be reinforced by ensuing practical activity). There may well be limits to the use some clients can make of this mainly verbal exchange—demonstrably so in the case of young children who have not yet developed the verbal skills or the mental concepts which are typically a pre-requisite for an ability to use the interview as an adequate means of communication. Here one may need that means of communication that have been developed in Child Guidance Clinics; for example, through the use of play-therapy.

Moreover, the typical interview situation where client and worker draw up chairs and settle down to talk may be inordinately threatening and more or less guarantee at best a stilted exchange; or be so outside a client's range of experience that they do not know how to use it. Here it may be far more profitable for the 'interview' to emerge in the interstices of an activity—whether this is over the washing up or at bedtimes in a children's home, or in the activity of a youth club or psychiatric social club; or over a drink in the local pub. For other clients activity itself may be the best means of communication they can utilise—and here, occupational therapists may have much to teach us in their use of craftwork, dance drama and so on. Groups that use touch and movement, however 'way out' they may seem to those of us steeped in the 'orthodox', have demonstrated the value of non-verbal methods of communication that may be of the most use to some clients.

Communication is an extremely complex matter. Social work students will, no doubt, be studying it elsewhere in their syllabus and utilising this knowledge in considering their interaction with clients. (See suggestions for further reading.) This dimension is endemic to everything in this text, though since there are limits to what may be contained between two covers, regrettably it cannot be explored in depth here. But though I now go on to focus on the interview in a 'traditional' way—and justifiably, for the interview is of tremendous value—I feel strongly that caseworkers should not utilise it in the automatic, unthinking way we may have done in the past. We have the professional responsibility to develop the skill of identifying where we can use the somewhat formalised interview which is implicit in many of the standard texts on casework; where we can still 'interview' but in a much more flexible way (for example, by taking a child out for a meal, or a trip to the park and utilising the opportunities such occasions may give us for a purposeful one-to-one communication); or where we need another way of communicating, entirely or in part. This third choice may involve caseworkers in adding to their 'interventive repertoire' with the help of those other disciplines which have developed such other means. There is, however, a limit to the knowledge and skill which any one profession can develop and narrower limits to those any one worker can make his own; while constraints of agency policy, time, premises and equipment may impose practical limitations. These limitations, however, do not absolve caseworkers from the responsibility of choice of means of communication on the basis of the client's needs and his capacity, and if even an adapted interview means cannot be used, then to make an appropriate referral and work as a member of a team with those who do have the communication means the client can use. One would hope that other workers would similarly refer and work with caseworkers where their particular interviewing skills were needed.

Whatever the means of communication used, however, I feel there are a range of basic needs which clients' bring which require a range of responses if those needs are to be adequately met. The needs may be identified as:

(1) to be treated as an individual;

(2) to be listened to;
(3) to be accepted;
(4) to talk in confidence;
(5) to be understood;
(6) to be helped.

I examine here these needs and the required responses in the context of the interview situation, but these needs and responses are common to all social work methods or means of professional communication. They are at the core of generic social work practice.

(1) To be Treated as an Individual

Social workers deal with their clients as individuals for three main reasons:

(a) Because they are individuals. This individuality applies in group and community work as well as casework, since no two groups or two communities are the same. In casework, this individuality has a variety of bases:

(i) Clients are physically unique; in body shape (tall, short, fat, thin, curvaceous, dumpy, handicapped, able-bodied); facial appearance (pretty, handsome, plain, disfigured); physical aptitude (manual dexterity or clumsiness, good at sports or a 'duffer' at them); intellectual capacity (bright, dull, particular aptitudes or blocks); metabolism (energetic, lethargic, hyperthyroid, diabetic). I am not suggesting that physical factors are the sole determinants in the examples I give: making full use of one's intellectual capacity, for instance, involves emotional and social factors, too. But physical factors may be of profound significance for the individual in terms of their body-image and how this relates to self-esteem; to the opportunities which are or are not available to them; and to their social relationships, in the sense that physical attributes may produce reactions in others which impinge deeply on the individual. This is demonstrably so in the case of the physically handicapped or facially disfigured; but even the most attractive girl, if she is unusually tall, may find her relations with the opposite sex rather an embarrassment, given our present conventions about the relative heights of sex-pairs.

(ii) They are emotionally unique; they have experienced a unique combination of relationships with others in the past and are currently experiencing relationships which are peculiar to them, with all this implies for the sort of people they are and the way they feel about and react to their particular situation.

(iii) Socially they occupy a position at the hub of a unique network of roles and relationships, with their family, neighbourhood, school or workplace, leisure activities.

(iv) They may be traumatically unique in the sense that no-one else has experienced quite the same combination of events (illnesses, accidents, deaths of members of the family or friends, moving home, redundancy, etc.) that they have.

(v) They are problematically unique in that while on the face of it their problem has much in common with other people's problems, no-one else experiences quite as they do.

(vi) Existentially they are unique in that they feel themselves to be individuals.

To stress this individuality it is not to deny that at times we all wish to be identified with a group. To be an individual all the time is an isolating, lonely experience and implies a rather frightening responsibility for ourselves. Perhaps the skill of the caseworker is in identifying where the client would rather be regarded as an individual and where as a member of a group—though assisting him might entail on occasions helping him to separate his identity from a group and on others helping him to identify himself with a group.

Nor is stressing individuality denying what psychology and sociology has to tell us about the way people behave: it is knowledge no social worker can dispense with. But this inevitably rather generalised knowledge needs to be particularised, helping us to understand *this* individual and *his* circumstances:

(b) Because it is part of a social worker's function to individualise;

Modern technological society has many facets, but there are three aspects which bear upon this individualising function.

(i) Modern society is typified by large scale organisations—not only in industry and commerce but in education increasingly, health, government, and even recreation. Such organisations employ specialised staff, are often bureaucratically structured, and tend to engage both with their own staff and with their consumers in highly particularised ways, on the basis of a pre-determined categorisation, and involving a plethora of form-filling. Both staff and consumers may end up by feeling partialised, dehumanised, bewildered, humiliated, frustrated and angry when there is no one person they can 'get at' in their attempts to find satisfactory remedies. They have been obliged to band together in other organisations such as trade unions, parent teacher associations, pressure groups and consumer associations in attempts to remedy feelings of loss of power, dignity, and generally being 'taken notice of'. But even these groups are sometimes large and only concern themselves with specialised aspects. To be able to feel a whole individual may still be at a premium.

(ii) Modern society is highly complex, involving us as individuals in engaging with a large number of people, in a wide variety of social systems, demanding both a degree of technical expertise and a wide range of social skills. We are caught up in complex network of expectations, and our failure to meet such expectations may have serious implications. We are bus passengers, income tax payers, vacuum cleaner owners, football pool coupon fillers; we are customers of banks, building societies, insurance companies, TV hirers, washing machine repairers, holiday camp proprietors, etc.

(iii) Yet at the same time, modern society offers us both greater opportunities and a wider range of choices than ever before. These can be enormously enriching, yet produce tensions and demands too. Failure may be felt more acutely, a knowledge of opportunities make us more restless, choices (accentuated by seductive advertising) harder to make.

In this situation, the individualising function of social workers may be seen as in (i) above:

making clients aware of what services exist, whether in terms of meeting need or providing opportunity. It means discussing these services, what they can offer and on what terms, with clients and assisting them to make a sufficiently realistic choice of what 'fits' them in terms of what they want and/or need. It means assisting them where this is necessary and possible, in effectively engaging with such services or organisations, whether their objective is to put their views, obtain some redress, or fill up the forms that will make

services available to them. It also implies social work intervention
with such bodies (again, where this is necessary and possible) to
help them to tailor their responses to this client in a way which
may more effectively meet need or create opportunity. Such intervention may concern itself with establishing effective communication
between the two, or restoring it where it has broken down; it may
mean making suggestions about the forms they use; it may involve
asking them to modify certain aspects of their regulations or procedures; or perhaps to take a more radical look at the whole way
they function. Some of these interventions it may not be appropriate
for an individual worker to make (or effective); it may mean involving
the agency, a professional group, a group of which social workers
are only a part, even a group of which they are not a part, but
try to influence. Such activity will be very much the concern of group
and community workers as well as caseworkers—perhaps more so:
but whoever does it and however it is done, it is part of this individualising function. Individualising may occasionally involve individualising the organisation to the client. Now and again clients are
unreasonable in their expectations and it could be part of our function to help clients come to terms with what is a realistic expectation
if they are to engage with and benefit from the organisation concerned.

As regards (ii) I feel we express our individualising function by
empathising with client's feelings engendered by their engagement
with social complexities; offering them practical help where this is
needed and acceptable (whether it is help we can give ourselves or
specialist help we can involve via say, a referral); offering our support
and encouragement when, with this, a client can successfully manage
for himself; or suggesting and discussing other ways of tackling situations where ways have broken down or the clients plans seem likely
to fail. We may need to assist our client to develop new technical
and social skills, and again, we may be able to undertake some of
this development ourselves, or involve others.

In (iii) social workers have the obligation again to make clients
aware of opportunities and choices they might not have otherwise
known about or considered, discuss and assist them to clarify the
implications, support them and assist them where necessary in carry-

ing through their choices where we can, and bear with them their feelings of disappointment and anger when, for perhaps a range of reasons, they decide to forgo certain opportunities or make choices which for them are not altogether their ideal. When clients have failed, we share their feelings about this, support and encourage them to try again, or try other ways.

(c) Because we cannot do our job without it.

Individualising is crucial to:

(i) The relationship. Individualising is tangibly demonstrated through our concern, empathy, understanding and courtesy. It is also demonstrated by making it clear to the client in interview that this time (however short it may have to be on occasions) is *his* time; doing our utmost to fend off interruptions and distractions. During this time, we give him our total attention: it diminishes that individual if we use his time to manicure our nails, try to write a report on another case at the same time, or stare out of the window. The relationship is vital to many of our objectives (the development of insight, for example); but even in instances where it may not seem so vital—where our service is restricted to material aid or referral, perhaps—the relationship we have with the individual client during our transactions will have a profound influence upon how he feels about having approached us in the first place, how he feels about using whatever we have provided, how he feels about approaching us on any future occasion, and the comments he will make to others about his experience of us.

(ii) To the diagnosis. If we are not individualising, then to some extent we must be either generalising or categorising. Should this occur, the client may well feel diminished to the point where he breaks off the contact. Even if he remains in contact (perhaps because he needs us badly) he may well be reluctant to communicate all the data we need to make an effective diagnosis; or our diagnosis may reflect our categorisations or generalisations. Either way, with what amounts to a mis-diagnosis, our treatment plans and goals are likely to be mis-directed, our efforts largely wasted, and the client's needs remain unsatisfied.

(iii) To the treatment itself. To be treated as an individual can do a great deal for a client's self image, his self-confidence, his motivation and therefore his chances of experiencing success. At least with us clients ought to be able to feel *whole* people.

Mr. and Mrs. Harrison had a spastic daughter Joan, aged five, their only child. Her spasticity was the result of a birth injury, which left her partially sighted, slightly deaf and with a degree of physical handicap. The question had also been raised of some mental retardation. The referral to the social worker was precipitated by the need to decide which would be the most appropriate form of schooling for Joan.

Both the Harrisons were initially extremely hostile to the social worker and went on at great length about the treatment they had received being sent from one specialist to another, each of whom was only concerned with one aspect of Joan's disabilities and who frequently offered advice about management which was contradictory to advice they had received from another specialist. They expressed strong feelings about the delays, the waiting, the bureaucratic procedures and what they considered the lack of caring of the people they had been involved with, and anticipated similar sorts of encounters now with educationists. They felt like ciphers not people. In the referral, reference was made to their being 'difficult'.

The social worker offered her sympathy, understanding and concern and was able eventually to arrange a case conference of those involved with Joan's physical disabilities and the Education Department. This took time, and the social worker had to sustain periodic outbursts of anger and frustration from the Harrisons. At the conference her physical treatment was co-ordinated through the General Practitioner and from the educational point of view, a period of assessment was agreed at the special care unit of a primary school catering for mentally handicapped children, where specialised teaching skills would be available.

During her contact, the social worker was able to explore with Mr. and Mrs. Harrison some of the guilt feelings they had about the birth of a handicapped child and the sense of stigma and social isolation that ensued, their feelings of disappointed expectations about Joan's abilities, their anxieties for her future, their problems of management of Joan, and their worries about whether they should have any more children—an opportunity they had not been given previously.

At the end of the contact, while the Harrison's problems had not fundamentally changed, they felt much more confident, capable and relaxed about them and knew that should difficulties occur later, there was someone to whom they could turn who knew them, recognised them and treated them and their daughter as individuals.

Individualising is not just a matter for the social worker, but also for the agency. A client will not feel respected as an individual if the waiting area is cold and dingy, the receptionist abrupt, and interviewing rooms are cramped and noisy.

Individualising is also an on-going process, and while it is probably most significant at the point of the initial contact with agency and worker, should we fail to individualise the changes during the contact (whether in the client, his situation, or in the relationship) and continue to deal with him as he was at the beginning of our contact, then once again we are risking mis-diagnosis and mis-treatment.

Finally, if we regard clients as individuals, it must be acknowledged that social workers are, too. We have our own prejudices (both positive and negative); particular abilities and disabilities; areas of knowledge and gaps; particular experience and lack of it. Training will help us to recognise prejudices, and lay them aside in our dealings with clients where they do not help; abilities can be developed, disabilities overcome; knowledge extended and gaps filled; experience enriched and new experiences undergone. But we will probably never be able to help all clients in all situations with equal competence. There are two implications here: for the agency, to utilise what we have to the full (at least as far as the workload of the agency permits)—i.e. a deployment policy which offers the chance of the best service to the client and the greatest satisfaction to the worker. For the worker, it means recognising his limitations. It is a strength, not a weakness, to ask others to assist those clients we acknowledge we cannot effectively assist.

(2) To be Listened to

Clients have something to convey to us, and do so both verbally and non-verbally.

(a) Verbally they may be

Talkative: pouring out material, almost oblivious of the worker; overwhelmed by their problems, their reactions, their reactions to being helped, or their reactions to having help thrust upon them by various external pressures: demanding of solutions—or for the worker to get out. They may feel helpless, angry, or bitter; may bluster or deny; may blame or denigrate themselves—or others.

Mrs. Charles was a married woman of 58, and suffered from an agitated depression. She poured out her feelings of despair, her fears that she would never be cured, and her anger that the doctors did not seem to be able to help, to anyone who would listen. Ultimately she so alienated her friends, neighbours and even her family that the social worker was about the only person who would listen to her. Interview after interview she would almost overwhelm him with a torrent of talk and a flurry of gestures, wringing her hands and pacing up and down.

Tentative: knowing what they want to say, but groping for the means to express themselves; wondering what sort of reactions they will get from the worker; or afraid to say too much in case the strength of feeling involved overwhelmed them, making matters worse or making themselves appear foolish.

Mrs. Phillips was a young married woman who was referred to the Mental Health service by her General Practitioner as suffering from a puerpural depression following the birth of her first child. For the first two or three interviews she chatted to the social worker about day-to-day matters, but then began to reveal certain difficulties in the relationship with her husband. A number of interviews later she suddenly revealed that she had been embezzling money from her previous employer (giving the proceeds in small amounts to her mother and sisters). On the birth of her child she had been forced to give up her job, no longer had the opportunity to cover up her embezzling, and now faced the prospect of being found out, prosecuted, and everyone getting to know about it. This prospect had overwhelmed her and was the reason for her depression.

Troubled: aware of discomfort, but not really aware of why; coming with some sort of presenting problem shaped to give some tangible form to the discomfort and express it somehow.

Mrs. Higson applied to a voluntary casework agency for a grant for shoes for her children. She was a quiet, shy, soft-spoken woman who clearly cared for her family, and managed competently on an admittedly tight budget. A grant was obtained for her through a Forces charity on the strength of her earlier service with the W.R.A.F. but all through this contact the social worker felt there was more to this application than just financial stringency. Mrs. Higson was gently offered the opportunity to talk about other matters but did not respond. The social worker felt this was not due to real reticence on Mrs. Higson's part but basically because although she was experiencing discomfort she was unable to identify it or express it other than in a tangible financial form. The Social worker was left hoping that the contact and the experience of being offered sympathy, concern, understanding and some practical help would have been enough to meet adequately the underlying discomfort.

Taciturn: denying any problem, or admitting only part of it; willing to be helped (if at all) only on his own terms.

Mr. Francis was approached by the social worker after his wife had contacted the agency in some distress regarding the marriage relationship which she felt left her deeply unsatisfied. Mr. Francis was prepared to acknowledge that there were one or two difficulties, but assured the social worker that since he was expecting a legacy under his grandfather's will shortly, he felt that a larger house, a car, a holiday, some more household equipment, etc. that he would soon be in a position to provide, would quickly resolve any difficulties there were.

Whatever their type of verbal communication (and these are only typologies), all our clients will be expressing two aspects of their situation: the objective (factual) and the subjective (feeling) elements, both of which are equally real, inseparable, and both of which need to be dealt with if the totality of their expression is to find an adequate response from us. There are times when the 'facts' are unalterable and to deal with the feelings is the only way we have to attempt to restore some sort of equilibrium with a sufficiency of satisfaction for the client.

(b) Non-verbal communication may be:

A matter of the tone behind the words, of dress, make-up or

grooming, posture, facial expression, gesture, or by indicators of emotive material such as foot-tapping, avoiding eye-contact, finger twisting, hair twisting, etc. We absorb an enormous amount in non-verbal
ways—largely without recognising it or acknowledging the part it
plays in our responses. It is important we should recognise where
non-verbal communication fits or is at variance with what is said.

It is equally important that we should recognise what we are communicating to clients by our own non-verbal factors.

Listening is active, not passive. The activities of listening may be
grouped as:

(a) Helping the client to communicate.

Ease of communication for the client will to some extent depend
on his physical comfort (type of chair, temperature, etc.), but his
emotional comfort will be crucial. Some of the elements of emotional
comfort are:

(i) Time—for the client's use.

(ii) A climate engendered by the social worker's attitude which
is warm, accepting, concerned and attentive.

(iii) A focus on the client—not on ourselves. It is so easy to obtrude
ourselves in a variety of ways: questions to satisfy our own pre-occupations; explanations and interpretations to demonstrate how clever
we are; false re-assurances because we are made anxious; advice
based on what we would do if we were in their place—all of which
either block, control, or disarm the client and what he wants to
communicate.

(iv) Skill to meet particular communication needs. Using the typologies above some of the skills might be: with the talkative client,
not to be overwhelmed by the volume or content of what he is
saying; not to be irritated by his self-preoccupation; not to meet
his reactions with unhelpful reactions of our own (anger with anger,
for example); not allow ourselves to be forced on to the defensive
by his clamour for his solutions. With the tentative to take special
pains to establish the climate, spell out our functions and the ways
we might be able to assist, deal with their 'kite flying' in a way
which will encourage further revelation. With the troubled, our pacing will be important not to rush them too early since this might
heighten any anxiety, to work our way out slowly from the tangible

problem they present, and eventually helping them to clarify just what it is that is troubling them. With the taciturn there may be nothing we can do, but at least we can handle our contact with them in a way which tries to leave them thinking well of us with the chance that any contacts in the future may be more productive. If they let us do something, undertake this with care, to keep open the possibility that slowly and gently we may develop a relationship with them that enables them to show us more of themselves and their problems.

(b) Hearing what is communicated.

This demands concentration and the development of the so-called 'third ear'. An enormous amount can be conveyed by the briefest communication—a few words, a tone of voice, a grimace, a shrug; and we need to comprehend the totality of this communication. There is a distinction, though, between comprehending and taking matters up. Much we may never take up: it may contribute to our diagnosis but when we come to formulate objectives the material either becomes largely irrelevant, or becomes not possible to use. A client may communicate to us (if only unwittingly) that he is a rigid personality. This may have nothing to do with the problems for which he asks our help, which may be quite practical. Even if his rigidity is related to his difficulties (for example, his relations with a teen-age daughter) we may decide that insight is not feasible as a solution to this problem, and for us to seek other solutions. What is communicated now, we may take up later rather than immediately, when the timing becomes more appropriate. The communication may relate to an underlying difficulty, but at this moment the client is in a state of crisis and immediate matters have to come first. It may take time before a client can face the significance of something they have said and to take it up at once may only make them bridle.

But of particular importance in 'hearing' significant communications may be:

(i) An association of ideas. Talking about a husband's death, a woman goes on to talk about her father's death.

(ii) Shifts in conversation. Having mentioned her brother's name a girl turns immediately to talking about her coming exams.

(iii) Opening and closing remarks. A client starts with 'A friend told me to come here, but I don't think you can help'; or just as they get to the door after a lengthy interview, a client says 'Oh, I forgot to tell you that ...'.

(iv) Recurrent references, whether specific ('He will go out every Friday.' 'I wish he would go out on another day of the week' 'I'd like to go out on Fridays.'); general ('I don't think its right that...' prefacing a number of topics); or of the 'merry-go-round' variety (always coming back to an incident of some months ago). At times, though, we can be grateful for recurrent references. Clients give us a second chance to pick up something significant we missed first time.

(v) Inconsistencies and gaps. A client relates an incident, later repeats it, but this time with a number of differences. A client tells his story, but at the end of it we realise he has confined it almost entirely to what other people did, and said hardly anything about his part in it.

(vi) Concealed meanings. Over reactions (whether to a comment of the worker's or indicated in an account of an occurrence); slips of the tongue (mixing up two people's names) or oblique references or hints.

(vii) 'Throw away' remarks. Asides or afterthoughts; half said, said casually, softly, quickly, sometimes with head turned away, or eyes lowered, or with a hand in front of mouth.

(viii) By the way solutions are presented. From 'I want...' or 'There's only one answer...', through 'Is it possible?' or 'What do you think ...?' to 'I don't like mentioning it, but ...'.

(c) Relating listening to purpose.

Without effective listening we will not understand the problem, the person it is happening to, the situation which surrounds him, his feelings about it all, or his feelings about us. In other words, we are again risking mis-diagnosis and mis-treatment.

In terms of treatment, we shall miss the opportunities afforded of relief through ventilating difficulties, the clarification which can occur through just the telling (and may be all that is needed to enable the client to deal with his situation himself), and the client may lose the benefit of a model of communication he could well use. We sometimes forget that talking about one's feelings with anyone is a rare occurrence—indeed for a few clients it may be the first time in their lives they have done so. If they can leave the interview appreciating how it has helped, they may risk the same thing with say, a marriage partner. If that partner responds, they may be well on the way to sorting out their tensions themselves.

In the relationship, 'cross purposes' communication—a product perhaps of not listening— is likely to lead to frustration and irritation, perhaps even a feeling that 'they don't care': effective communication should lead to a greater sharing and a consequent development of the relationship.

I have put the onus for listening on the worker, where it lies. But the client is also listening, and every social worker needs to be aware of what he is 'saying': to recognise where his communication is not helping, or to pick up where what he is 'saying' is being misunderstood. Words, gestures, clothes may mean one thing to us— they may mean very different things to our client.

Effective, purposeful communication does not always mean encouraging our clients to talk, however: it can, on occasions, mean limiting it. The grounds for limiting may be threefold:

(i) Agency function. There is little point in delving into matters which are really the concern of other agencies. If among a client's complaints is the way the road outside his house has been resurfaced, the technicalities of tarmacadam is the province of the Highways Department. Help him formulate his complaint to them, but the intricacies only they can deal with.

(ii) The worker's skill. If we have some evidence of a psychotic illness, for example, which is beyond our professional competence to treat, there is no point in encouraging a client to go on communicating his symptoms to us in the way a psychiatrist would be justified in doing in order to establish his diagnosis. Our task would be to work towards an appropriate referral.

(iii) The client's needs. There are a number of possible reasons where it would not be in the client's best interests to encourage communication—clearly so if in talking he is getting more and more anxious and there is a risk he may not 'hold together'. The client might be obtaining some masochistic or sexual gratification from his telling which it may not help to indulge. Emotionally charged material may sometimes be produced by an hysterical client as a kind of bait to manipulate the worker into a course of action detrimental to the client's interests in the long run. Demonstrably irrelevant material might properly be gently closed off and the client brought back to the point. When faced with making some decision, a client may go off at all kinds of tangents to postpone the decision-making. If a decision really ought to be faced and the client is capable, then to be gently brought back to it may well be the most helpful thing to do. If a client is bringing a great deal of material— more than you can both reasonably 'chew at' in one session, then it could be more profitable to suggest we leave certain matters to next time and focus on what we have. Occasionally one can sense that a client is bringing so much highly charged material early in your contact that you possibly risk a reaction setting in after the interview, when on reflection, the client will feel so embarrassed by what he has said that he will be reluctant to say anything more. Limiting communication is, in effect, helping the client to pace matters in a way which is more productive in the long run.

(3) The Need to be Accepted

Essentially, acceptance is taking the client as he is—not on condition that he is like we, or anyone else would like him to be; or even what he would like to be himself. Acceptance has the connotation of taking the 'bad' in the client; but I feel it is just as important to take the 'good' in him, otherwise we are not taking him as he is. It may be especially important to acknowledge his potential.

Acceptance sounds rather sloppy and passive, but it is both tough and positive; tough because it entails the laying aside aspects of our own reactions (both positive and negative) where these hamper our professional objectives; positive in that acceptance is essential to attaining these objectives, for three main reasons:

(a) It is essential for the relationship. Many of our clients have already been the object of various social control mechanisms—legal condemnation, ostracism, avoidance, belittling, nagging by others or by their own conscience. Demonstrably, these methods have failed or they would not be clients and it would therefore be absurd for us to try the same methods. We would get the same result, probably: failure. We offer the new approach of acceptance and it is out of this that a useable relationship grows. Acceptance involves not only the absence of the various forms of moralising, but the positive offering of empathy—feeling with the client, born of our concern, knowledge, and skill.

(b) It is essential for the diagnosis. Moralising will severely inhibit the client's expression of the negative elements of himself even if, as a result, he does not break off the contact. An elaborate game of the pretence of 'goodness' could develop, which will mean that the social worker will never get at the realities of the situation. Acceptance, therefore, is essential to our full understanding which, in turn is essential to our helping effectively.

(c) It is essential for important aspects of therapy. While our clients come to us for many different reasons, most of them (in their initial approach, at least) are likely to wonder what sort of reaction they are going to get from you and be sensitive and defensive. To moralise is very likely to add to their problems or strengthen their defences. Acceptance demonstrates that with us, at any rate, their defences are unnecessary, while it begins the process of dealing with their problems. There can be a release of psychic energy, previously locked up in defences, but now available for tackling the difficulties; there can be a rise in self-esteem, which in turn, can lead to a rise in the motivation to deal with the problem; there can be the beginnings of self-acceptance in those clients whose difficulties include guilt. In these circumstances both client and worker are then engaged with the reality of the situation and can work on it.

When negatives are out in the open this is a welcome sign that the relationship has begun and the problem-solving work started.

Acceptance is not earned as though it were a 'good conduct' hurdle race. This is not to imply that methods based on learning theory —'rewards' for 'good' behaviour—have no place in social work. In practice, behaviourists or not, we are all using them, if only through grunts, nods and facial expressions. But even behaviourist methods need a sufficient degree of acceptance both initially and thereafter if they are to be of any use. Nor is acceptance condoning or excusing behaviour, with the implication that a double standard exists (with the client on the 'lower') or that, with this client 'you can't expect anything else'. Acceptance does not mean that we abandon standards and go on putting up with negative behaviour indefinitely with its connotation that the client is a 'hopeless case' with no potential. The client may have little enough faith in himself, and if we lose ours his situation then becomes truly hopeless.

Nor is acceptance ignoring behaviour, suggesting it is unimportant, when it is maybe very important to the client (certainly in terms of consequences) or to others. Ignoring it in these circumstances can only lead to confusion. The client knows full well that the social worker is involved because of his behaviour. Ignoring it does not help the client to engage with social realities, either. It may be that the client's behaviour is justified by his realities, but whether this is so or not, it is important for us to continue to accept his feelings until the reality is clear to us and we can plan with him how to remedy matters.

Mrs. White was a young married woman with four children—two at primary school, two still at home. Mr. White was in steady employment though he earned only a low wage. Home for the family was a council house on a pre-war estate. Mrs. White had been the subject of many complaints from the neighbours and the school concerning the state of the house and the state of the children; and had been the subject of a good deal of attention from a range of social agencies. A social worker was called in at the point where complaints had changed to demands for the children to be taken into care on the grounds of neglect.

During the first visit, Mrs. White was sullen, reticent, very much on her guard and her hostility to the social worker was only thinly veiled. She clearly saw her as another one of 'them'. The social worker was careful to demonstrate her acceptance, avoid criticism and indicated her understanding of Mrs. White's feelings about her visit. After one or two visits, she offered some tangible help, but in a way which tried to show her concern and wish to assist, recognising that the offer could be seen as a judgmental reflection on Mrs. White's capacity as a wife and mother. Reluctantly, Mrs. White accepted free school meals for the two older children, and with the social worker's help, she and her husband applied for Family Income Supplement. It was some time, however, before she accepted a twice-weekly place in a playgroup for the older toddler.

In the background, the social worker was still under considerable pressure to 'do' something about the situation, but she resisted these with growing confidence as her relationship with Mrs. White gradually relaxed and Mrs. White began to talk more freely about the children and her husband. It became clearer that despite their difficulties there was a good deal of affection and stability in the family relations.

After some weeks, the social worker brought up the question of the complaints that had been made. Mrs. White's reaction was to be furiously angry with the 'nosey parkers' who were always 'down on her', constantly criticising and nagging. She vigorously defended her care of the children, and angrily went on to demand how 'they' would manage in her place. The house was 'rotten', the neighbours 'stuck up', she couldn't afford things on the money they got. Coping with four small children was 'no joke', and she had no-one to help her. Her relatives lived miles away, and even if they were here she would get nothing out of them. She never had even when she was a kid.

The social worker tried to convey her understanding of Mrs. White's feelings, but the next one or two visits were rather difficult, Mrs. White having returned to something like her original sullen-ness and reticence. On the next occasion, though, she suddenly blurted out that 'it wasn't fair on the kids. I know I feel rotten in the mornings, but that's no reason for them to have to go without any breakfast'. In a tearful rush of feeling she went on to say how tired and rundown she felt, how inadequate she felt, how hopeless everything seemed, that everything got on top of her. The social worker offered her sympathy, understanding, comfort and reassurance, while in practical terms she arranged a physical check up which revealed Mrs. White was anaemic for which treatment was begun.

Following this interview, Mrs. White was rather embarrassed by her outburst, wondering rather sheepishly what the social worker would have thought of her. Again, acceptance came into play, and

Mrs. White's embarrassment eased. The social worker now began to notice a slow but steady change in the situation. Mrs. White began to make an effort to tidy the house up a little before the social worker came, was clearly making an effort to see that the children were fed and reasonably clean and tidy before they left for school, and was beginning to take more of an interest in her own appearance. She bought herself a lipstick, even though she said she felt guilty about spending money on 'luxuries'. She seemed to be gaining more self-confidence, was a good deal more cheerful and obviously felt much more able to cope.

The social worker commented on the change and asked Mrs. White how she thought it had come about. 'I do it for you, not for 'them'. You didn't tell me off', she said.

But, as I implied, we cannot ignore behaviour since we are employed to deal with it—and typically with behaviour seen as negative (by the client or others). The 'crunch' issue then becomes where acceptance ends and our intervention begins—our attempts to modify a situation. This presents social workers with a dilemma which is both ethical and practical.

Attempts to resolve this dilemma have often involved splitting of different sorts. Hollis[1] attempts to split 'sin' and 'sinner': we are enjoined to always accept the latter even while disapproving the former. This is a difficult position to maintain. While there are some clients who feel that aspects of their behaviour are not 'them', but a result of alien impulses or invading compulsions; others will feel that 'what I am I do', or at least that 'what I do is justified'. In everyday life, anyway, what people do is taken for what they are and their reputation stands or falls accordingly; and when we are on the receiving end of criticisms of our actions, we typically experience them as criticisms of ourselves. 'Sin' and 'blame' (that is, culpability) are in any event, concepts which are undergoing rapid social change in society and about which there may be little universal agreement. As concepts they may be of little help in some circumstances.

Biestek[2] attempts to split non-judgmental agencies (in which he includes social work agencies) from judgmental (such as the law and the church) which have the authority to condemn illegal and/or immoral behaviour and thus determine culpability. Quite where this leaves the probation service in this country, or aspects of local authority work in the areas of child care and mental health, is unsure. Indeed, at one point Biestek suggests that the functions of a mental welfare officer in relation to compulsory admissions are nothing to do with non-judgmental social work and properly a function of a judgmental (perhaps legal) agency. He supports the view that social work is basically neutral and that ours is an objective, diagnostic approach to behaviour. Halmos[3] has effectively demolished the 'moral neutrality' claims of the counselling professions, demonstrating that values are endemic in them. Even if social work could substantiate its claim that it deals with its clients on the basis of their need and not on a basis of deserving (acceptable) and undeserving (unacceptable) behaviour, it would be foolish to suggest that such distinctions are not still extant in society and that it may be part of our task to assist clients to come to terms with this. Judgment, in this societal sense, is certainly not (as Biestek seems to assert) the prerogative of certain institutions—in practice, at any rate.

In Britain, given social workers' involvement with statutory functions, a split along judgmental/non-judgmental lines does not seem tenable. We are even caught up in morals in that we become involved in situations even where no statutory obligations arise, where we are expected to intervene, and for our intervention to work towards certain ends. Intervention is justified for the protection of the client, for the protection of others, or for the protection of society as a whole. Ideas about justification may differ, and the objectives of intervention; but whatever our ideas, the implication is that there are limits of some kind to what is acceptable behaviour, so the dilemma exists whatever our ideology. It would remain quite proper for us to weigh up what such intervention might imply for our future work with the client and where the balance of advantage/disadvantage lies for *all* the parties involved.

I am not sure that Biestek's other 'split'—between basic and secondary issues as guidelines for what to accept and where to intervene—are much help in practice. There may be little unanimity of view about his groupings (including the client's view): and I cannot totally accept (as he seems to do) that law and morality are 'basics', always to be upheld by the social worker. There can be occasions when we may well need to question both, at least.

If, as I have argued, social workers do have certain judgmental functions and have been authorised and trained by society to exercise them, then I feel it is up to us to use them as responsibly and impartially as we can. This may be uncomfortable for the client, uncomfortable for us, and uncomfortable for society; but if we are expected as part of our judgmental functions to pin 'blame' (at least by implication) through the form and direction of our intervention, then society has no right to grumble (though grumble it will) if we pin the blame where sometimes it will rightfully belong—on certain malfunctionings of society. We shall be ignoring aspects of our professional responsibility if we fail to do so.

There are, however, perhaps two circumstances in which we may have to appear un-accepting.

(i) Some clients seem to need to test our acceptance out before feeling able to commit themselves to us and the task. They produce their worst behaviour— even going beyond what they would normally do— just to explore our reactions, and perhaps reassure themselves that the structure they seek is a safe, strong one. We do them no service if we merely absorb it all like cotton wool. We can best demonstrate that we care in such cases, by 'putting our foot down'.

(ii) Some clients can get overwhelmed by the strength of their feelings and impulses, and become extremely frightened by this loss of self control. By again putting our foot down, we can be, in effect, lending our ego-strength as a reinforcement for their own until such time as their own develops sufficiently. This is no more than good parenting involves, and amounts to an acceptance of their wish to be more mature, self-directing people.

Finally, acceptance is communicated non-verbally as well as verbally and has implications for agencies (for example in the provision of decent reception facilities) as well as social workers (for example whether we accept that cup of tea even though the cup is not particularly clean).

Acceptance may be particularly crucial at the beginning of a contact, or where clients are hyper-sensitive about it: but it has implications all through our work.

(4) The Need to Talk in Confidence

Confidentiality usually implies not giving information; it also encompasses the *getting* of information, since both involve a revelation of the client. In other words, we should get the client's permission before obtaining say, a social history or approaching another agency for information, unless one of the factors discussed below obtain.

Confidentiality involves both ethical and practical aspects: ethical, in that 'secrets', as Biestek[4] terms them, are a possession and clients have a right to determine how they shall be used; practical, in that we cannot do our job without it. Confidentiality is necessary to:

(a) Diagnosis. If clients feel they cannot reveal material they think could be damaging, we will never get the total picture. Treatment based on partial information is unlikely to be successful.

(b) Treatment—especially ventilation, with the opportunity this affords for the relief of unburdening, and the opportunity to gain new perspectives (whether through obtaining new information in response to the telling, or new perspectives just through the telling); or the chance of acceptance through the telling (the therapeutic benefits of which we have previously discussed). The opportunity to talk in confidence is one that many of our clients will specifically mention as of value to them.

They feel they cannot really talk to friends or neighbours for fear of damaging gossip being spread about them; even with family they may be afraid that what they tell may upset relationships which are important to them and on-going. Either way, they will have to face living with the consequences of telling—consequences which may involve large areas of their 'life space'. It is a tribute to the reputation that social work has that clients frequently assume that they are talking in confidence and do not very often need a specific re-assurance about this. Clearly this is a reputation we should jealously guard if our work is to be effective.

(c) The relationship. Confidentiality is essential to the development of trust, which is fundamental to our work and our relationship. It is also a measure of our respect for clients, and therefore a key quality of the relationship we offer—therapeutic in itself and an important part of the model we inevitably offer clients. To breach confidence carelessly will damage the client, may ruin our work, and reflect upon the whole social work profession. It is also suggested by Perlman that the exchange of emotionally charged material (which often means confidential material) is a vital aspect of a deepening relationship.

Mrs. Cox was admitted to a maternity hospital for the delivery of her fifth child. The admission was unexpected and occurred at seven months because of medical complications. She was immediately referred to the medical social worker since there were clearly emotional and social difficulties around the premature admission.

Earlier in her pregnancy, Mrs. Cox had been referred to a psychiatrist for a possible abortion to be considered, but ultimately a termination had been decided against. A psychiatric social worker had been asked to make a social report for the psychiatrist.

As it happened, the psychiatric social worker and medical social worker were husband and wife, and when Mrs. Cox heard the name of the medical social worker she enquired whether she were any relation. When the medical social worker told her that the psychiatric social worker was her husband, Mrs. Cox commented that she supposed the medical social worker 'knew all about her'. She was reassured by the medical social worker that she and her husband never discussed their clients in any way that would identify them, nor would she do so unless Mrs. Cox gave her permission for this. Mrs. Cox responded immediately and went on to talk about aspects of her situation and feelings which in other circumstances might have taken her several interviews to reveal. Her relationship with the psychiatric social worker (to who she was referred on discharge) also developed rapidly.

Unfortunately, Mrs. Cox' opinion of nursing staff slumped when she overheard a nurse tell the obstetrician as she opened the door of the side ward for him 'This is our psychiatric case'.

The right to confidentiality is not absolute, however. For example, the law only recognises two occasions for privileged communication (and in each it is the client, not the worker, who claims the privilege): between client and lawyer, and between client and probation officer engaged in matrimonial work. By custom, however, privilege is extended to doctors and priests, and occasionally to others. Social workers (like other citizens) can be subpoenaed (and their records, too) and if they refuse to give evidence may be held in contempt of court. In criminal cases (like other citizens) we may be liable to proceedings as accessories if we do not tell.

Conversely, it appears that clients may, in certain circumstances, have the right to sue for damages if we disclose prejudicial information; so legally, and much more often in practice, we are caught in a web of conflicting obligations to disclose or not to disclose. There would seem to be three questions we have to ask ourselves:

(1) With Whom do we Share what Information?

Clearly, the 'golden rule' should be to get our client's permission before passing any information on. If the request to pass information originates from us, make sure the request is justified. This is good practice in that it underlines our respect for the client and also involves him in decision making. But there can be circumstances where to get permission is not possible or perhaps, always necessary.

(a) Where the client is in no position to give or withhold consent. Hamilton suggests this situation exists where the client is psychotic, critically ill, delinquent, or a menace to himself (for example suicidal), but while I think we can all imagine circumstances within these categories in which the 'no position' argument applies, I feel they are far too broad and within each we need to consider carefully before determining that the client is really in 'no position'.

We may have confidential information about a client's family circumstances, for example, which has little or no bearing upon a mental or physical illness however critical. While we may feel it is important, in the client's best interests, to pass on information to doctors, psychiatrists and others which has a bearing on the illness without his specific permission, I do not consider we have *carte blanche* to pass on all the information we hold about a client just because he is in no position to say 'yea' or 'nay'.

(b) Where the client's consent may be assumed. Here there may be two sets of circumstances:

C.I.C.—G

(i) When the client's approach is to an *agency*, we may assume that confidentiality extends to the staff of that agency, since they will inevitably become involved.

(ii) Where the problems the client presents to us and asks for our assistance will inevitably involve a team or a range of agencies. It is possible here to include as 'team', 'significant others' in the client's social orbit, and as 'agencies', employers, landlords, etc. (But see below.)

But in neither of the above circumstances do we have the right to tell all we know. I feel the limits are:

(i) To that information which will enable others to perform their functions adequately. Examples might be:

Medical information (or information bearing on treatment) to doctors;

Financial information to the Supplementary Benefits Commission;

Factual information to charities, etc. when we apply for grants;

Sufficient information to our own administrators to enable them to carry out their tasks;

Information to courts to enable them to make 'good' decisions;

Information to parents to enable them to be 'better' parents;

Sufficient information to colleagues, successors, substitutes, etc. to enable them to take over from us effectively.

(ii) To that information which enables us to perform our function adequately. Again, examples might be:

To typists, enough information so that our records, reports, etc. are effective instruments in furthering the problem-solving;

To supervisors, enough information so that we develop skills, get sound advice, etc. to more effectively assist the client.

There are a number of other points to be borne in mind in determining what information to share with whom. A prerequisite is a clear understanding of our own functions, the functions of others involved and the relationship between them. Those occasions which involve people with on-going, intimate and/or pervasive relationships with clients (for example, relatives, employers) as compared with occasional and specifically limited interventions (such as doctors, the Supplementary Benefits Commission) may need particularly careful handling. It might be as well to get a specific permission to disclose rather than assuming permission, and to discuss with the client the precise nature of the material to be disclosed.

We may need to weigh up whether the other people or other agencies involved may be regarded as sympathetic, neutral or potentially hostile to our client's interests. With the latter we may, again, need to handle matters carefully, but I do not think this extends to the point where information when given is so selected or slanted that it becomes misleading; or is presented with such a thick wrapping of mitigating circumstances that, again, it is tantamount to being misleading. Such action could amount to conniving with a client; or so jeopardise our relationship with others involved that our work with them is hampered to the detriment, eventually, of this client and other clients in the future. Even when the client agrees to a disclosure and we feel it is justified, we may hesitate because we feel such a disclosure may not be handled by others with appropriate discretion. In such circumstances we can only weigh the advantages/ disadvantages to our client of disclosure/non-disclosure. It may pay us to get to know other people involved and perhaps, educate them informally if necessary.

(2) *When do we Breach a Confidence?*

The books seem to suggest five circumstances when disclosure without the client's prior consent is justified:

(a) Where keeping the confidence would conflict with the client's 'higher duty to himself' (Biestek)[5]. While this concept may be clear to a religious, others may not find it of much help.

The British Association of Social Workers' discussion paper on confidentiality[6] specifies where the client's life is in danger. This seems to limit matters to only physical existence, but could be construed to include aspects of life considered vital to the quality of that existence (marriage, parenthood, etc.). While the risk of death is universally regarded as adequate justification for breach of confidence, beyond this the worker must exercise his discretion, it seems.

(b) Where retaining would conflict with the rights of others (Biestek); or involve 'serious danger to other persons' (BASW). While danger is not spelled out, the implication is again physical—but I am not sure many social workers would leave it at that, especially where the adequate care of children was concerned.

(c) Where keeping the confidence would represent a 'serious threat to the person of the worker' (BASW)—again, not worked out, but with physical overtones. Biestek extends this idea to 'conflict with the rights of the worker'; to include damage to his professional reputation, to circumstances which might involve him as an accessory, or where he would not have bound himself voluntarily had he been able to do so.

(d) Where retaining would conflict with the rights of the agency (Biestek) or (BASW) where there would be a threat to the reputation of the agency. The issue here seems to be whether retention would damage the work the agency might do on behalf of other clients.

(e) Where keeping the confidence would conflict with the rights of the community (Biestek); or be a 'serious danger to the community' (BASW). Again, such statements are vague and leave almost everything to the discretion of the worker, but at least they do underline the *social* aspects of our obligations.

It may be possible in practice, to 'smell' a confidence is coming which we would not be able to keep. If so, we can spell out our obligations beforehand and leave the client with the choice to tell or not. But if he does tell before we can stop him, we are left with the problem of how to handle matters. There may be a number of stages in this.

(i) Determine the seriousness of the issues to all concerned. If the consequences of a breach are very serious for the client while the consequences of keeping the confidence involve only slight damage to others, the worker may well decide, on balance, not to press the matter. But not all issues are simple. Perhaps, too, we ought to look at our own motivations in this process of deciding what is/is not serious and to whom.

(ii) While the nature of the confidential material may not warrant a breach of confidentiality whether the client agrees or not, it may be that further work with him, or on his behalf may be so seriously jeopardised that we feel constrained to make it a condition of such further involvement that he agrees to information being passed on. Obviously, we would explain fully to the client why we had come to this conclusion.

(iii) If we decide we cannot keep the confidence, then initially we try to get the client to tell the appropriate person or agency. If he will not, try to get his permission for you to do so. Should he refuse, explain fully why you have to do so.

(iv) Convey the confidential information with decency and despatch leaving the client with the maximum of dignity you can. And go on trying to work with him. Later, the client may see things your way; but even if he does not he will have had to engage with reality and may learn something profitable from this.

Mrs. Terry, a married woman in her early fifties, came to a mental health agency, complaining about her husband's behaviour towards her over a number of years, but particularly since their children had left home. She accused him of neglecting her, keeping her short of money, always being out drinking and verbally abusing her. She wanted the social worker to come and 'sort him out'. She was adamant, however, that the fact that she had asked the social worker to call to see him should not be disclosed to him. She wanted the social worker to call in casually and offer as an explanation for his visit that he was 'in the neighbourhood and thought he would drop by'. If her husband knew she had precipitated the social worker's call, she thought he would become very angry with her and assault her.

The social worker sympathised with her distress and acknowledged the dilemma she was in over disclosing the source of the information which led to the social worker's visit. He explained however, that to bind himself never to disclose this information might put him (and Mrs. Terry, too) in such a false position at some stage, that it might well negate any assistance he might be able to give to Mrs. Terry and her husband. He expressed the opinion that it might be better to risk her husband's anger right at the beginning. At least he would know that Mrs. Terry was concerned enough about him and their relationship to have sought help to try to save a marriage that was threatened. Mrs. Terry still refused permission for a disclosure.

This refusal left the social worker in a dilemma and with three choices:

(i) He could accede to Mrs. Terry's condition, risk his work with Mr. Terry and possibly his work with Mrs. Terry too, since it was possible she was manipulating him, using him as a 'big stick' to beat her husband with, a position he would have to recover from if he were to be of real assistance.

(ii) Perhaps unethically, he could appear to accede to her stipulation but at some stage make a disclosure, but again seriously jeopardise his work with both of the Terrys.

(iii) He could make it a condition of his intervention with Mr. Terry that he was not bound to confidentiality about the source of the referral, though he recognised that to make this condition might preclude any further work with Mrs. Terry as well as her husband, given her persistence regarding confidentiality in this matter.

In considering alternatives, the social worker had to take into account the risks to Mrs. Terry. The situation with her husband was of long standing and he ascertained that nothing had changed recently except her understandably increasing 'fed-upness' with it all. The social worker did not feel, in these circumstances, that the risks to Mrs. Terry warranted being bound to confidentiality when weighed against the risk to successfully working with this couple that remaining bound represented. He made intervention with Mr. Terry conditional upon being released from Mrs. Terry's insistence on confidentiality about the source of the referral.

Mrs. Terry refused this condition, refused the offer of further meetings with her, and left the agency saying she would get help elsewhere.

(3) How can we Guard the Information we Possess?

Both agency and worker are involved in this guarding process. It is the agency's obligation to provide facilities enabling clients to talk in confidence, to keep telephone conversations away from those not involved (especially other clients), and to keep recorded information away from those not concerned. This applies to agency staff not concerned as much as others. This not only involves lockable cabinets, and perhaps, differentiated filing systems, but also clear instructions about access to them. It is also to be expected that agencies employ staff who know what confidentiality means (or instruct them in it) and devise administrative systems which assist: for example depersonalised typing pools may not be the best way. In smaller, tight-knit communities, it may reduce pressures on staff if there was a rule that they did not handle material involving people they knew socially. In all agencies there ought to be someone to whom workers can turn when confronted with difficult decisions about confidentiality, and to assist the staff generally by making at least general policy about confidentiality clear. As part of an agency, a social worker shares these obligations—perhaps by bringing issues and inadequacies to the attention of those responsible for the agency's management, by gently assisting others to keep the rules, helping in any staff training programmes about it—and by being scrupulous about it himself.

. As far as the worker is concerned, we have already examined the circumstances in which information may be passed; but often we are asked for information by others in a context which may or may not have a bearing on the work we are trying to do with our client. While we may be able to respond to the enquiry under our 'assumed permission', we may have to decline until we have obtained specific permission. While we may risk being considered 'cussed', it spells out to others that we consider confidentiality important. People sometimes approach us for information when they would never dare approach a doctor for medical data in the same way.

The whole question of confidentiality becomes more complicated where records (including reports) are involved, since they are permanent and risk their use out of context over time: they are specific statements which we may not be able to qualify verbally when they are used; we may have little control over who has access to them especially where material leaves our agency in the form of reports, etc., and we may have little control over the use to which information they contain is put. The amalgamating of filing systems can produce problems here, while computer banks can be quite a threat. What we record and how we record it must therefore be shaped by the purpose of those records and who may have access to them.

Internally, it is proper that the administration should have access to information required to evaluate agency performance (statistical material, etc.) and also to safeguard the appropriate allocation of resources (for example, in submissions for material aid); but they will not need 'professional' material and this might be kept in separate files. 'Professional' material will be needed by colleagues, should they be involved, and supervisors: but even here they may not need everything and a summary be enough (or even more useful).

Externally, reports need to be prepared with care and shaped to the purposes of those who will use them; but at least reports mean that you can select (if necessary) the information which goes out in a way that allowing others to examine your files does not. Only very exceptionally should any 'outsider' see our files.

Breaching a confidence is not always a matter of passing on information which the client has given to us. We sometimes acquire information about a client which he has not told us; or even information which he does not know about himself (for example, a medical diagnosis). In such circumstances we can only ask ourselves

(i) Whether the information is relevant to the work we are trying to do with the client;

(ii) Whether it is in his best interests, taking all the circumstances into account, that he should know.

As long as we are satisfied on either count, then I feel we have a professional responsibility to press the source of our information for disclosure. But the question of 'best interests' is often hard to determine. We might get to know of a proposed, but still confidential road widening scheme, involving the possible demolition of a client's house among others. Forewarned, those involved might get together to resist the proposal, fight effectively at a public enquiry into the scheme and/or wring rather better compensation terms from the local authority if the proposal is implemented. But premature disclosure could involve a highly damaging 'planning blight' situation for which there is no compensation if the proposal turns out to be only one of many ideas for dealing with traffic flow, and a 'rank outsider' at that in terms of possible implementation. Disclosure to the client that he was suffering from a terminal illness would have to take into account the client's likely response to knowing, which can at best be only a professional opinion. The situation here may be complicated if relatives have been told, but asked to keep this from the sufferer, yet they come to the social worker because they are so distressed by what they feel is an intolerable situation for them.

Should our representations to those who know to tell (or for their permission for us to do so) fail, we are again left to weigh up the consequences for all the parties concerned—not forgetting the consequences of a breach on our relations with others which could have repercussions for other clients. Agonising as it may seem, I feel we have little alternative but to abide by the decisions of other professionals, though making it clear to them why we disagree and that the consequences of their decision must be their responsibility. I say this because we would expect no less from other professionals if the responsibility for disclosure were within our professional competence; and we cannot apply one set of expectations to ourselves but another to professional colleagues.

Finally, I think it is always worth while asking ourselves why a client has disclosed confidential information. There can be occasions when he tells us, 'knowing' that we will be under an obligation to disclose the information. Even if he protests when we indicate we cannot retain the confidence, he may still indicate his relief in some way. At a pre-conscious level he may have been asking us to help him disclose or at least resolve his conflict over telling or not.

(5) The Need to be Understood

Understanding is clearly essential for the diagnosis, and the objectives and the means to attain them will hinge upon a good understanding. Understanding is thus crucial to an effective outcome. But it is also crucial to the relationship: if the client feels misunderstood his irritation about this is bound to colour his reaction to the worker; while if the worker feels that he is not understanding, any anxiety he may have about this will communicate itself to the client—again affecting the relationship. Understanding also impinges on treatment in other ways: to meet with understanding can be a tremendous relief in itself and so valuable therapeutically; while if one of our objectives is to add to a client's understanding, we can hardly do this unless we understand ourselves. In this process we shall be making use of both our knowledge (whether psychologically or sociologically based) and our empathy.

Understanding may be looked at along five dimensions: what it means for this client to ask for/be given help; what the problem is; what the problem means to the client; who the problem is happening to; and the context in which this person-with-a-problem is functioning.

(A) WHAT IT MEANS TO THIS CLIENT TO ASK FOR/BE GIVEN HELP

Contact with a social worker usually only happens after a complex process involving both personal and social factors has been gone through. Though no studies have been made of this process in social work, some useful analogies may be drawn from studies in the medical field of becoming ill. The stages in the process have been identified as the transition from health to illness; accepted illness and convalescence.

(a) *Transition* may be sudden or gradual into *accepted illness*—the stage when the patient, family, significant others and the professionals agree. There can be difficulties where there is no agreement—for example where the family is not 'allowing' it, or the patient is 'claiming' it invalidly. While the sick role produces problems for the sufferer (debility, anxiety, threats to previous methods of coping, dependency) they will be 'allowed' relief from their normal role expectations provided others are convinced they are submitting to, and co-operating with treatment and demonstrating their wish to recover.

Both personal and social factors will determine how the transition is managed. Even the symptoms will have varying significance; while transition to a stigmatised sick role may be particularly resisted. But most symptoms will produce anxiety, since they represent a threat to self-image and suggest vulnerability. Reactions to symptoms may be denial, welcome or inertia; on the part of the patient, his family or others.

Denial is likely where there is a threat to self-esteem, guilt, a sense of failure, or the symptoms involve the security of others; where there is a fear of setting off a train of events over which the patient has no control, such as a visit to the doctor leading to a hospital admission and surgery (a fear which may be reinforced by mythology or past experience); or where the professionals are seen as unhelpful. (A helpful professional is active, quick, efficient, competent and kindly—with again, mythology and experience contributing to the image.)

Denial may be reinforced by the reactions of the family (if these add to the patient's difficulties)—but reactions may also lead to a 'gift exchange' (extra attention, care, support) which enable the symptoms to be contained; or 'allow' or 'push' the patient into the accepted illness stage. A family reaction of anger is likely to lead to most difficulty.

The influence of the culture will depend on whether the symptoms are seen as natural or exceptional; blame-worthy, or to be sympathised with. Either way the patient's and/or family's efforts to deal with the symptoms themselves may well be supported initially, but where the point is reached when it is more dangerous to do nothing than to do something, cultural pressure may be exerted to contact the appropriate professional.

Welcome is likely if the client enjoys dependency, or the attention produced, or the control over others illness may bring; or if in a chronically distressing situation, symptoms are the 'last straw' which allows them to opt out. Such patients are likely to be difficult to get out of the accepted illness and/or convalescent stages.

The family may welcome the patient's move into accepted illness if this relieves tensions for them or they derive gratification from a nursing, nurturing function. (Again, this may influence how easily the patient is 'allowed' to recover and assume their normal roles once more.)

Inertia (knowing something is wrong, but doing nothing about it) is likely if the symptoms are regarded as 'normal'; tolerance levels are high or expectations low. Again, personal and cultural factors are involved: they can reinforce each other, or produce tension where discrepancies exist. Much treatable sub-health persists through inertia—and perhaps many social problems, too.

Typically, the stages of transition will have been, through: trying personal ideas/remedies; getting advice from other significant 'lay' figures; and only after these fail will they get professional help.

(b) *Convalescence* (mentioned here since the professional may get called in at any one of the three stages) may be coloured by how effective the treatment was in the 'accepted illness' stage; or may be prolonged by the secondary gains of it—even though prolonging illness may produce adverse family and cultural reactions. But convalescence may be difficult anyway since there is no defined 'disability role' to guide patient, family or culture; there may be swings between 'allowing illness' and pressurising for a return to full responsibility— the uncertainty producing irritation and frustration all round.

David, aged five, was enuretic at night; he had been dry for a while around the age of three, but bedwetting had recurred with the birth of a younger brother when David was four. His mother was anxious about his bedwetting thinking it might be a sign of emotional disturbance connected with feelings about his brother or a reflection on her handling of the rivalry situation. She read some books on child rearing problems to try to find out how to handle matters, but found these contradictory in the advice they offered. David's father tended to 'pooh pooh' his wife's anxieties, saying that David would 'grow out of it'.

Mother sought the advice of an older neighbour who tended to reinforce father's view, saying that she had had similar problems with two of her boys at that age and they got over it by the time they were about seven.

David himself had seemed relaxed enough about his wetting originally, but had become increasingly anxious about it, perhaps as a reflection of his mother's anxiety even though she tried to conceal this from him.

Mother also discussed matters with her own mother, who added to mother's anxiety by being rather upset adding that 'all of you were dry by the time you were two'.

David had started school a few weeks earlier, and on a school visit, mother mentioned his problem to David's schoolteacher. She thought it was nothing to worry about yet, but added that David might be embarrassed if the other children in his class got to know about it. Mother subsequently asked David whether he had said anything at school. He hotly denied this, but he had clearly 'got the message' (whether from school or from mother's asking him was not clear) that he had a problem which involved some shame or stigma.

Eventually, risking her husband's displeasure, she took David to the doctor. The doctor expressed his concern and arranged for David to see a consultant paediatrician. The consultant played matters down, suggested mother relaxed about the matter, and gave her and David another appointment for six months time. Mother was not very happy about this outcome, but did her best to cope and relax until the next appointment. This time, with the problem little improved, the consultant rather reluctantly arranged for David to be supplied with a 'pad and bell' device, being influenced by mother's continuing anxiety and David's evident heightened embarrassment.

The device helped David to become dry after some six months, but in the early stages father expressed in no uncertain terms what he felt about being woken up almost every night by the bell. David's younger brother, who shared a bedroom with David, also added his complaints. David was acutely aware of the disturbance the bell created, but was very relieved when his bedwetting finally cleared up.

Asking for/being given help, therefore involves the clients feelings about the problem; their feelings about others feelings; their feelings about help; their feelings about what others feel about getting professional help in; their feelings about your help. But they may also well come with some relief about having made a decision to come at all; and with a varying degree of hope that you will be able to do something. (Similar feelings may exist even where it is not a self-referral.) The worker responds to such feelings with warmth, acceptance, respect, and understanding which helps the client to deal with them, allows his expression of them, and indicates the worker's appreciation of the particular difficulties his intervention has produced. It is important that the worker does not jump to the conclusion (on the basis of this initial contact) that the client is always like this, nor should he be anxious about the ambivalent feelings which typically exist in the client. Both positive and negative feelings can be used in the casework process, since motivation is often a

balance of discomfort and hope, both of which may need to be kept
going for progress.

(B) WHAT THE PROBLEM IS

We have already seen some of the problems for client and worker
regarding the communication of the difficulty, but to understand it
is important to begin where the client is—his view of the difficulty—
and to respond to this with understanding, by feeding in information
and discussing ways in which we might help.

This latter is important, since it gives us the opportunity of clarify-
ing our role, so assisting a realistic engagement between worker and
client; and also begins the client's thinking (if this is needed) about
possible solutions—an important part of the casework process in
itself. We do this in a way which will allow the client to bring out
any underlying problems (if they exist) and so proceed to a *re-definition* of the problems (a process which may occur a number of times
in the course of a case). It is essential, if the outcome is to be successful, that client and worker agree about what the problem is and
how it is to be tackled between them—though this will possibly take
time; but some fairly quick agreement about 'preliminaries' will be
useful. Until this 'contract' is made, the 'engagement' process has
not really begun.

Problems arise, however, when the worker feels that in order to
help effectively, he would like to re-define the problem and renego-
tiate the 'contract' and the client is reluctant to do so. Here we
have to ask ourselves whether the product of the client's definition
would be an adequate or feasible solution; or whether our motivation
(for example to do 'deep' casework) is not influencing us. We might
also ask whether our 'contract' terms do not demand too much of
the client's capacity, might involve complications in the client's situation, or involve demands on resources (whether of worker, agency,
people in the client's environment, or materials) which are inordinate.

I feel we need to ask these questions even where the client appears
to be asking for a re-definition (for example, 'What makes me do
these things?'). Such questions may be more rhetorical or a plea
for control rather than a request for insight. Interpretation needs

to be incorporated emotionally by the client, not merely intellectually, to be useful. 'Intellectual' insights might be incorporated into an 'intellectual' defence system. Insight is better worked towards by the client and worker together, rather than offered by the worker.

I am not suggesting, however, that it is not important at times, for the worker to understand underlying difficulties even if these are not acknowledged by client and so not incorporated into the 'contract'; their existence are factors to be reckoned with in the diagnosis, the selection of goals and treatment methods.

(C) WHAT THE PROBLEM MEANS TO THE CLIENT

We have already seen that the meaning of a problem will be along the three dimensions of personal, group (family and significant others) and cultural meaning—in both objective and subjective terms. It is important to acknowledge these dimensions since problems come to us not so much because of their severity, but because of the degree of social disturbance created within these dimensions (for example not the 'strength' of the phobia but what it is of; not the mild dementia, but the reactions of family or neighbourhood). It is as much the inter-action effects which trouble people as the 'problem' as such. Clearly, too, we need to keep these dimensions in mind not only for diagnosis, but for selecting goals and treatment methods.

(D) WHO THE PROBLEM IS HAPPENING TO

We need only enough about the 'who' to deal with the problem; to try to get more is an intrusion into privacy—unethical, and bad practice in that it may well produce a hostile reaction. We may well need to know more about a person than that area we are actually dealing with in the sense that it contributes to our diagnosis and subsequent treatment goals and methods; but much of this material the client may give us anyway (without our 'fishing' for it) since, on the basis of our knowledge, we may be able to make inferences without the client always being conscious of quite how much he has told us.

With the above in mind we may need to know:

(a) The sort of person he ordinarily is—his needs, drives and motivations and how he usually copes with or expresses these— his 'ego functioning', in effect: how clearly does he perceive situations realistically, what range of factors in a situation can he encompass, how far can he appreciate other's points of view, how far can he select and focus upon relevant factors; how far can he tolerate frustration, appropriately control or channel the expression of his own feelings, how persistent is he, how far is he in touch with his own feelings, and able to acknowledge them, how far can he recognise the impact his own feelings and actions have on others.

(b) How his 'normal' personality is being influenced by his current situation: given his needs and drives and motivations, how far are these being met or unmet, frustrated or fulfilled, understood or misunderstood in the 'here and now'; and how his coping mechanisms are contributing to a successful management and resolution of his difficulties or are exacerbating them either by failing or even producing further complications through a 'negative feedback' of some kind.

To understand him fully, both in terms of what he ordinarily is and how he is currently functioning, we may need to know something about how his past has shaped him, or may have a significance for his particular reactions to particular aspects of his present situation or difficulties.

(E) THE CONTEXT WITHIN WHICH THIS PERSON WITH A PROBLEM IS CURRENTLY FUNCTIONING

We have seen the way in which the family group, significant others and the culture impinge on the situation: to which one more factor needs to be added—the material circumstances. Many of our clients have to contend with material circumstances (poverty, bad housing, unemployment, etc.) which would severely tax even the most mature of us.

We need to understand this complex for a number of reasons. The problem may be in the context and not in the client at all; or part of the problem may be there and part within the client. Even if the problem should be entirely within the client, the reverberations of it extend into the context. Thus wherever the problem lies, the context becomes involved within the orbit of treatment. Where the problem is entirely within the client but we are using indirect methods of treatment, the context is very clearly involved. Many of the resources needed to deal with the problem may lie in the context and their existence (or lack of them) may very well need to be taken into account when planning treatment goals and selecting treatment methods. Contextual resources may well need to be worked with in order to make them effectively available to our client.

Perhaps above all we need to understand it since as social workers it is our function to do so, given that the focus of our work is the area of interaction between the individual and his environment, the feedback which each contributes to the other.

To sum up: to comprehend (and convey to the client that we do) we need to understand along these five dimensions. If our understanding is partial or lopsided the whole process of our interaction and intervention is likely to be abortive or only partially successful at best. If the client appears to be 'keeping us in the dark' along one of these dimensions, this could be telling us something.

(6) The Need to be Helped

It is an over-simplification to suggest that all those with whom we come into contact have a need to be helped as they see it. Some reactions might be:

(a) A refusal of help because the client does not acknowledge a problem exists.

'I have had an attack of multiple sclerosis, but I am now cured and that is the end of it.' (This in a not untypical period of remission.)

(b) A refusal because, though acknowledging a problem exists the client chooses to deal with it himself.

'I know I have multiple sclerosis, I know I may have another attack in the future, but I am alright at the moment and while I can I will manage myself, thank you.'

(c) A refusal because, though acknowledging a problem exists which is beyond his ability to deal with, a client does not want the sort of help you are offering.
'I know I have multiple sclerosis, but I don't want your talk and I don't want your gadgets; what I want is a cure and as you are not a doctor you can't help me.'

(d) A refusal because, though acknowledging a problem exists which is beyond his ability to deal with and for which your help is appropriate, the cost of that help (in terms of time, effort, awareness, the repercussions in his contact, etc.) are too great.
'I know I have multiple sclerosis, but talking about it only makes me even more depressed; the gadgets tire me out using them; and visits from social workers in this neighbourhood mean only one thing and I am not going to risk getting that sort of reputation, thank you.'

But where our help is accepted (if only to some extent), good practice involves two elements and a process: the elements are the agency and the worker; the process that of engaging the client.

(A) THE AGENCY

It is primarily to the agency that the client turns for help; the worker is part of a range of resources offered by the agency (though many of these other resources may be channelled through the worker). It is the agency which determines the focus of the work, and shapes it through resource provision, policy determination, etc., so it is essential the worker understands it and his position within it. Imagining the agency were an onion, the layers (beginning from the outside) might be considered as:

(a) *The societal framework* which 'produced' it and within which it operates—aspects we have already examined.

(b) *The legal framework*—provided by statute or charter, outlining the general aims of the agency (or aspects of its work) with perhaps some detail about more specific duties and methods to implement them. The legal framework will also indicate the source of funds of the agency. Thus the legal framework has important repercussions for the nature of the service, accountability for the service and the setting of the service.

(i) The nature of the service may be public or voluntary. In a public service, availability is usually to all who come within certain categories (with implications for caseloads), though typically with a distinction between mandatory and permissive services—mandatory being those considered important, often with an 'emergency' element, to which the worker is expected to give priority; while permissive services have a lower priority and fewer resources, involving the worker in resource allocation and waiting list management. The voluntary agency takes up those obligations it chooses in terms of category and numbers within that category, which may mean limited caseloads for the worker, but also limitations of resource.

(ii) Accountability is usually carried by a constituted committee. In a public service the committee typically comprises elected representatives (or their appointees) of central or local government. Inevitably political considerations come in—though the degree may vary widely.

The ideas of political parties about how much should be allocated to say, a Social Services Department, or how that allocation should be distributed as between functions, can be quite varied—though every party will have one eye over its shoulder on the electorate (and particularly the ratepayers). Changes in political power may have repercussions for the whole Department. Not infrequently, though, discussions at Committee level will cut across party lines and reflect the individual personalities of the councillors. It is when matters get to full council that party lines may become more apparent, especially when the whips are on—a matter that will be determined at the pre-council meeting of the councillors of that party. Inevitably a certain amount of 'horse trading' will go on of the 'if you will back me over this, I will back you over that' variety.

This situation will present the Chief Officer of the Department with some difficult tactical issues: should he use the formal and informal channels open to him to try to 'sell' a matter he regards as important though he knows that influential people will accept his proposals only reluctantly—or should he 'slant' his proposals to what he anticipates will be acceptable and therefore more likely to be implemented. The degree of influence which a Chief Officer carries—and therefore the balance of power as between officials and elected representatives—is a very subtle matter and sometimes calls in to question where accountability really lies—especially as councillors are to some extent dependent on the advice of the Chief Officer in matters in which he is the expert, and also somewhat dependent on the information which he provides for them to come to a decision. The information could be selected in such a way that a decision can virtually go only one way—at its worst, an unethical manipulation of the decision making process. On the other hand, there may be councillors who regardless of evidence will still decide matters on the basis of their own prejudices or political expediency.

The committee of a voluntary agency may be technically elected by a very circumscribed number, but may in practice be a self-perpetuating group with considerable autonomy.

Even here 'politicking' may play its part in terms of the personalities of the committee members, their influence, the sub-groupings; and the balance of influence and power between them and the head of the full-time staff be a delicate and complex issue.

While what happens at the top of the Department or agency may have a considerable influence upon the autonomy of the individual worker just how much accountability he will be left with can still vary widely depending on the ethos or style of the organisation—a matter which may stem from tradition or the style of the particular Chief Officer.

(iii) The setting may be primary or secondary. A primary agency is one with social work objectives in which social workers have the primary professional place; a secondary setting is one in which a social worker or social work agency is incorporated in another, non social work agency, and uses social work skills to deal with the psycho-social problems of clients of the 'host' agency where these are blocking the attainment of the objectives of the 'host' agency with these clients. Such psycho-social problems may be grouped as:

> Problems of causation (for example, psychosomatic complaints in a hospital setting, giving rise to the opportunity for the social worker to be included in the treatment team);

Problems of incorporation (whether these are blocks preventing a necessary engagement with the 'host' agency, or problems of fully utilising the agency programme after the commencement of engagement—for example, school phobia or learning difficulties);
Problems of discharge or transfer (typically, to ensure that the work of the 'host' agency is not vitiated).

But the setting does not pre-determine the mode of working, but rather the predominant need of the client. Thus in a primary setting a social worker may be working in a secondary mode in that the predominant client need is medical and he has to shape his work to that of the 'primary' profession involved—the doctor; while even in a secondary setting, the social worker may be working in a primary mode if the predominant client need is psycho-social, and other professions are shaping their work to support the social worker's objectives. (for example, where a patient remains in hospital for a while, not because he needs further medical treatment, but to give an opportunity for suitable accommodation to be found, or arrangements made for adequate aftercare.)

(c) *The policy framework* This turns the general aims of the legal framework into a programme via the determination of priorities and the allocation of resources, and is a committee responsibility. Usually, the committee seeks the advice of its professional staff; not infrequently, the staff will bring policy matters to the attention of the committee. But as we have seen above, what finally emerges as policy is a complex matter involving that committee itself, its relations with other structures, and its relations with professional staff.

(d) *The administrative framework*—is essentially the 'nuts and bolts' needed to implement policy. This is a very complex matter detailed consideration of which is left to Chapter XI.

(e) *The procedural framework*—the forms, rules and regulations on which successful administration rests.

It is, therefore, primarily the agency which will determine for the worker who he helps, in which way, on what conditions, with what resources, and where the worker's help fits in with other help needed by or being given to, the client.

(B) THE WORKER

Essentially, the client comes into contact with the worker because the worker is seen as competent to deal with this sort of problem whether by the client or others. In other words he has the professional authority to deal with it.

Of these two aspects (professional and authority), I examine authority here—profession warrants a chapter of its own (see Chapter XII).

Authority has three aspects: knowledge, position and relationship.

(i) Knowledge. We are regarded as 'experts' (by clients and others) in, perhaps, three areas:

the social services;
psycho-social problems;
aspects of the setting in which we work.

(The last may on occasions be unreasonable for example, if we are asked for medical information by a client rather than the doctor: but it may be reasonable to act as intermediary or interpreter.)

Our information and advice in these areas should be available to those who seek or need it.

(ii) Position. There are three aspects to this:

Because we work in agencies which express certain social values and belong to a profession with an ethical system, clients and others will expect us to behave in accordance with certain principles and to direct our work in a way that upholds certain values. These expectations may not always be realistic; and they may or may not help us in our dealings with the people who hold such expectations; but they exist.

Our position gives us a certain command over resources (more particularly, those of our own agency). Clients reasonably expect us to use our authority in this respect on their behalf. Others will too, though their view of how we are exercising this authority may be coloured by their view of our clients.

As a derivative of our position we may have a statutory power and responsibility to act.

Our positional authority will be reinforced if others respect our knowledge-based authority. Positional respect does not come automatically.

(iii) Relationship. You will carry weight (authority) with others if your relationship is good, again reinforcing the knowledge and position aspects of authority. The competent exercise of knowledge and position authority can also reinforce the relationship authority. A 'good' relationship in social work is the professional one—one that serves the *purpose* (problem-solving) and includes those elements which will assist the purpose and excludes those elements which will not. It is a *directed* relationship—a term I prefer to Biestek's 'controlled emotional involvement'. There are, perhaps, five ways in which the professional relationship may differ from customary social relationships (for example, friendship).

(1) Duration. While social relationships are open-ended in this respect, the professional relationship ends when the problem is solved, and this ending is implicit from the beginning.

(2) Time. Typically we see our clients for a limited time on limited occasions: we do not just 'drop in' for a chat, or spend long hours in their company. (I do not want to over stress this: we can have friends we see rarely, and it may be justified for a worker to adopt a 'drop in' mode of working, while occasions may arise when we are in clients' company for many hours.) But our use of time has to be justified for professional reasons, not because we happen to enjoy the other's company. In other words, the time we spend with clients (or with others on their behalf) emerges from the needs of the clients and the objectives of our involvement—nothing else.

(3) Place. Typically we see clients either in our office or at home (their home) rather than inviting them to our home or joining forces with them to visit elsewhere (pub, cinema, or dance hall). Again, though, I do not want to over stress this since it could happen that we properly see clients other than in their home or our office as I indicated earlier. Where we see people will be determined, as far as is practicable, by the venue which is most helpful in furthering our professional purposes—not because we happen to prefer it.

(4) Focus. The focus of a friendship is a mutual satisfaction of a range of needs—emotional, social, intellectual, aesthetic, and so

on. This makes it a very open-ended relationship. It will presumably last while both are at least getting sufficient out of it to make it worth their while continuing to give to it (which is unpredictable); while the range of need to be met within it will vary with the individuals and how they negotiate this matter. Close friendships may become very pervasive and involve a considerable area of the 'life space'. Thus there is the opportunity for friendships to become rich, diverse and satisfying; but also the risk that a disruption in one area of the friendship may have repercussions over a wide area of the 'life space', leading to a situation in which reticences appear in some areas for the sake of consequences elsewhere. The focus of the professional relationship is not mutual, but the client's needs—the problem solving work. Wide aspects of the client's life and feelings may be examined or brought into play, but since the focus is specific, not generalised, this may be done without undue fear of the repercussions. The very 'limitations' thus make the relationship usable.

(5) Role relationship. Rather than mutual, the relationship, in casework anyway, is that of helper and helped. The fact that the worker comes from an agency cannot be denied. But the mode of expression of helper/helped has been questioned in the past by the functionalist and diagnostic schools of social work. The functionalists saw the contact as basically an exploration, jointly undertaken, with differing contributions from each, but essentially on a footing of parity. They accused the diagnostic school of aping medicine by themselves determining the problem, what the treatment was to be and applying it, which was not only ethically insupportable but also impracticable. People could not be 'treated' like this and their co-operation and involvement in the process was essential, making mutuality the only possible basis. The diagnosticians accused the functionalists of being unrealistic in that people came to social workers because they saw them as experts, with the sort of help they wanted; and that it was little short of inhuman to expect a mutual contribution (with the degree of capability and responsibility that implies) when clients were bowed by problems and needed help, protection, guidance and nurture. We now recognise that both arguments contain part of the truth, and are not mutually exclusive.

[If I might interpolate here, I tend to use the terminology of the diagnostic school, but do not consciously identify myself with any one school in particular.]

We are sometimes made anxious when we feel the client is attempting to 'socialise' the relationship. Such anxiety can be defensive on the part of the worker anxious not to become really engaged with his client; but if attempts do originate from the client they may stem from genuine ignorance, a testing out of the worker, or a need to know something about him before he commits himself, or an inappropriate handling of role relationships indicative of similar problems in other social spheres. An expression of feeling in the relationship is sometimes indicated by the client's offering of 'gifts' (material or service).

The giving and accepting of gifts is a characteristic of mutual relations such as friendship, and a social worker anxious about socialising is often in a dilemma whether to accept gifts or not. To help solve the dilemma, I feel it is important to try to recognise the motives behind the offer. Some offers are only politeness (cups of tea for example), others may be placatory (should clients have felt you have been cross with them), others may be attempts to disarm (to ward off anticipated anger on your part about something they have done), some may be an expression of guilt (some compensation for what they have done to you), some are a genuine thank you, (a token of appreciation for what you have done). Some clients almost have a need to give: it is the only way they know of securing a relationship. Others may offer you something to restore their own dignity in a kind of way, since they find it irksome to their self esteem to always be on the 'receiving end'. Some gifts have a sort of symbolism for clients—an offering of something good when there is so much about themselves they feel is bad. Some gifts symbolise the meaning of the relationship—like the client who gave her social worker a gift for Mother's Day even though the worker was much younger than she was. Some gifts are an attempt to manipulate: for the 'I've done this for you, now you do this for me' variety. Some are genuine attempts to mutualise or socialise—perhaps because your social work role with its implied focus, is threatening. Mutualising defuses the threat, becoming an avoidance technique.

An idea about the motive may well help us to decide whether

to accept or not (within, obviously, any rules our agencies have about this). We may be able to avoid rejecting an offer where this would hurt, but de-personalise it to some extent, by accepting it for the agency rather than ourselves.

Socialising is sometimes confused with informality; but in essence it is an attempt to involve the worker in other 'life areas' without a problem-solving focus, thus giving rise to the sort of constraints mentioned above and so controlling to a degree the problem solving area—to the detriment of the problem-solving work.

The helper/helped relationship is endemic to casework, I suggest; but people also need satisfying mutual relationships (or perhaps, mutual relationships to fill specific needs/gaps in their life areas). In such circumstances an alternative method of social work (for example, groupwork) may be called for, or the use of volunteers.

Relationships are never static: they grow, wither, and fluctuate with mood, circumstance, motivation, progress or lack of it. Nor can they be taken for granted, but need working at.

To return to authority, Hollis suggests there are six gradations in the use of authority; but these gradations have implications for the roles and relationships involved which apply whether we are using authority towards clients or directing it towards others on behalf of clients. We may need to bear in mind that having used one of the severer forms of authority, it may be very difficult for us to return to the use of the less severe afterwards—often because of the effect on roles and relationships. (See also the discussion on compliance systems in Chapter XI.) As a rule, therefore, we use the least amount of authority that is likely to be effective, remembering that authority is more likely to be accepted where the relationship is good.

(a) Underlining. This means, basically, taking up and confirming suggestions made by others (including clients). It demonstrates a unanimity of view and implies mutuality and partnership. It involves the worker in the role of conferee—a person to discuss things with, and applies whether the 'conferor' is a client, colleague, another professional, official or relative.

(b) Suggesting. Here the initiative is more with the worker: the mutuality is less, but the partnership remains. It implies the 'conferor' is uncertain and is looking to the worker for ideas and opinions; or the worker feels it would be helpful to offer them to relieve some uncertainty. The role is still that of conferee, but may merge into that of broker if the suggestions are taken up and require making links with resources or opening new lines of communication; together, perhaps, with assistance in making and sustaining these. Suggesting (or merely underlining) may involve us in some discussion of the implications of this or alternative courses of action—both in practical and feeling terms. Some degree of partialising may be involved, too; since suggesting may have connections with what we consider needs to be tackled in terms of saliency, or tackled first in terms of urgency.

(c) Advising. This may be merely a matter of providing information but more usually involves a concrete opinion on a course of action. It still assumes a common bond, though in this case the bond may not be so much mutual as indicating a complementary interest. Here the role is one of mediator—helping the parties concerned (worker/ client, client/others, worker/others) to identify the common interest— perhaps by identifying what is standing in the way of it: by defining the limits and constraints operating in the situation. Advising techniques typically involve the marshalling of argument and evidence.

(d) Advocating. Hollis terms this 'urgent advice'. While there may still be some appeal to at least a complementary interest, the basis of this has become tenuous and we are here bordering on a conflict situation, with the advocate firmly committed to one side of it. When using advocacy to a client, his reluctance to concur may almost be assumed, given he is almost by definition, identifying with the other 'side' of the endemic conflict. The risk to the relationship in this situation is self evident. When advocating on behalf of a client, Middleman and Goldberg ask us to remember that it may be very hard for a client to contemplate a conflict situation, especially if this means risking becoming vulnerable (i.e. exposed to retaliation by the other party to the potential conflict). Whether matters are taken this far, they suggest, is a matter for the client to decide. They have much at stake—the worker has little, probably. Demonstrations are among advocacy techniques, which typically require marshalling support.

(e) Deterring. Here the conflict is in the open, the basis of consensus has gone and something of a power game is on. This may be enough to contain the situation, of course—though on the basis of one party's submission. The implication here is that, should a submission not be forthcoming, recourse will be had to coercion. The risks here (to the client/worker relationship or the worker's with others; and for the client in terms of his vulnerability) are greater—but the worker is now also beginning to be at risk, too. He certainly should not expose himself through the use of deterrence unless he is sure he has a watertight case (including legally): that is, he should know that he will win (or at least, not lose ignominiously) should it come to coercion. Should he fail to deter and also fail badly to coerce, he will have lost a great deal of standing—with clients, others and his agency, too, perhaps. Deterring, since it involves power, may mean the use of such techniques as bans, prohibitions or injunctions besides threats.

(f) Intervention. Hollis's word, but meaning the use of law and the application of sanction. Here the conflict is overt and unresolved, either by agreement or submission. The law invoked and the sanction applied will vary with circumstances, of course. When the law or sanction is applied to the client (such as their compulsory removal to a psychiatric hospital or the removal of their children to a place of safety) the threat to the relationship is severe and the possibility of continuing to work with them in jeopardy. This will be a factor for the worker to bear in mind before determining upon the use of coercion; but he will also need to remember that the law he is typically required to operate is designed to protect—either to protect the client against himself, or to protect others from the client's actions. The need to protect may far outweigh the need to maintain the opportunity to work further. The use of coercion does not always sever relationships, anyway. Some clients, afterwards, will acknowledge that the worker 'did the right thing', that he took action because he cared, and the relationship emerged all the stronger. We should never assume that just because we have used coercion the relationship is severed; but always try to continue working.

When taking coercive action on behalf of clients, the worker should always remember the probable stress and cost (including financial) to the client; so again, the decision whether to use this ultimate form of authority has to be the client's—and the case watertight. Authority may be used directly by ourselves, or indirectly by our utilising others better placed (whether for expertise, position or relationship reasons). Occasionally clients may manipulate us into using authority unnecessarily: perhaps as an easy way out for themselves— or to prove us wrong with a relished 'I told you so'.

The engagement process

Assuming the presenting problem at least, falls within the scope of the agency, the engagement process involves working out with the client what is to be done—negotiating the terms of the 'contract' previously discussed. A joint approach in this matter is both ethically sound (in that it embodies our values of worth and democratic rights) and practical. Imposed help is likely to be resented (thus vitiating treatment) as well as fostering dependence. Plans worked out with the client are likely to be seen by him as more relevant; he is more 'ego-involved' with them and is, therefore, more likely to try to implement them. The working out is growth producing—involving examination and decision; while if the plans succeed, the client can take some credit for this, with all it implies for additional competence, satisfaction, esteem and motivation. The engagement process is a microscosm of the whole casework process.

In the process of determining what is to be done and arriving at the contract, we shall also be deciding the distribution of the work between client and worker. This distribution will be effected by the function of the agency, the nature of the problems, the capacity of the worker and the capacity of the client—factors examined in the next chapter.

Nothing in this chapter negates the unitary approach to social work practice. What I have written about interviewing and communication, the needs which clients bring and the responses required from the worker (as well as the dilemmas sometimes involved), the influence of the agency on practice, the authority the worker utilises, his use of his professional self and the idea of contract are all common to all forms of social work practice. It is true that I have framed what I have written with individual work in mind; but a shift of emphasis (for example, a community worker might put more into the context within which the person-with-a-problem is functioning) or some amplification (for example, a group worker would need to negotiate a contract between members of a group as well as between the group and himself) would be sufficient to make this chapter applicable to any form of practice.

References

1. Florence Hollis, *Casework: a Psycho-social Therapy* (Random House), 1972.
2. F. P. Biestek, *The Casework Relationship* (George Allen & Unwin), 1967.
3. Paul Halmos, *The Faith of the Counsellors* (Constable), 1966.
4. Biestek, *ibid.*
5. Biestek, *ibid.*
6. *Confidentiality in Social Work*, Discussion Paper no. 1 (British Association of Social Workers), 1971.

Further Reading

No consideration of interviewing is complete without reading one of the classics of social work literature, *Common Human Needs* by Charlotte Towle (George Allen & Unwin), as well as one or two of the other standard works such as *Interviewing: its Principles and Practice* by Anne Garrett (Family Service Association of America), *Some Casework Concepts for the Public Welfare Worker* by Alan Keith-Lucas (University of North Carolina Press), *Interviewing in the Social Services* by Elizabeth and Karl de Schweinitz (National Council of Social Service); while *Interviewing Children and Adolescents* by John Rich (Macmillan) has a valuable contribution to make in a neglected and difficult area of practice.

The interview is considered in all the standard casework texts and these should be explored by all students, if only to see the value of the variety of approaches used in them. Typically, a student will feel more at home with one approach rather than another, but it would be a pity if his reading were confined to just this one. The texts I have found most useful are:

A Primer of Social Casework, E. Nicholds (Columbia University Press).

Social Casework, E. H. Davison (Balliere).

Social Casework: a Problem-solving Process, Helen Perlman (University of Chicago Press).

Casework: a Psycho-social Therapy, Florence Hollis (Random House).

Theory and Practice of Social Casework, Gordon Hamilton (Columbia University Press).

Social Casework: Principles & Practice, Noel Timms (Routledge & Kegan Paul).

Although not a typical standard text, a contrasting view based on a very different psychological approach, is given in Derek Jehu's book *Learning Theory and Social Work* (Routledge & Kegan Paul).

I still think (as my references to him infer) Felix P. Biestek's *The Casework Relationship* (George Allen & Unwin) is a 'must' for any student. The use of relationship is considered by Margaret L. Ferrard and Noel K. Honeybun in *The Caseworker's Use of Relationship* (Tavistock) and in a number of the articles, collected and published in book form by George Allen & Unwin, under Dame Eileen Younghusband's editorship, in their National Institute for Social Work Training series. I would especially commend the volumes *Social Work with Families* and *New Developments in Casework* which are full of material relevant to this chapter.

For the student who is interested in casework practice in particular settings or with particular groups of clients there are a considerable number of texts, of which the following are a sample:

Social Work in Child Care, Elizabeth Pugh (Routledge & Kegan Paul).

Casework in the Child Care Service, Noel Timms (Butterworths).

Social Work with Children, Juliet Berry (Routledge & Kegan Paul).

Adolescence and Social Work, A. J. Laycock (Routledge & Kegan Paul).

Social Work in Foster Care, Robt. J. N. Tod (ed.) (Longmans).

Social Work in Adoption, Robt. J. N. Tod (ed.) (Longmans).

Social Work in Medical Care, Z. Butrym (Routledge & Kegan Paul).

Social Work in General Practice, E. M. Goldberg & J. E. Neill (George Allen & Unwin).

On Death and Dying, M. Kuhbler-Ross (Collier Macmillan).

Family Influences and Psychosomatic Illness, E. M. Goldberg (Tavistock).

Parents and Family Planning Services, Ann Cartwright (Routledge & Kegan Paul).

Without a Wedding-ring: Casework with Unmarried Mothers, Jean Pochin (Constable).

Casework and Mental Illness, E. E. Irvine (ed.) (British Association of Social Workers).

Mental Illness and Social Work, Eugene Heimler (Penguin).

Psychogeriatrics, Brice Pitt (Churchill Livingstone).

Social Work with the Mentally Subnormal, F. J. Todd (Routledge & Kegan Paul).

Social Work in Marital Problems, Family Discussion Bureau (Tavistock).

Husband, Wife and Caseworker, Mark Monger (Butterworth).

The Work of the Probation and After-care Officer, Phyllida Parsloe (Routledge & Kegan Paul).

Casework in Probation, Mark Monger (Butterworth).

Casework in After-care, Mark Monger (Butterworth).

The Psychology of Human Ageing, D. B. Bromley (Penguin).

Welfare in the Community, E. M. Goldberg (National Council of Social Service).

Social Work with Immigrants, Juliet Cheetham (Routledge & Kegan Paul).

Counselling in Education, Patricia Milner (Dent).

For the clients' view of social work (essential reading, anyway; but particularly in connection with the idea of the contract between social worker and client) I suggest *The Client Speaks* by John E. Meyer and Noel Timms (Routledge & Kegan Paul) and *The Receiving End*, edited by Noel Timms (Routledge & Kegan Paul); together with an excellent article by Stuart Rees which appears in the *British Journal of Social Work*, Autumn, 1974, called 'No more than contact'.

For further reading about specific matters raised in this chapter I would suggest for communication, Peter Day's book *Communication in Social Work* (Pergamon) and *Interviewing and Communication in Social Work*, edited by Crispin P. Cross (Routledge

& Kegan Paul). On authority, I would recommend *Authority in Social Casework* by Robert Foren and Royston Bailey (Pergamon), while for a discussion of the professional social worker's task I would suggest *The Professional Task in Welfare Practice* by Peter Nokes. The ethical issues which arise in practice are examined in Raymond Plant's *Social and Moral Theory in Casework* (Routledge & Kegan Paul).

For those students interested in the process of becoming a client, I suggest they look into David Robinson's *The Process of Becoming Ill* (Routledge & Kegan Paul) and *Health and Sickness—the choice of treatment* by M. E. J. Wadsworth, W. J. H. Butterfield & R. Blaney (Tavistock); while there is also some interesting, relevant material in Erving Goffman's *Asylums* (Penguin).

Discussion

In this long and complex chapter there is material for at least half a dozen seminars.

Students at the beginning of a course often have a stereotype of interviewing deriving from their stereotype of casework as an 'in-depth', quasi-analytic, one-to-one session in an office setting. Some students try to emulate the stereotype, others are hostile to it; both may need help to recognise that the way a social worker 'interviews' needs to be thought about and selected.

Individualism as a concept usually presents few difficulties as almost all students are sympathetically concerned for clients as individuals, though sometimes they do not extend this to colleagues. Expectations based on stereotypes emerge in discussions concerning them—doctors and the Supplementary Benefits Commission appear to be the main 'victims' of this process. Any problems about individualising clients tend to emerge in students' practical work, though discussion can greatly assist individualising through an extension of their knowledge and their imagination.

Listening is again an acceptable idea, though students tend to see it as a passive rather than an active matter. The seminar discussion of this topic might be used to illustrate the wide range of factors involved in mal-communication and the feelings this generates—provided always the group is cohesive enough at this point to tolerate a process which can be quite painful. This is one way in which college based teaching can replicate in a way, what will be taking place in fieldwork teaching.

Acceptance of the client is also an approach that has the natural sympathy of students, though in any discussion some of their own biases may show up. Two areas of difficulty often emerge; one is students' tendency sometimes to be non-accepting of those who express non-accepting views of their clients. While I sympathise with their anger, I feel that even the non-accepting have to be accepted at least to the point which enables working relationships to be maintained if clients' interests are not to suffer; utilising what opportunities we have for informal education to try to modify hostile views. The other is the students' thoughts and feelings about the hazy and agonising situations in which they have to act judgmentally because of their obligations as social workers yet struggle to maintain a workable relationship with those they feel they have acted against. Their function of social control (as they see it) is one that troubles students frequently—as it does the whole profession. Discussion can help to clarify a great deal.

Confidentiality is another issue which can become a highly emotive one in discussion. It is not the keeping of confidences which gives trouble (since almost all students see this as important) but where we breach a confidence. Like most of us, students would feel easier if the confidentiality rule were absolute, and they do not like to acknowledge that we may have obligations to pass on information given in confidence. Even where they accept we may have to, they would prefer clear guidelines and they sometimes find it hard to tolerate the ambiguity of what guidelines exist and sometimes the lack of agency policy to help them. The responsibility that accrues with professional status is often hard to bear, much as we enjoy the authority that goes with it.

Students often get extremely angry (rightly) at what they see as lack of regard for confidentiality in their agencies—poor interviewing facilities, overheard telephone conversations, records accessible to all and sundry, etc.—even jocular conversations in the staff room. If such conditions obtain in their practical work placement agencies, they feel particularly angry and helpless given they are 'only students'. The only answer here is for college staff to acknowledge their responsibility here, take matters up with the fieldwork teacher concerned, and the agency if necessary—though the only ultimate sanc-

Casework in Context

tion the college may have is not to use that agency again. In any meantime, the student should be supported in his own stand as far as his own work is concerned. But perhaps of equal importance for discussion is to clarify ways students might have when subsequently employed to take such matters up constructively within their own agencies. The handicap, often, is workers' feelings that they cannot change anything when frequently they can.

Students are typically reaching out for further understanding. A great deal that is happening elsewhere on the course will be furthering understanding and discussion here can add to this in a usefully interdisciplinary way, particularly if case illustrations are used. The implications of the process by which one becomes a client is a fruitful area for discussion, often overlooked. In understanding others students will sometimes come to a fuller, but painful, understanding of themselves—a factor that should not be forgotten in any discussion of feeling or interaction.

In the section of helping I have focussed on the agency and the worker's authority, looking particularly at the nature of the professional relationship. Discussing the agency often brings up students' feelings of frustration and constriction about agency focus, policy, resources and bureaucracy. It might be better to defer too lengthy an examination of these factors until consideration is given to the relations between professional staff and administration (see Chapter XI); but discussing the agency does give the opportunity to look again at the societal context of both agency and social work practice.

Authority is not an easy topic to discuss; many students do not like to think of themselves as carrying authority, with its negative overtones, and have an innate (and very valuable) preference for an egalitarian approach to their clients. Being considered as experts rather frightens them when, as students they are aware of their lack of knowledge (in general, and in particular about their agency or field of work should this be new to them); though they readily appreciate the value expertise can be to their clients. The value to their client of their positional authority (and especially their command over resources and influence) may need underlining when again, some students dislike the thought of positional authority—and it is a difficulty in dealing with some clients. Students at times enjoy positional authority when it means they can provide for their clients or influence matters positively; but get uneasy when this authority means they have to deny clients for a range of reasons, or their influence proves insufficient.

Looking at the nature of a professional relationship is also quite a painful and confusing matter for some students. Three issues typically arise:

(1) The question of involvement. Some students have an endemic fear of over-involvement (whether as a factor of personality, through having been 'warned off' by colleagues, or their own concern not to make a mess of things); while others regard the typical social worker as uselessly stand-offish and want to plunge in. The concept of a directed, purposive, involvement may assist both groups.

(2) The differentiation of the professional relationship from friendship. Many students would like to think of themselves as befriending clients, especially those who are isolated and friendless. We all need friends, but it is hard for some students to accept that we cannot be both a professional and a friend at the same time. I see them as mutually exclusive relations. The professional task with the friendless is to help them to make friends with others, not ourselves.

(3) The differentiation of professional *style*. Here again we are often up against a stereotype of professional behaviour with feelings for and against it. To consider a selection of style to best serve the purpose is the most helpful approach to students feelings and anxieties, I feel. A formal approach is not necessarily cold and an informal not necessarily risking socialising.

The discussion about professional relationships is likely to recur when relations with voluntary workers are considered (see Chapter XIII): but a second look at a later stage of the course is frequently very productive.

All through my discussion with students of this material, I tend to emphasise the functional necessity for and the purposiveness of factors such as individualising, acceptance, the professional relationship, etc. I feel this assists students to a clearer identity as social workers. They can explain to others why they act in certain ways, distinguish what they can and cannot do, and comprehend the functional necessities behind others' actions—an important step towards good teamwork. The bulk of students come to professional training with the natural aptitudes and attitudes that make for good professional practice but until they have identified why these are functional they may tend to use these qualities indiscriminately and not always most effectively; or they may promote them into quasi-principles of behaviour that everyone ought to follow, irrespective of their function, which could be seen by others as quite unreasonable at times (and therefore also spoiling good practice).

CHAPTER IV

Diagnosis

We now turn to diagnosis, treatment goals, methods and plans—the operationalising of earlier material. While for theoretical purposes we have to isolate these aspects, in practice this is difficult to do, and they may be going on concurrently, though with perhaps a differing emphasis given to them through the stages of our contacts with clients.

Diagnosis has been defined by Perlman[1] as 'an organising of the facts of person, problem and place (agency) in a casework situation and coming to some judgment of their meaning for what is to be done and how best to do it'. Diagnosis (despite its rather awesome medical overtones) is no more than making conscious and formalising a process which inevitably takes place at the intuitive level anyway; but making it a structured process enables thoughtful consideration to be given to the evidence (and therefore, a better balanced view) and also enables any bias on the part of the worker to be identified (and therefore a more objective view). With this greater accuracy more effective work can take place. A diagnosis gives boundary (focus), relevance (purpose) and direction (suggests immediate and ultimate goals and methods to achieve them) to our work; in other words, tells us what is needed, what is possible, and how best to tackle it. Diagnosis not only makes material (objective and subjective) more useful for ourselves, but also makes it communicable (in whole or in part) to clients and other team members as necessary.

Mrs. Potter was admitted to hospital suffering from appendicitis. She was 37 years old, married, with two daughters aged 11 and

8. Her operation went normally and her subsequent recovery, but towards the end of her planned hospital stay, the ward staff picked up that she seemed to be fretting and so referred her to the medical social worker.

After the introductions and some preliminary exchanges, Mrs. Potter rather reluctantly admitted that she had been worrying, but felt that she was being rather silly, did not want to bother the nurses or doctors who had much more important things to do than listen to her and felt apologetic even about taking up the social worker's time. She explained that this was the first time she had ever been seriously ill, it was her first hospital admission and her first operation. She knew she had had appendicitis, but could not help wondering whether, when they operated, they had found 'something else' they were not telling her about. She hated the thought of a scar, too, and wondered what her husband would think about it and if this might not have some effect on their marriage. She had also thought the operation might have some effect on her menstrual cycle or her own wish for the physical side of marriage; or even on her ability to have children—though they were not planning to have any more children, anyway.

Mrs. Potter had the natural concern for how things were going at home in her absence and how the children were taking her being away; but of most immediate concern to her was how she would cope when she got home. Her husband, who was now 45, had had a slight heart attack some months before. She knew she would not be able to do any heavy lifting, and so on, for some time and she was afraid that if her husband had to do it instead he might have another heart attack and perhaps die this time. Her mother had been able to stay to look after things while she was in hospital, but she could only stay for a few more days at best because of commitments she had in her own home—father being far from well.

During the interview, the social worker ascertained that, though inclined to be a bit anxious, Mrs. Potter managed very competently ordinarily. She had a stable, affectionate relationship with her husband (who was a schoolteacher), enjoyed her children, had a number of outside interests, a circle of friends, and got on well with her own and her husband's relatives. There were no financial problems and she liked the house they lived in, which they were buying on a mortgage. From the interview, the social worker felt that Mrs. Potter was able to acknowledge her feelings, and though she tended to mask them to the point where she found them a little frightening, at least she did not deny them. With a little encouragement she could talk about them, focus upon them meaningfully, and relate comfortably enough to others while she was doing so.

With Mrs. Potter's permission, the social worker subsequently discussed matters with the Consultant Surgeon and the Potters' General Practitioner. From the consultant she learned that this was a straightforward case of appendicitis with no complications, no suggestion of any other condition, that within 3/4 weeks Mrs. Potter should be functioning normally, and that any residual scarring would be minimal. From the G.P. she learned that as long as Mr. Potter kept an eye on his diet and weight and did not indulge in any prolonged unusual exercise, there was no reason why he should not live a completely normal life. In the course of her conversations, the medical social worker had explained a little of the background to her enquiries and the reasons for her professional involvement.

On the basis of her material, the social worker considered there were no problems that warranted her intervention other than those Mrs. Potter had herself raised. She felt that having ventilated her difficulties, Mrs. Potter's needs might be adequately met by offering the reassurance of the medical information she had obtained, plus the practical assistance of a home help during her convalescence.

When the social worker saw Mrs. Potter next day, she seemed a good deal more relaxed and accepted the medical re-assurances, though in a way which indicated they were now only confirming what she herself believed. She said how stupid she felt that she had let things get out of proportion and that she had felt a lot better just by talking about them. She admitted that as regards the home help, she did not relish the idea of a strange woman coming into her home and running it, but that she would not really mind as she badly wanted to get back home now. She proudly showed the social worker the bunch of flowers her husband had brought her at visiting time the previous evening and the 'get well' cards her daughters had painted and brought too.

A diagnosis is never static: we shall be constantly adding to it as we get to know more about a person/situation. It will always be tentative, since we cannot know everything (nor do we need to); but it can too, be a touchstone—helping us to identify areas where we need to know more to help effectively.

The books identify different types of diagnosis: a *dynamic* diagnosis is an analysis of current interaction which is always needed since it is this situation we shall be constantly dealing with. But we may not understand the current functioning without a *clinical* diagnosis, i.e. a study of personality structure, whether of the client and/or 'significant others' in the situation. (A clinical diagnosis is not to be confused with a medical diagnosis.) We may not even understand current personality structure without an *aetiological* or historical diagnosis to help us understand the factors in the development of the problem, their duration, consistency and pervasiveness, and how the client has previously dealt with them. A *categorical* diagnosis is a broad 'labelling' of the problem (marital, housing, personality disorder) used primarily for statistical purposes or 'short-hand' communication—but should be used with care. Labels tend to stick, and their vagueness means they can be interpreted so differently that they become nearly meaningless as a way of understanding *this* instance of marital disharmony, housing problem, etc.

The process of making a diagnosis has been broken down into a number of stages: gathering the data, the diagnostic study, the diagnosis itself or the evaluation, and the diagnostic product. These stages will be involved whether the matter is straightforward or complex, but to press for diagnostic material on the assumption that situations always involve complex personal factors is an unwarrantable intrusion likely to be resented by the client. Even where there are complexities but the client does not wish to discuss them, pressure may be resented. Broadly, we only seek that information we need to deal with the problem—the problem being that negotiated and contracted between worker and client. Problems should always be handled, though, in a way which allows the client to re-negotiate, bearing in mind that occasionally we may need to encourage this process.

(1) GATHERING THE DATA

There are many sources of data: referral reports, the agency's records of previous contacts, reports from other members of the team such as psychiatrists or psychologists (the results of I.Q. tests, personality tests, or projective tests such as the Rorscharch), or collateral sources—other agencies, schools, etc., or relatives (whether obtained formally through a social history or informally through our contacts with them). A home visit will tell us much—the client's material and social circumstances, the way the home is run, and may also provide the opportunity of seeing our client in interaction with the family or others. But quite the most important source of material is the interview—what and how the client communicates and what the worker understands from this.

Gathering the data involves many facets of social work skill—individualisation, acceptance, communication, the handling of issues of confidentiality; and will depend often on the way the relationship develops, to allow of the expression of emotionally charged material where this is necessary, and therefore, probably needing time for this to happen; perhaps four or five interviews. Data gathering is important, though, since no diagnosis can be better than the material it rests upon.

(2) DIAGNOSTIC STUDY

Gathering the data has been described as 'opening one's eyes to look' and the study as 'closing one's eyes to think'—a process which sometimes does not happen in the press of day-to-day agency 'busyness'. But in the long run it saves time if it means the difference between work which is focussed and structured and work which is a flurry of unfocussed, unstructured activity. Broadly, the study attempts to identify the problem areas which are to be the focus of the social work involvement, and these problem areas and the factors which relate to them are then carried over and organised in the following.

(3) DIAGNOSIS OR EVALUATION

Broadly, this means looking at the nature or character of the problem, its organisation and extent, and the people to whom it is happening. Generally, a situation is likely to be a combination of factors, but they may be grouped as under:

(a) Physical. Problems may arise directly out of the illness or disability itself—its implications for the sufferer and/or their families; and/or the derivatives—problems of management and accommodation of the physical factors for all those involved.

Physical factors themselves have both their objective and subjective side—how the sufferer feels and how his family and others feel. There is no scope here to go into the multiple facets of the work of medical and psychiatric social workers; but just to mention subnormality, schizophrenia, dementia, congenital deformity (spasticity, blindness, deafness, spina bifida), acquired deformity (stroke illness, amputation, disfigurement), deteriorating conditions (arthritis, multiple sclerosis), heart attacks, etc. is sufficient to indicate the objective medical, practical management (with all this implies) and the emotive elements (for the sufferer and all those involved). The relevance of physical factors is irrefutable, even if they are only part of the problem. Bear in mind that there can be many indirect effects of physical factors in that while people ordinarily cope sufficiently well, because they are ill (not always recognising that they are) they are not able to do so. Pain, anxiety, feeling 'below par' can make people narcissistic, dependent, tired, irritable, depressed; affect their self-image, disrupt communication between people, and distort relationships. It is always an important part of assessment to get the physical aspects checked.

(b) Psychological. Where psychological factors have a bearing on problem areas (in the client or others) it is often crucial to determine whether these represent a 'steady state' (on going behaviour patterns), a reaction to stress, or attributable to a transitional developmental phase (adolescence, climacteric, for example). But it is also important not to think of psychological factors merely as a 'list of defects' contributing to the problems, nor even as a 'list of strengths' which might be utilised in coping with the problem areas (though they are both), but as a complexity in an interactional situation which will have a bearing on the total social work process.

The approach to the assessment of psychological factors will be coloured by the social worker's preference for a particular school of psychology. None has a monopoly of the truth in interpreting anything as complex as human behaviour, and my hope would be that all social work students would be introduced to the main schools of psychological thought. To be exposed to only one would risk a doctrinaire interpretation and a treatment approach the client might find totally unacceptable. If I now use psychoanalytic terms it is largely because of their familiarity and their comprehensiveness, but I repeat there are other explanations for the behaviour mentioned. But it is this compass of behaviour which may (and I emphasise may) need to be taken into consideration, depending on the nature of the problem.

Analytic psychology hypotheses that man has certain instinctual drives (sex and aggression-self assertion-self preservation) which are carried through certain developmental stages described as the oral phase (focussing on the mouth and feeding), the anal phase (focussing on urination, defaecation and toilet training) and the genital phase (focussing on sexuality). Adult maturity will depend on how successfully drives and stages are managed, particularly during infancy—with success dependent on the responses of parents. These responses will be in part culturally determined but deeply influenced by the way their own instinct-through-stages development went. The child, therefore, is not interacting in a neutral atmosphere but one heavily charged with feelings—some of which his parents may not recognise in themselves since they have been pushed down into unconsciousness by means of repression or disassociation—ways of defending ourselves against feelings which are unacceptable (typically dangerous) or developmental needs which still exist unmet. The emotions still exist, however, and the child will sense them. Any of his feelings which he senses will be dangerous, given his dependence on powerful parent figures, he will deal with by repression or by other defence mechanisms such as projection (attributing to others unconscious feelings in himself that he cannot accept or deal with: handling them as though they were 'out there' rather than 'in here') or sublimation (transmuting unacceptable feelings or impulses in himself into socially acceptable forms of activity). Those feelings directed towards him which he feels threatening will be resisted by assertion, withdrawal or perhaps some form of reaction formation (a hyper-sensitivity to certain forms of threat producing exaggerated defensive responses).

The stages of development may leave certain needs at stages unfulfilled; particular fears at certain stages might develop because of particular parental responses (for example, at the anal stage because of parental feelings about the dirtiness of it); or a child may be trapped in one stage, afraid to progress to the next because of parental feelings in that area. Freud suggests there may be considerable difficulties at the genital stage for boys since their sexual drive towards the mother is inhibited by their fear of castration by the father—their rival for the possession of the mother. This fear is said to be negotiated by identification with the powerful father figure.

As the child's social life develops to encompass not only the mother but both parents and subsequently siblings and peer groups, new opportunities are created for significant relationships, new socially derived needs emerge (for companionship and play, for example) calling for new social skills. But analysis would suggest that how these widening relationships, needs and skills are developed depends a great deal on how successfully the primary relationships within the family have been handled. There will be a carry over into relations with parent surrogates or authority figures, such as teachers, attitudes derived from relations with parents; while peer relationships may reflect how relations with siblings have been experienced. There may be connections between these two in the sense that if relations with parents have not been sufficiently satisfying a child may experience siblings as a threat to relations with parents—a sibling rivalry situation—reflecting not only tension in relations with parent figures but with peers, too.

Out of this interplay of very primitive feeling, the super-ego develops: that part of our unconscious life, in analytic terms, which attempts to counteract those aspects of the drives and stages development which are deemed dangerous to survival. It is perhaps the super-ego which then becomes identified as the 'good' side of our emotional life with the 'id' (the drives-through stages) the 'bad' side. The super-ego may thus become a source of certain drives or needs connected with self-security such as the needs to be thought well of, to be popular or liked, or the need to nurture others—all in some way a reflection of our need to secure the nurture of others for ourselves since we are never totally independent and have an on-going need for support and contact with our fellows.

This drives-through-stages process and super-ego formation is accompanied by a developing awareness of self, self-identity, constantly exposed to and influenced by the feedback received from interaction with a widening social circle. Also accompanying this process are the child's developing cognitive skills, and out of this interplay of inner and outer factors the ego—what most of us would understand as self, emerges.

The ego has to contend with and mediate between the inner world of the unconscious (id and super-ego) and external realities and responses. The influences of past interactions remain with us, colouring our views and reactions. This is not to suggest, however, that these influences are immutable. New relationships, especially the intensive ones such as marriage and parenthood (and, on occasions, a relationship with a social worker), while 'digging up' feelings and reactions from the past, will provide the opportunity for re-living old relationships in a way, and so the opportunity for re-learning; for resolving (re-solving) tensions and conflicts former relations left with us. This is what makes these new relationships so dangerous, painful and challenging, but potentially so rewarding and enriching too.

In a previous chapter I outlined some of the ego qualities such as tolerance levels, perception and being in touch with feelings. But it is understandable that in the tri-partite interaction of the inner emotional life, external reality and the self, that some people's tolerance levels are low, perception is distorted by a turbulent inner life and that contact with inner feelings is broken off.

As social workers, our concern is often for people who are in psychological difficulty:

 those who are withdrawn from almost any meaningful contact with others since contacts involve danger for them;
 those whose emotions are shut away or seriously inhibited;
 those who 'blow their top' too readily;
 those who get 'walked over' by others;

those who eat compulsively since ('orally') they are still emotionally
hungry;

those who are revolted by any contact with dirt;

those who can only find sexual gratification through homosexuality, pornography, flagellation, promiscuity or masturbation;

those who avoid contact with the opposite sex altogether, or whose
relations are troubled by impotence or frigidity;

those who are plagued by guilt or masochism;

those who are so desperate for affection or popularity that others
shy away from them, sensing needs that might engulf them;

those so suspicious of others that they push them into the very
actions they were originally suspected of;

those that are perpetually dependent or inordinately independent;

those whose self-esteem is so threatened that the slightest hint of
even unwitting denigration produces a totally disproportionate
reaction;

those with defences so tightly drawn or inflexible they seem perpetually at breaking point;

those with defences so rigid that they are creating difficulties for
others that redound on the rigid to make his situation worse.

It is more likely, however, that we shall see people in conflict:
between expression of drives and super-ego fear of them and repression of them; between a thrust for maturity and a fear of loss of
dependency; between a continuing dependency but an underlying
resentment of loss of independence. This is not to suggest that we
will deal directly with unconscious material (though it may become
modified in the course of our work) but it will tell us much about
the way people relate and their capacity to do so, which will be
of importance in identifying the limitations within which we must
work and indicate areas bearing on the potentiality for movement
within the situation.

But given that social workers are not analysts, but concerned with
people in interaction with themselves or others, social work may
be more indebted to the ego-psychology approach rather than
psycho-analysis (though ego-psychology is a derivative of analysis).

Ego qualities are many: among them are abilities of perception
(accurate/distorted), judgment (rational/irrational, considered/hasty),

reality testing (working at things as they are, or resorting to fantasy), self-image (realistic, inflated/denigrated), impulse control (too little, too much), and executant ability (can they do things, organise themselves to achieve, persist). Thought processes may be logical/illogical, informed or ignorant. We may need to take into account identifications (models); fantasies (distinguished as such, or lost in them); affects (cold/intense, appropriate or inappropriate affectual responses); anxiety levels (realistic or not, how pervasive, persistent, how anxiety is dealt with); guilt (realistic or not, coped with by denigration, reparation, projection or how); what defences are being used (denial, projection, introjection, evasion, rationalisation, regression, manipulation, seduction, etc.); whether defences are excessive or few (leaving people vulnerable, rigid or flexible) and how far they might allow of insight or modification. (For a discussion of the nature of defences see Chapter VI.)

As I have stated, ego and unconscious developments take place over time in response to situations, and it may be significant to ascertain how people relate to their past—relations with parents and siblings, the impact of trauma (separation, death, illness), the circumstances of their upbringing and what it meant to them (poverty/ wealth, membership of a particular sub-cultural group, or ethic group, etc.), the opportunity or otherwise that education and/or employment offered, the significance of their experience of marriage and parenthood.

All this will help us to understand their general outlook on life: the way they see it as basically good, unjust, or a perpetual battle. People may be 'locked up' in their past, brooding over it; or they may be able to view it dispassionately, or in a considered way, learning from it; or they may blot it out. All this will effect the way they may be currently functioning and influence our approach and assessment. There may be little need to 'dig' for this material—much of it will emerge in the course of our contact.

Any 'digging' that may be done (and this is only done if the problem-solving warrants it) needs to be handled with exceptional care, since opening up aspects of the past or the present may release material the client may be unable to cope with subsequently, making their situation worse rather than better.

How much of this psychological material is incorporated into the diagnosis will depend, of course, on the problem areas being dealt with. The evaluation of the material will also incorporate our knowledge of what is appropriate to the particular developmental stage (in human growth terms) or the place in the life cycle. The understanding of the developmental stage might be crucial in work involving children. Diagnostically it would be significant to know what might be expected at a particular age in order to evaluate whether behaviour is typical or atypical—reflecting retardation or disturbance. If behaviour were typical, but the parents regarded it as atypical this could indicate that the focus of the work needed to be on them rather than the child. Also in handling say, an admission to care it would be vital to understand what the likely effect of separation at this age would be and how much the child might be able to comprehend in the way of explanation of what is happening to him. A child of two has little appreciation of what 'next week' means. If he does not see mother for a day or two he is likely to be convinced she has gone for ever; but a child of eight would be able to understand and tolerate separation with less distress probably since he would ordinarily understand more and have a greater appreciation of what time meant. To plan the admission anticipating some of the likely difficulties derived from our knowledge of child development may enable us to minimise any possible damage—if only from the point of view of the frequency of parental visits.

Our general awareness of behaviour appropriate to life cycle stages, or the difficulties associated with particular stages (marriage, parenthood, climacteric, 'mid-life' crises, loss of function in older age and so on) would help us to evaluate behaviour, understand reactions and give us a lead in to problem areas.

(c) Social. No-one operates in a physical or psychological vacuum, but always in interaction with an environment. The part this environment plays can be crucial. Again, it has many facets which may come within the diagnosis. Among these may be income level (high, low, consistent, uncertain, with its source often of great significance— earned by employment or insurance right, or unearned and therefore dependent on company directors, spouse, parent or Supplementary Benefits); housing (whether owned or rented; a house or a high rise flat; whether spatially adequate, too much, or overcrowded; whether well-equipped or lacking basic facilities); neighbourhood (tolerant or intolerant; supportive or 'none of our business'; its 'fit' to the client(s) in terms of social class, ethnicity, mores, etc.); employment (job satisfaction, or in cases of unemployment or 'mal'employment, job availability, prospects, remuneration levels, security, status, conditions of work; the qualifications, skills, experience, mental or physical aptitudes called for—and how the client 'fits' with these); religion (active membership or not; offering support—consolation, expressive outlets, sublimation—or reinforcing problems around guilt, birth control, etc.—or affecting tensions around identity, primary loyalty); availability/quality/attitudes of, and client(s) attitudes to a wide range of social organisations and services (medical facilities, schools, shops, transport, playgroups, youth clubs, recreation facilities, courts, credit organisations, legal advice centres, post offices, social security offices, etc.); social groups (do they exist, formally—Women's Institutes, Mothers Unions, Working Men's Clubs, Scouts, Guides—or informally—pubs, launderettes, bingo, neighbouring coffee mornings; are they typically insular or welcoming; can the client manage them in terms of cost, time, ability to manage relationships appropriately, client(s) attitudes to them); and above all, extended family relationships (their existence, availability, and quality—supportive and assisting problem solving, or destructive and contributing to the problems).

A local situation will not be divorced from the wider society, of course: local employment may reflect the national economic position or national policies regarding say, development areas; local housing reflect national emphases on clearance or rehabilitation of older property, on the incentives for owner occupation, private renting or public renting; or the priorities for hospitals, schools, roads, transport, the encouragement of voluntary action, immigration policy and a multitude of other facets. Local situations cannot be divorced from national attitudes about class, colour, creed, crime, and a welter of culturally determined expectations and the control/reward mechanisms that support them, the degree of consensus about them, or conflict concerning them.

All this indicates social work's profound concern for the nature of the society we live in and the derived institutions (political, educational, economic, familial, etc.) which have such a crucial bearing upon the quality of the life of individuals within that society at local and national level.

In examining these three aspects, we are trying to assess the nature of the *transactions* our client is engaged in and to identify where the misunderstandings, inappropriate responses, or inadequacies (personal, social or material) lie. As Hollis[2] suggests, we shall be analysing whether this is basically a problem of deprivation, frustration or provocation; whether we are dealing with a 'normal' person under inordinate stress (and many of our clients are struggling with circumstances that would defeat us and all but the most mature); or with a troubled person who cannot cope with 'normal' demands. We shall need to make this analysis in conjunction with what we know is 'normal' in terms of the stage of development, place in the life cycle, and subcultural patterns of behaviour of those groups with which our client(s) have been identified in the past and is currently engaged with. But clearly, the conclusions we come to will have a profound influence on how we will handle matters.

(4) DIAGNOSTIC PRODUCT

Having identified the problem areas and the factors which relate to them, the product begins to turn towards possible solutions; but before these can be determined, we need to think about the potential contribution to solutions of the client, others, the agency and the worker.

Clearly, from the point of view of producing growth and avoiding dependency (as well as, perhaps, avoiding waste of the worker), the objective is for the problem-solving work to be left to the client as far as this is possible and reasonable. But to determine how the work is to be distributed in the immediate and more distant future, will require an assessment of the client's 'workability'. Workability is a compound of capacity and motivation. Perlman[3] discusses capacity under three headings:

Emotional—the ability to relate to others, and the ability to feel—
　　without either shutting down on feelings or being overwhelmed

by them; in touch with them, experiencing them, but containing them.

Social intelligence—not so much a matter of I.Q., but of basically ego qualities—perceptivity, ability to focus attention and communicate, plus a general 'know-how' about self management and the management of situations.

Physical—which may be the easiest to assess in objective terms but also needing assessment as to how much the client has 'left over' to work on problem-solving.

In looking at capacity, we are not only concerned with the client's existing capacity but also their potential capacity, given help from us in terms of the treatment methods available to us: whether capacity may be extended with release from the stress through the worker's use of psychological support or material aid; whether modifications in attitudes, responses and so behaviour might be achieved through the use of reflective discussion or consideration; whether resources exist to develop the client's range of skills, and so on. It is this potential capacity which will be the basis, perhaps, of our long term goals; immediate capacity will need to be the focus of immediate goals and guide the distribution between worker, client and others of the current work. I feel it is important to have the long term goals in mind, though, even in the here and now situation to ensure that what we do immediately does not impinge detrimentally on the long term objectives.

But capacity is of little use if motivation is absent. We shall get some clues about motivation level when the client tells us something of how he came to the agency in the first place—of his own volition or under duress from events or other people. His presentation will also tell us much, with motivation likely to be low if the presentation is either apathetic or the client is seeking 'magic wand' cures, more wish-fulfilment than reality based. Clearly, there is much for the social worker to do to assist motivation on a realistic level—through the use of support and encouragement; the discussion of the reality situation, even the stimulation of anxiety occasionally, or even direct confrontation: so motivational capacity may also need to be assessed in the long term (will it evaporate when the stress is lifted, can we stimulate it, or make it more realistic?) as well as in the here and now. Perhaps the balance is achieved when we can work out with the client achievable goals at a tolerable cost.

We shall learn much about capacity and motivation from the material which has already gone into the evaluation, of course; but again, the interview will be the main contributor to our knowledge: how clients present the problem (narrow, specific, broad, tentative); how they present their solution (in material or personal terms); how they indicate their involvement in their situation (their fault, others fault, 'bad luck', with little feeling, or a great deal, appropriately discharged or not); how much of themselves they reveal in this process; whether they expect the worker to assume full responsibility for their problems, or whether they are prepared to work at the situation with him; how far they have been able to modify their view over the course of the interview (or do they go out with the same feelings, attitudes, views of the situation, the worker and solutions, that they came in with?); how do they react to the tentative views and ideas the worker puts forward, or what he offers in the way of help (which almost inevitably means a degree of delay if nothing else, and so requires the tolerance of least a degree of frustration)—and so on. We shall probably end up with a range of factors which are not modifiable, others which are—in the short or longer term; and our goals and methods will need to allow of both.

We need to examine the social factors included in the evaluation, not so much now in terms of their relation to the problem areas, but in terms of the opportunities they afford or the constraints they put around the situation in terms of possible solutions. Again, we shall probably be faced with immovable and modifiable factors which need to be allowed for. Even those factors which are modifiable may take time, and mean that stop gap measures may need to be employed in the interim. Parental attitudes to children are not changed overnight: the damage to the child goes on, and we may have to think in terms of a residential placement at least as a holding measure until parents attitudes have been sufficiently modified. Housing policy and provision is inevitably a matter of years; social attitudes involving say, class or colour may take even generations to alter. The problem about the use of interim measures (as I indicated in my opening chapter) is whether in at least ameliorating current suffering we may be reducing the pressure for the more radical changes needed. This operates at a number of levels: parents with a 'problem' child away may have only a reduced incentive for changing themselves; an individual family's housing problem solved reduces the pressure of the housing list and so the pressure for housing action; class accommodated may be class perpetuated.

Besides the social factors, we need to examine what other individuals, groups, institutions or agencies, or other methods of social work could contribute (or need to contribute) to the problem solving; and finally we need to examine what our agency and we as social case workers can contribute. This process must begin with the functions of our own agency—determining what of the problem areas is the agency's responsibility. In the light of this responsibility, the availability of the agency's resources (whether of cash, kind or social worker's time and skill) must be assessed, since given these, certain solutions may or may not be possible. Having identified the agency's area of responsibility, we will then have also identified the problem areas which more properly belong elsewhere. We will need to consider where a referral or intervention by us may properly be made; and from our knowledge try to gauge how others' procedures, resources, etc. are likely to effect matters, and whether this may not call for modification of our own possible programme. Very occasionally, all the problems may come within the orbit of our agency; very occasionally we may refer the whole problem elsewhere; but in the majority of cases a joint approach is necessary, involving ongoing co-operative work—the team approach; or pressure applied—a basically conflict approach.

It is perhaps at this stage of diagnosis that I find the systems approach such a useful tool of analysis.

It is out of this total diagnostic process—data, study, evaluation and product—that our subsequent selection of goals and treatment method will emerge.

References

1. Helen Perlman, *Social Casework: a Problem-solving Process* (Chicago University Press), 1957.
2. Florence Hollis, *Casework: a Psycho-social Therapy* (Random House), 1972.
3. Helen Perlman, ibid.

Further reading

Most of the standard casework texts mentioned at the end of the last chapter, contain sections on diagnosis; but also of fundamental significance are the 'unitary approach' books by Perlman, Pincus and Minaham, Goldstein *et al.*, mentioned at the end of Chapter II—quite apart from the books being studied in other discipline areas, of course.

I would add two items of reading specifically related to diagnosis here: Peter Sainsbury's *Social Diagnosis in Casework* (published by Routledge & Kegan Paul) and Jonathan Bradshaw's seminal article 'The concept of social need', which appeared in *New Society*, 30th March 1972.

I would also suggest students read E. M. Goldberg's 'The normal family: myth and reality' which appears in *Social Work with Families* edited by Eileen Younghusband, published by George Allen & Unwin.

For those students interested in other approaches to understanding a look at Neil Leighton's 'The act of understanding' (*British Journal of Social Work*, Winter 1973) or Ben H. Knott's 'Social work as symbolic interaction' (*British Journal of Social Work*, Spring 1974) would be very useful.

Discussion

Diagnosis is a term which some staff and students dislike, considering it pretentious, even god-like. I merely use the term since it is in common usage and if a term such as assessment is preferable to them, I have no quarrel with this. It is the process rather than what it is called that is important.

Obviously, diagnosis is a matter which draws upon practically the whole knowledge base of the course: human growth and behaviour, psychology, social psychology, sociology, and social administration, and as such may be one of the best integrative topics for the whole course. There is a very good case for involving staff from other academic disciplines in seminars on this matter.

If consideration of diagnosis takes place fairly early in the course it may help those students who are having a little difficulty in recognising the relevance of learning in other discipline areas to the social work task; but perhaps at the risk of their feeling a little overwhelmed by the knowledge implications when they may also be feeling inadequately equipped in terms of knowledge. But consideration presents the opportunity at least to begin shaping their approach in a way which enables them to go on developing their skill in diagnosis as they acquire further knowledge, with support in this process being offered both in tutorials and field practice supervision.

Generally speaking, though, I have not found much difficulty in thinking about diagnosis with students. They frequently come on training courses feeling they are deficient in diagnostic skills, that they have not got the measure of all the factors extant in cases they have been handling, and keen, for the sake of their clients, to develop this area of practice. This motivation makes them avid to learn.

Perhaps one of the most fruitful teaching media here is the case study.

CHAPTER V

Treatment Goals, Methods and Plans

(A) Treatment goals

Goals are necessary to make our work effective. Without them our cases may drift aimlessly, prolonging them unnecessarily, adding to our caseloads and cutting our availability to others. Goals are essential to treatment planning and the selection of treatment methods.

Goals are not ideal solutions or complete cures. Social work rarely cures in the sense of producing re-organised, perfectly functioning personalities with all problems gone. Because of this, social workers often compare their achievements unfavourably with say, medicine— forgetting that much of medicine is aimed at controlling symptoms, reducing vulnerability, and arresting deterioration: and that doctors, too, can often do little but alleviate when they are up against poor housing and sanitation, low income, unco-operative patients and families. What emerge as goals usually represent a compromise between what is desirable and what is feasible: what is achievable. Since we tend to get 'ego-involved' with goals, to set them at unrealistic levels will only waste time and end in disappointment and self-doubt.

Hamilton[1] suggests that our goal in general terms is to prevent breakdown, conserve strength, restore social functioning, make clients' life experience more comfortable and compensating, to create opportunities for growth and development, and increase capacity for self-direction and social contribution.

Mrs Preston was left a widow at the age of 29, with the care of four young children (two still under school age) when her husband, an Army Officer, was tragically killed in a road accident. With the

142

generous financial help of her husband's former colleagues and a grant from a Services benevolent fund, Mrs. Preston had been able to purchase a reasonable house in a town not far from the base, managed to maintain their small car and was, with her widow's allowances, in no immediate financial difficulties.

Some months later, however, she was referred by her General Practitioner to a social worker since she had become severely depressed and was not responding particularly well to treatment with anti-depressant drugs.

When the social worker met Mrs. Preston her main complaints were of her utter exhaustion, her feelings of complete isolation, and a feeling of hopelessness that she would never be able to cope with all the pressures she felt she was under. She feared for the future of her children and for her own sanity.

Mrs. Preston attributed her tiredness to lack of sleep. There was only her to go to any of the children when they woke at night and once woken up she could not get to sleep again: she lay awake, her mind churning, feeling terrible by the time she got up. She could hardly bear the children near her, constantly snapped and nagged at them when she could not avoid them, could hardly make the effort to feed them decently, neglected the housework and never played with them now as she had done. She felt inordinately guilty about what she was doing to them—especially as she recognised they missed their father dreadfully, needed her more than ever, and that they were desperately upset by the change in her. She loved them very much, though: indeed, it was only the thought of what might happen to them that had stopped her 'ending it all'.

Mrs. Preston had hoped originally to keep in touch with her friends at the camp, but the ties of the children made this hard from the beginning. Increasingly she had felt 'out of it' at the camp. Social relations had become awkward among married couples now she was 'unattached' and conversation, especially about current events at the camp, now that neither she nor her late husband were part of the scene, tended to reinforce her feeling of exclusion. Because she had tried to keep in touch, though, she had developed virtually no contacts in her new locality, and as her depression had increased, camp contacts withered and she could not make the effort to make any new. She had increasingly withdrawn into the home, till even shopping (accompanied by two demanding children) had become a nightmare. Her mother and a married sister were alive, but lived too far away for much in the way of visiting or practical help. They had worries of their own and when she wrote she deliberately put on a brave face.

As she talked of her earlier life, the social worker formed the impression that Mrs. Preston was a lively, outgoing young woman with a range of interests (many of them artistic) and a full social life; that she was a warm and competent mother and an affectionate wife with a stable married life. The social worker determined that Mrs. Preston was a mature person, overcome by her grief at the loss of her husband and the heavy demands of trying to bring up a young family on her own. It was undeniable, however, that she was severely depressed, and experienced suicidal ideas and the worker was obliged to consider hospitalisation as a possibility. She decided, however, that this might create almost as many problems for Mrs. Preston and the children as it would solve and that there were enought latent strengths in the situation to warrant trying other ways of assisting first—focussing on the needs for practical help, reducing Mrs. Preston's social isolation and helping her to come to terms with her bereavement.

As an immediate first step, the social worker arranged for the two younger children to attend a local playgroup four sessions per week, which gave Mrs. Preston some relief as well as social contacts with other mothers in the group. She had ascertained that Mrs. Preston was at one time an active member of the Methodist church and had missed her church contacts lately. The social worker contacted a member of the local congregation (with Mrs. Preston's permission)—a warm, active, outgoing person with a wide range of social contacts, and several children of her own. Through her, Mrs. Preston was given a good deal of practical help—baby-sitting during the day to enable her to get on with shopping and housework, some evening baby-sitting so she could take up her interest in art again and go to the occasional supper-party, plus some 'man about the house' help with repairs to household equipment, toys, the car, some gardening and bits of decorating.

As Mrs. Preston's depression slowly lifted, the social worker was able to explore her feelings about the death of her husband and also helped her to see that some of these at least were related to the death of her father. This had happened when she was 14, but she had never really been able to express her grief since her mother had taken his death rather badly at the time and Mrs. Preston had felt constrained to be a prop to her mother during her mourning period.

Mrs. Preston continued to improve and though her life was still an arduous one in many respects, she coped and derived a sufficient satisfaction from her life, even though she was widowed. She became able to reciprocate some of the help she had received from others.

The social worker learned a couple of years afterwards that Mrs. Preston had remarried, and though there were some repercussions from the children, they were working through these themselves without a need for further intervention.

Goals will derive from considering the physical, psychological and social factors involved; the capacity and motivation of our client(s); and the available resources in the community, other agencies, our own agency and in ourselves. Often at this point we realise that the 'desirable' element of the goals involves other methods of social work—group, community or residential—and we need to ask whether these are available (to make a referral), whether we ourselves can use these methods, or at least press for their introduction. This is not to suggest that casework has not a unique contribution to make to problem-solving, whether used alone or in conjunction with other methods; but there may be times when casework goals have to be modified by the non-availability of other methods, or modified because other methods (especially community work) take time to effect change.

The McDermott family were referred to the Social Services Department of a small County Borough by the Housing Department. The family lived on a temporary caravan site owned by the Local Authority, but were in danger of eviction for non-payment of the site rent (the rent collecting being a Housing Department responsibility). There were three children involved and as the parents were maintaining they had nowhere else to go, the matter was referred to the Social Services Department since the possibility existed of the family having to be admitted to temporary accommodation or the children taken into care. The Education Welfare service was also involved because two of the children were not attending school (the third was under school age).

After two or three interviews with the family, the social worker came to the conclusion that the McDermotts were capable parents, with warm ties with their three lively children. Both parents had been brought up in 'travelling' families, wanted to remain travellers and wanted their children to be so, too. Mr. McDermott dealt in scrap metal, but also did some seasonal agricultural work; while Mrs. McDermott supplemented the family income by making pegs and artificial flowers which she hawked.

The McDermotts had been living on the site for four months, but were refusing rent because of the poor facilities on the site. There was only one standpipe to supply water to 15 caravans, the toilets had largely been destroyed, there was no provision for Mr. McDermott's scrap metal dealing and there were frequent quarrels with others on the site about pilfering metal. The hard standing provided was quite inadequate, and got into the caravans on people's shoes, making keeping the places clean even more difficult. The whole area was low lying and often under water in wet weather. Earlier complaints had brought no action and the McDermotts, together with some other families on the site, had felt constrained to try the only way of protesting they knew to get something done.

With regard to the school, the McDermotts wanted their children to learn to read and write even though neither of them could; but they were deeply suspicious of schooling since they felt convinced the schools would try to turn their children into 'house people' and alienate them from the travelling way of life. This they could not accept, and if it meant that the children would remain illiterate, well, 'they had managed all right without'.

The McDermotts also complained of the attitudes of the local community who, they felt, disparaged and belittled them, though did not go as far as actual harassment. The local residents at the time the temporary site had been opened, had protested about the unsuitability of the site, its proximity to housing, and its adverse effects on local amenity and property values.

With the McDermotts' permission, the social worker contacted other residents on the site, with the idea of forming some sort of group to represent the residents in negotiations with the local authority to secure improvements to the site. The transient nature of the residents and a lack of unanimity among them, however, meant this idea never materialised, so the social worker contacted the Regional Representative of the National Gypsy Council, for him to act as spokesman.

The social worker also contacted a sympathetic councillor to see whether he could use his influence on the Borough Council to try to secure better conditions. The councillor undertook to do what he could but explained that he was not optimistic about getting additional money spent on what was officially a temporary site. The Borough was short of land within its own boundaries, knew at the time the site was opened that it was not really suitable and had tried to deal with the problem of travellers originally in co-operation with the three surrounding Rural District Councils who had more land available and one or two potentially useful sites. The negotiations with the R.D.C.'s had broken down largely, since none of them wanted the problem on their territory. The Borough had provided a temporary site as a holding operation, pending further negotiations.

The attitudes of the local residents remained unchanged despite the social worker's discussions with their representatives. The site was unsuitable and they wanted it moved.

In the education sphere at least, the social worker had some success. She had been put in touch with a member of the Education Committee who had at one time run her own pre-school playgroup. With her active interest, the support of staff and students from the nearby University's Departments of Social Work and Education, plus voluntary helpers organised through the local Council of Social Service, a group was formed which bought (with the help of a grant from a charitable foundation), converted, equipped and staffed a caravan school. Originally intended as a pre-school venture, in practice it served the educational needs of a wide range of children from the site in a way which won the acceptance of many of the resident parents as well as children.

The situation continues to be an uneasy compromise. Some improvement has been made to the site, but the local authority still regards it as a temporary one and is still engaged in negotiations with both local Councils and the Central Government. The Education authorities have left education matters to the caravan school. The social worker continued to support the McDermotts during these protracted moves, though she felt limited to offering her sympathy, and what encouragement she realistically could; giving such practical advice and help as was needed; and bearing with the family's inevitable feelings of tension and frustration, given the slow, limited progress that was being made in other ways. She had persuaded them, with great reluctance on their part, to resume paying the site rent, which at least staved off the eviction. Some consolation was the fact that it was at a slightly reduced rate, negotiated between the local authority and the Gypsy Council representative.

Eventually, with summer seasonal work available elsewhere, the McDermotts moved on.

These examples serve to underline, though, one of the characteristics of goals—the distinction between ultimate and intermediate goals. While the worker must have an idea of what his ultimate objective might be, this very often needs to be worked towards by a series of steps, for a number of reasons:

(1) Under the stress of the immediate situation, ultimate objectives may seem so remote and impossible of attainment that the client loses all motivation to attempt the objective.

(2) It is often from the encouragement, confidence and developing skill derived from attaining an immediate objective that a client is strengthened to attempt the next stage.

(3) There may well be a need to deal with an immediate situation to prevent breakdown, deterioration, or to achieve some degree of stability before any work can be done on factors which precipitated the situation.

In other words, we begin where the client is: and in considering goals we use initially the objectives the client presents, discussing with him both how desirable and how feasible they are, their implications for all those concerned, what achieving them might call for, and how they might be attained. Such a discussion should get three essential processes going; engaging the client in the problem-solving process; establishing the *sharing* of the goals (or at least the initial or intermediate ones) without which the contract between worker and client cannot be concluded; and allowing for the renegotiation of the contract where this needs to be done for realistic problem-solving work to be undertaken.

Care needs to be taken that immediate or intermediate goals do not militate against the achievement of ultimate goals—though in practice this may be difficult especially where a case presents as a crisis and immediate steps have to be taken before there is much real opportunity to ascertain what ultimate objectives might be achievable.

Perhaps one of the most useful questions we can ask ourselves in ascertaining goals is what is modifiable. Much may not be: the birth of a mongol child, an amputation, an irreversible progressive disease, bereavement, past events, entrenched attitudes, may be 'facts' neither we, nor the client can escape from and we have to look elsewhere—to what is modifiable in personal or environmental terms for our solutions (which might be little more than containment). But among the modifiable factors there are likely to be those which are more immediately accessible to treatment (for example, some form of practical help) while others (such as modifications of attitude) are likely to take longer to bring about change. Such an analysis could prove very useful not only in helping us to establish ultimate goals, but also in suggesting the intermediate goals.

Goals (like diagnosis) are often fluid and tentative: while the desirable may be clear fairly quickly, it is often only as the work develops that what is feasible becomes clear (for example through the way client and worker are able to deal with intermediate goals) and the ultimate goals modified.

(B) Treatment methods

According to Hamilton[2], treatment is the sum of all activities and services directed towards helping an individual with a problem. The focus is the relieving of the immediate problem and, if feasible, modifying any basic difficulties which precipitated it. Typically treatment methods are grouped as direct and indirect.

DIRECT

Perlman[3] sees direct treatment as the provision of a systematic but flexible way in which the client can work over his problem, his relation to it and possible solutions. Hamilton sees direct work as a series of interviews with the purpose of inducing or reinforcing attitudes favourable to the maintenance of emotional equilibrium, constructive decisions, growth or change. She goes on to distinguish between two types of interviews:

(a) Counselling, which she sees primarily as a rational discussion of issues, focussing on clarification, but embracing feeling as well as intellect since learning (old and new) involves an emotional element and this may imply a degree of abreaction (a re-living of emotions experienced elsewhere).

(b) Therapeutic interviewing—of which casework is one form. Therapeutic interviewing is indicated, she suggests, where intrapsychic conflict is projected or displaced on to the environment or neuroses or behaviour disorders are acted out. In casework, though, unconscious material is not used but the derivatives of it, with the focus on effecting appropriate (i.e. problem related) adaptation through emotional readjustment rather than fundamental change.

But perhaps the most useful analysis of direct treatment methods is that of Hollis[4], who distinguishes six forms.

(1) SUSTAINING TECHNIQUES

These involve expressions of interest, concern, sympathetic listening, acceptance, realistic reassurance, realistic expressions of confidence in the client's ability, encouragement, and 'gifts'—for example, extra time, extra interviews, home visits, and practical services. (In work with children, quite tangible gifts may be used—for example, Christmas and birthday cards and presents, taking them out for meals etc., since they cannot comprehend as adults can, the significance of less tangible gifts.) Sustaining techniques may be of particular value at the beginning of a contact to foster the development of the relationship; but will be of value all through in helping the client to deal with anxiety, to support them when the going gets 'rough' (during the development of insight for example), and to maintain motivation.

In some cases, sustaining techniques may be all that are required. With this amount of support, the client may be able to cope with his situation himself. This can happen in brief contacts (where for example, someone is asking for assurance that they are 'doing the right thing'); and in certain long term cases where the security of only an occasional contact is sufficient to give a client enough confidence to manage. The existence of a 'life-line' is enough to ensure that it does not become necessary to use it.

(2) DIRECT INFLUENCE

By this Hollis[5] means, basically, the use of authority in its various forms. As we have looked at authority in Chapter III, I will not elaborate here. Hollis suggests that direct influence is used where the client needs direction—perhaps from ignorance, anxiety, in a crisis when they are floundering badly, where ego strengths are weak, or when we are dealing with a borderline psychosis. As we have seen, the degree of influence we are able to exert may depend on the relationship, so she suggests influence should be coupled with sustaining techniques; but she also counsels discretion in the use of both methods since they tend to produce dependence—though a period of dependency may be a necessary stage on the way to independence, of course.

(3) VENTILATION

As a method, we have already covered this in that part of Chapter III which examined the client's need to be listened to, so again, there is no need to reiterate.

(4) REFLECTIVE DISCUSSION OF THE PERSON/SITUATION
CONFIGURATION

Hollis suggest four subdivisions of this method:

(i) Reflective discussion of the situation. The aim here is to assist the client towards a realistic appraisal. The introduction of new knowledge may be sufficient here (should gaps exist); but we may also need to stimulate and extend the client's comprehension (even imagination) to help him to see a wider range of the factors involved; or to explore with him any distortion which may exist in his view of the situation. If this does assist a more realistic view, this may be sufficient in itself to prompt the client to a solution he can then implement himself, or work towards with help. The focus here is on the objective elements in the situation.

(ii) Reflective discussion of the effects of his actions on others. This may crop up either in connection with discussion about the onset of difficulties or about possible solutions; but would typically be used where just a discussion of the situation did not produce satisfactory results in identifying problems or answers to them. Again this means stretching the client's imagination and comprehension and beginning to assist him to examine his inter-actions with others.

(iii) Reflective discussion of the client's feelings and reactions. Discussion of the inter-*actions* with others may not be sufficient for the worker or client to establish sufficient in the way of identification of problems or solutions without some examination of the client's feelings. Here we are moving into the subjective area of the situation. This examination (as well as discussion of actions under ii) needs to be handled with care. An appropriate timing is needed and the appropriate degree of relationship, since whether feelings are hidden from the worker (because the client is not ready to discuss them) or hidden even from himself (because he is not ready to acknowledge them), the worker pointing them out (or pointing to the possibility of their existence) may provoke anxiety, hostility or a precipitate rejection of such 'explanations'—making the whole task more difficult, or even impossible. It is usually far better for the client to come to such realisations himself in discussion even if this takes a little longer. A positive, accepting relationship will assist this, together with the use of 'neutral' leads or oblique references, such as 'people sometimes feel...' which leave it to the client to pick these up. (Even if he ignores such leads at the time, he may use them subsequently, inside or outside the interview.) But it may also be necessary to gently pick up material the client gives (perhaps by bringing together for him to examine, material from different parts of the interview, or different interviews) which indicates inconsistent, inappropriate or unusual reactions—though in a way which promotes clients comments and exploration rather than interprets.

(iv) Reflective discussion of clients reactions to worker and agency. This may assist clients towards a realistic view of the agency's or the worker's functions and establish the worker's role—a necessary preliminary if effective use is to be made of the casework. But uncertain irrational elements in the client's view may also emerge which may be useful diagnostically or provide an entry for relevant discussion. In any event, the opportunity will be given to the client to ventilate his feelings about agency, worker, and being a client which could be very useful.

(5) REFLECTIVE CONSIDERATION OF DYNAMIC FACTORS

Where reflective discussion is not sufficient to deal with the problems, and provided the client has the capacity (including ego-strength) to do so, worker and client may venture into consideration of dynamic factors—an examination of both the feelings and motivations behind interactions and relationships with others, including a degree of focus on his own contribution. This brings us near to his own intra-psychic conflicts, though we shall not deal with these as such, but rather with the conscious and pre-conscious manifestations of them and the defence mechanisms being employed. This sort of consideration again needs to be handled with considerable care (and calls for a clinical diagnosis) and will typically be used only where:

(a) It is necessary for effective problem solving;

(b) Where the client acknowledges the validity of this exploration for problem-resolution and really seeks this understanding of himself. In other words, where goals of at least a degree of self-awareness have become part of the contract and where not only capacity but motivation are sufficient. Material emerging with this method is referred to current functioning problems, and not encouraged just for its own sake. As previously mentioned, since here we are developing insight, this method should be used in conjunction with sustaining techniques, since the process may be a painful one for the client.

(6) REFLECTIVE DISCUSSION OF GENETIC OR AETIOLOGICAL FACTORS

If exploration of dynamic factors should prove still insufficient, this final method can be used—but with even more care. Here the aim is to help the client's thinking about the past in order to make connections which illuminate the current difficulties, so they may be dealt with. Again, consideration of the past as such is pointless: clients may even use it to block consideration of the present or use it to justify present behaviour. We may, on rare occasions, take up aspects of behaviour in the client/worker relationship and use these as illustrative material about past and present functioning, but this is likely to stimulate transference, which we may or may not wish to do, depending on our goals. 'Explanations' of aetiological or dynamic material can only be tentative, since there are usually a number of possible explanations of behaviour, and again, connecting events and feelings are best left to the client to make (though perhaps with our assistance) rather than explanations being made by the worker. Explanations imposed in this way may be rejected (even if accurate), be rationalised, or accepted at only an intellectual level with no real emotional shift or development.

One important 'direct' factor which is not often discussed, is that of identification by the client with the worker. The obverse here (if we could regard it as a treatment method) is that of 'offering of model'—though I am not sure we can properly consider it as a method in that we can consciously vary its use depending on the needs of the case.

But at least there is some room for manoeuvre here. For example, if part of a client's problem is that they see all authority figures as strict or condemning (and provided we are an authority figure for them), we could offer them a model of at least one authority figure that does not behave in this way—even if the client tries to get us to. Experience of this 'new' model may help them view other authority figures more realistically through 'transferring out' their experience of us. Similarly in say, a marital problem, if we can demonstrate the relevance and success of examining feelings reflectively in our work with the couple concerned, this may encourage them to employ similar techniques in their communication with each other outside the interview situation which they had not previously attempted. In this way they might very well be continuing the work and the healing begun by the casework. In family therapy at least, this sort of use of the worker as a model for communication is not only advocated but is seen as an integral part of the on-going work of the family between sessions and an essential ingredient in progress.

But method or not, the significance of identification cannot be overlooked, and a number of our clients may use us as 'reference people' in handling situations and responses. They will pause to consider how 'Miss X' or 'Mr. Y' would deal with matters—using this as a guide to their own performance. In any relationship with clients, therefore, it behoves us to examine just what sort of model we offer, and to consider the consistency of what we say, what we suggest and what we do. It is not unknown for our clients to carry identification as far as wanting to be social workers themselves, and identification may be a particularly significant factor in dealing with young people or the immature. Clearly, identification can assist if the clients subsequently internalise it appropriately and make it part of themselves; but if it remains something 'borrowed', it may perpetuate dependency. Clearly, too, identification with us may be deliberately rejected healthily or unhealthily.

Indirect

Indirect treatment involves the use of what Hamilton terms the social resources. These are usually grouped as referral, material aid and environmental manipulation.

(1) REFERRAL

Hamilton[6] reminds us that social workers are trustees of *all* community and agency resources. We therefore have a responsibility to know them, see that they are used by those who need them, and used appropriately. Referral is a prime element in meeting client need since needs are almost invariably complex and beyond the function of one agency to deal with. Making a good referral is not a simple matter always and may involve a number of stages:

(a) It may involve a careful diagnosis of needs, an awareness of how these needs might be met (particularly when they fall outside agency function), and making clients aware of the resources that exist.

(b) It involves helping the client to choose the resources to be used, and preparing the clients for the referral. Often in this process we will be dealing with anxieties aroused by the suggested referral, and occasionally these can be profound and involve much direct work. Independence and pride may be felt to be at stake by a suggested referral to Supplementary Benefits; fears of mutilation or fear of unconsciousness may be aroused by a suggested medical referral with surgery a possibility; many fantasies or a feeling of profound inadequacy and failure stirred by a suggested referral to a psychiatrist or a child guidance clinic.

It may also mean assisting the client to ventilate his feelings about the referral as such—including, perhaps, feelings that we are rejecting him, or that he is being 'moved on' yet again in an elaborate bureaucratic game. It means acquainting him with the realities that may await him elsewhere, and settling issues around confidentiality.

(c) It may mean stimulating motivation to take up the referral, and/or supporting him in the use of the resource, which might mean an on-going function for the social worker as part of a total team involved.

Even in referral we should remember our aim is to foster self-direction, and this may have a bearing on what suggestions we make about resources he might use among the possible selection available; how free we leave the client to make his own choice or attempt to guide him in the light of the problems and his capacity; and how far we go in bringing client and resources together (for example do we arrange everything, or leave the client to do all or part of it)?

(2) MATERIAL AID

The use of material aid (in cash and in kind) often engenders strong feelings in the groups involved—the providers, the receivers and the dispensers. The way aid is handled by each of these groups is frequently diagnostic in itself.

Providers motivations may be many: real concern (though this is not infrequently for groups in which they are particularly interested, or which are generally felt to be 'deserving'), a sense of obligation or commitment, a wish to be thought well of, for status, as a bribe to gain the affection of the beneficiaries, or perhaps via material aid to fob off, or salve their consciences about their inability to respond to closer, emotional demands. Material aid can be used to smother others' anger, to disarm criticism, or the power to give or withhold, used as a lever to manipulate others' behaviour in the desired direction, or control situations (with all the potential satisfactions this can bring). Withholding can express our anger or disapproval; but sometimes we withhold through a fear of turning towards ourselves and encouraging an appetite we feel may be insatiable, or creating a perpetual dependency. Some enjoy such a dependency, of course, and may use material means to foster it. Others see dependency as undermining self-help and material help for the 'feckless' as undermining the work ethic—unfair to those who help themselves and earning the disapproval of the hardworking. Some do not like the responsibility being a provider entails and try to push it elsewhere; and even providers have their problems when it comes to allocating resources among competing and equally deserving ends. Considerations such as these may come in whether the providers are central or local government, voluntary societies, or individual parents or spouses.

Receivers may enjoy their dependency or their freedom from responsibility, or get a 'kick' from constantly demanding their material 'rights'— for various unconscious reasons of their own, or with justification. Many will accept help sensibly as realistic and reasonably due to them; while others will feel shame, inadequacy, humiliation and a sense of failure, perhaps reacting with anger or apathy—feelings which will be reinforced or eased by the way in which help is given. Many will feel that in accepting help they have surrendered

their independence to a degree and put themselves under an obligation—some perhaps refusing help they are entitled to because of the
strength of their feelings on this score. Perhaps worst of all is asking
for help and not getting it, with the implications however veiled,
that they are 'unworthy'. Their original need goes unmet with the
additional burden of having humiliated themselves by asking all to
no purpose.

Social workers, in their role as dispensers, have often disliked being
in a position to give or withhold. Toren[7] goes as far as to suggest
that it is impossible to combine the function of a material aid dispenser with that of social caseworker. The power in the hands of
the dispenser mean that the client is going to slant the presentation
of himself and his situation in a way which appears to him to give
the best chance of securing the material aid he may desperately need.
This inevitability is flatly contradictory to the need for openness,
frankness and reality in the casework relationship if it is to be successful. Many social workers share Toren's view and are concerned
about developments in social policy which give social workers increasing power—especially in the area of resource control.

Dispensers, too, may share some of the human feelings of providers
and utilise their position to manipulate, bribe or fob off clients or
to bolster their egos. They may have favourites they reward with
material aid or clients they dislike and punish by withholding. They
may also have fears about the insatiable client, enjoy control, or
enjoy dependency; or get enjoyment from colluding or conniving
with the client getting material help by 'beating the system'.

Whether this is so or not, however, dispensers are inevitably the
go-betweens. They carry the responsibility for administering provision, making recommendations or decisions about allocating it within
a policy laid down by the providers, and within the limits of what
is actually provided. Often they have to act within the constraints,
too, of 'public purse' accountability. At the same time they have
to bear the reactions of the recipients since they meet them face
to face. While they may derive satisfaction when they are able to
meet material need and they receive the client's expression of gratitude, they also have to endure the frustration, anger and humiliation
of clients when they have to tell them 'no'—a decision to which

they may have contributed, or for which they may well be held responsible by the client anyway. Additionally, they have to go on working with them, to help them to bear these feelings. Sometimes, even where they have 'provided', they may have to bear with, and try to understand a client's ingratitude; or stand by and watch what they have 'provided' mis-used—whether from incompetence or perhaps an unconscious wish to destroy what is given because of the underlying anger at being forced into the position of having to ask for it.

In this tense, intermediary position, there are sometimes pressures within us to quietly sabotage a policy we disagree with, whether by withholding where the rules allow giving, or by giving by manipulating the rules which indicate we should withhold. We can quietly turn a loan into a grant by 'forgetting' to collect the instalments. Often we are not helped by policies and guidelines which are unclear, or by the blocks or manipulations of those further up in the hierarchy with problems similar to our own, and to whom we must refer requests for aid. Such uncertainties can only ultimately be reflected in our own uncertainty in dealing with an applicant, to the detriment of the whole process. Where we have little to offer anyway, there is a real temptation not to raise the matter of aid at all, or where the client raises it, to deal with it with evasions, excuses or glib promises we know we cannot fulfil. This is poor casework, however, and it is far better to have the matter out and face the client's feelings with him.

The situation is not helped by the confusion of present provision, the administrative complexities involved, and local variability. In broad terms provision can be regarded as either basic and unconditional (their right to food, shelter and clothing) or—in Hamilton's terms—diagnostic: i.e. an addition to the basic dependent on an assessment of some kind. Difficulties sometimes arise when the basic is so meagre that the diagnostic addition becomes almost an essential; where the basic or diagnostic present such complexities that the administrators of it, let alone the clients, get confused by it all; where what is basic and diagnostic can be provided by various organisations; or where the diagnostic element produces variations in the way applications are dealt with. We tend to think that basic provision = the social security system but much that say, a Social Services Department provides (especially in the way of residential accommodation) may be arguably basic. While more typically what Social Services Departments provide is diagnostic (and, incidentally, without the 'A' code and appeal system of the Social Security System), we can find ourselves caught up in arguments over say, clothing grants for children, as to whether these are the responsibility of the S.B.C. as an exceptional needs grant, the Education Department as part of their Welfare provision, the Social Services Department (under the provisions of the 1963 Children & Young Persons Act to prevent children coming into care) or even a charity.

In this welter, I feel that certain obligations rest on social workers:

(1) To know *what* material help is available, *where*, the *conditions* (if any) of entitlement, and the *administrative means* of obtaining it— whether it is the sphere of welfare rights, education grants, 1963 C. & Y.P. grants, residential accommodation, housing, charitable trust funds, or what; and to assist the client through with his application.

(2) Where help is given/withheld as a reflection of mistaken underlying attitudes, to educate.

(3) Where help given is inadequate, to use all the available means to get it augmented.

(4) Where help is adequate, but the administration so complex or dehumanising that applications are discouraged, to get the system simplified and humanised.

(5) Where there is confusion of responsibility or lack of clear guidance, to get these sorted out.

(6) To examine our own work, to see whether our biases are coming in.

(7) To see that our own use of material aid (basic or diagnostic) is adequately geared to meeting the needs within the overall problem solving process. Hamilton suggests that in casework, the following are the criteria:

(a) To help clients improve situations (grants for furniture, clothing, etc.) or to change them (get adequate housing for example). On rare occasions, where the clients can do little for themselves, it may be up to us to change them—perhaps radically where urgent practical needs exist which cannot be met in any other way in the currently existing situation (be this an old people's home, a hospital, a place of safety, a children's home or foster home, or accommodation for the homeless).

(b) To create opportunities to develop capacity or improve health (clubs, therapeutic groups, educational courses, convalescent homes, etc.)

(c) To help them to retain independence (appliances, adaptations, home helps, vocational re-training).

(d) To protect in a crisis (emergency payments for food, to settle debts for rent arrears, prevent disconnection of gas or electricity).

(e) To create a special living experience (holidays, pay subscriptions to Scouts, etc.).

We discharge these obligations within the context of the relationship we have with our clients—a relationship which is not only sensitive to their needs, but also sensitive to their dignity. Material aid often involves feelings of loss: loss of control over aspects of the environment and associated feelings of inadequacy (given the social mores about self-sufficiency); the loss of independence when one becomes beholden to others for income or accommodation; or the profound feelings of bereavement and separation when one loses one's home on admission to residential care. This is not to suggest that the provision of material aid will not also bring feelings of relief and security; but a degree of ambivalence is bound to exist—if only because that relief has been secured through another's agency—yours. The relationship should be sensitive to this ambivalence, especially where we are dealing with clients who have in the past experienced a great deal of loss or indignity. Material aid is never easy to accept.

In addition, it may be quite justifiable to use material aid to help us establish the relationship we need to assist a client; but remember the possible detrimental effects, too, on our further work if a relationship is established in this way. It could set up certain expectations or cast the social worker in a certain role which might not help in the long run, given that goals other than the provision of material aid are being worked towards.

A request for material aid may or may not be a presenting problem: but even if it is not, the handling of a straightforward request for aid, given the often strong feeling involved, can be vital and either enrich or demean the applicant. Well handled, it can be real preventive work. In addition good relations established on such occasions can lead to earlier referrals in future (with the greater chance of success), goodwill on the client's part which will be a further asset, and add to the reputation of the Department through the recipient's speaking well of the service. Very occasionally in meeting a practical request well, we may be assisting with a much deeper but inarticulated need quite adequately—again good preventive work which may save the client subsequent suffering.

The way we handle requests is as important (at times, perhaps, even more important) than the aid itself.

(3) ENVIRONMENTAL MANIPULATION

Manipulation is not a word I like—management might be a preferable term. As I have indicated elsewhere we are almost invariably involved with the client's environment: either causative or pressure factors are there, or the environment needs support because of the difficulties the client is creating; while the environmental resources may well be elements we will look towards for assistance in problem solving—therefore needing us to seek and support that involvement. Work with the environment will typically be coupled with and complementary to, any direct work we do; but occasionally we may only be able to work through the environment.

Much of what I have considered under the heading of material aid (aids, adaptations, clubs, homes, workshops, housing, etc.) are regarded by some as environmental management—and I have no strong feelings either way. But what is undoubtedly environmental management, is the emotional support of, involvement with, attempts to release feeling in, and change the attitudes of, the people in the client's environment which form part of our problem solving—be they family, friends, neighbours, workmates, officials, teachers, councillors or other professionals. In our diagnosis we will have made an assessment of what environmental help is needed and how 'workable' the environment is; but in extreme cases, we may feel that the client's situation in terms of relationship resources, even coupled with our own efforts, is so damaging or so unable to meet the needs/ demands of the client that the only alternative is a new environment, hopefully more able to sustain him. This may entail trying to arrange a shift from home to lodgings or a hostel, for example; or to a children's or a foster home.

Hollis[8] suggests environmental manipulation is neither simpler nor very different from methods of direct treatment and that in dealing with the people in the client's environment we will be using the techniques of sustaining, direct influence, ventilation and reflective discussion—much as we would with a client. The inference here is that it is only when we get to using dynamic or aetiological consideration that such people become clients in their own right, as it were.

Although the occasions when we acquired a new 'client' via our attempts at environmental management are rare, they can present difficulties, especially where they develop over the course of a contact and we do not start out with the understanding that, say, a married couple (rather than one spouse) or the whole family are involved on a client basis—as they would be in matrimonial work or conjoint family therapy. Occasionally we come to realise ourselves that the client carrying the symptoms is not really the 'sick' one, but one of the 'environmental' members and we would like to shift the focus of our work. In this sort of situation we can be anxious about the implications of the new situation for our relationship with our client, be apprehensive of possible 'sibling rivalry' situations, or fear for the tearing of our loyalties between now two clients. We realise the greater possibility of misunderstandings and complications as well as potential problems around confidentiality. We may also wonder how we can get on to a new footing with the 'environmental' member if we have not already done so. There would seem to be two possibilities here: if we can 'smell' the 'environmental client' situation coming, to involve another worker (always with the proviso that the person concerned is prepared to accept help in their own right). If another worker is already involved, perhaps we might re-distribute the focus of what we are doing between us. Secondly, we can clarify the new situation with the people involved and so open the way to re-negotiating the contract. Such a negotiation, even if it can be achieved, is likely to produce some upheaval at least temporarily, but perhaps rather this than to let the matter drift in uncertainty and potential confusion, with the likelihood that little will be really achieved.

We have already mentioned that certain people in the environment may be in a far better position as resource people for the client than we are ourselves. If we can 'recruit' them for this task of being resource people, then it is our obligation to support and assist them in it, as well as to assist the client to use them appropriately, perhaps. Relatives, teachers, neighbours, health visitors, doctors, solicitors, volunteers—perhaps even foster parents and the staff of residential homes—could be regarded in this way. Children caring for an elderly relative, a wife caring for a chronically sick husband, parents caring for a physically or mentally handicapped child or a child suffering the repercussions of prolonged hospitalisation—these could be examples of people far better placed than we are to meet clients needs, but who seldom get the help and attention from us that they merit. Too often, with our focus on the client, we treat them as mere adjuncts.

We tend to see ourselves as the prime carers when (as fieldworkers at any rate) we are rarely in this position. Nine times out of ten in fieldwork, the focus of our work is to try to assist the prime caring of others—a social work task that is both difficult yet inordinately worth doing if we can see what it would mean to the client should that prime caring break down. Not only might there be a devastating sense of loss, but the subsequent demands on resources required to replace the prime caring would be severe—whether in material terms or in terms of the demands on the social worker and/or other services. The most difficult cases for us are those in which the client is almost completely isolated and heavily dependent on us.

It is here that we see some of the fundamental differences in casework in the field and residential settings. The residential worker is in much more of a prime carer role. While this may give him a great deal more scope for therapeutic intervention, it also means he may well face much heavier demands—especially in terms of transference (given a resident's greater dependency)—a matter I consider later in this chapter. I would only interpolate here that where a need exists for a re-learning of intensive emotional experiences arising in other, earlier relationships involving dependency, the residential worker may be in a much better position to offer this sort of case-work help than the field-based worker. This surely is part of the rationale for say, residential placements for maladjusted children—and one of the reasons for field-based caseworkers recommending such placements.

(C) Treatment Plans

From diagnosis and methods, we put together treatment plans: i.e. that selected *blend* of methods which most appropriately meet *identified* needs and assists towards *goals*; with the blend changing over time as *movement* takes place—i.e. a *sequence* of use.

From the diagnosis we will have identified where the problems lie (in the client, the environment, or typically, a combination of both) and the workability extant in the situation. We may well begin the treatment planning, bearing these factors in mind, by asking our-selves can the client with our help, deal with the environmental fac-tors himself—in which case we can make our selection of the direct methods available—or are there at least some environmental factors he cannot manage and which therefore require our intervention to some degree with indirect methods.

Even where the problems are the client's rather than environmen-tal, we may need to ask which area—client or environment—is likely to be more responsive, and perhaps to decide (for example, in the light of limited client capacity and/or motivation) on indirect methods (environmental management for example) rather than direct as the only way of achieving a tolerable solution, if not the 'ideal'. Since direct work may be slower in achieving results, too, we may be obliged to use indirect (for example, material aid to stave off an eviction) in order to stabilise a situation sufficiently to enable us to have the time for more protracted direct work (on marital disharmony for example) which was at the bottom of the trouble (rent arrears). Again, it may be a question of selecting between direct methods: using direct influence rather than consideration of dyna-mics for very similar reasons.

In terms of sequence, where the problems originally involve, say, weak ego strength, we may need to use direct influence; where anxiety, sustaining techniques; where guilt, ventilation. But hopefully, we would later be able to switch to other methods—with a strengthening ego, to turn more to sustaining the developing capacity to make decisions and assume responsibility; with anxiety subsiding, begin reflective discussion to explore the clearing, more realistic view of the person/situation configuration; with guilt lessening, begin examining the dynamics of it—always given, of course, that using these methods is valid in terms of the ultimate goals (the intermediate having been achieved).

Again plans need to be flexible to meet contingencies and match the flexibility of diagnosis and goals.

(D) The use of Relationship in Treatment

While we have seen the importance of relationship in earlier chapters and discussed the qualities of a professional relationship, I would like to tie in here, relationship and treatment methods. Relationship has been described as a condition in which people with a common interest interact with feeling and is established when emotion moves between them. The emotions need not be similar, but involve expression and response—and we have already examined aspects of this in social work, especially in Chapter III. Obviously, the casework relationship emerges out of the *task* being undertaken by the client and worker—and so clearly has connections with treatment methods. Obviously, no two casework relationships will be the same: not only are the clients different personalities, presenting differing problems, with differing needs, but the worker's responses will differ— as indeed, they need to. While the nature of the relationship cannot be controlled by the worker entirely, he can at least offer that which he hopes will stimulate a response in the client which will assist the problem solving; while the feeling or responses he receives from the client he can direct or channel in a way which, again, furthers the purposes. But limitations will remain which will have a bearing on both goals and methods.

As examples, we may be involved with clients who cannot relate at all (the very withdrawn psychotic, the severely demented and some might add psychopaths), and the only methods we will be able to use will be the indirect methods. Clients very frightened of relationships would shy away from anything other than a very gradual development of relationship at a pace they could tolerate, so direct methods might only be usable late in the casework process. Others might be open and we could use direct methods straight away; a few might be so emotionally labile or have such an insatiable need for relationship, we would need to control our feeling responses so as not to be overwhelmed by the client, playing down the direct methods initially. The inference of this is that in order to use certain methods, we need the relationship before we can introduce them.

Another factor in relationship and treatment method, is to remember the developmental stage of the client—for example the more direct and intense emotions of children: and also to bear in mind the cultural determinants of expression of feeling (stereotypes though they may be, perhaps)—the open working class or West Indian expression, the greater reserve of the middle class; the differences of expression between the sexes within cultures, as well as the differences between cultures—the more egalitarian Western and the less egalitarian Eastern. All these will have a bearing on the style of our relationship, but also given that relationship, what we might be able to achieve within it and how we go about it.

Hollis[9] distinguishes two types of relationship—the basic and the special: the basic being the warmth, concern, etc. the worker brings to all relationships coupled with our confidence in our ability to help and function as a worker (the latter an important element in giving the client confidence in us). This basic relationship may have certain similarities in quality with some social relationships; but the special relationship has a particular therapeutic element which we bring to bear in cases where this is needed. This distinction may be illustrated when examining relationship connected with at least the direct methods of working (with many similar points to be made about indirect methods, if Hollis' arguments about the common ground are valid).

Sustaining techniques are very much the basic relationship in action while, as we have seen, direct influence may not get very far unless a basic relationship exists. Much of reflective discussion will need the basic relationship too, for effectiveness; but perhaps it is here that we begin to move into the area of the therapeutic relationship—and more demonstrably so when consideration of dynamic and aetiological factors are the methods being used. It is here that transference elements may begin to emerge, and the relationship itself becomes part of the treatment, with perhaps identification coming in.

Hamilton[10] defines transference as a carrying over of irrational elements from other relationships, particularly in the past, displaced on to the social worker, reflecting unconscious motivation. Hollis stresses that this is a quite natural phenomenon: we none of us come to a relationship 'new born'; but I feel there is a distinction to be drawn between such a natural and generalised transference and the particularised transference to the social worker that can emerge. Its emergence may be quite spontaneous and unsought; but it may be more likely to occur in dependency situations where the client feels especially helpless and we are therefore in a quasi parental position— though it can happen, too, over a period of time as we become very important people for the client through the work we are doing with them, and our relationship therefore of deep significance.

Should this sort of transference emerge, it will inevitably involve some distortion of the client's perception of us, since we will have become the recipients of feelings and attitudes which belong elsewhere—to other people and relationships. To that extent the client's perceptions and responses will be unrealistic. We may be regarded more as parents, children, siblings, spouses or lovers than social workers. To be on the 'receiving end' of such a transference (perhaps, particularly a sexual one) can be a frightening experience for some workers—frightening in terms of the responsibility of being such an important figure for someone else; frightening in terms of the potential damage we could cause to someone who may already be damaged if we mishandle the situation; and frightening in terms of the possible complications this unrealistic perception of us might entail. Seductive invitations, for example, would be professionally reprehensible to accept but if rejected could conceivably lead to accusations of professional misconduct.

The value of an able consultant in situations involving transference is indisputable, if only to assist with feelings of being trapped in a situation we can neither accept nor get out of. My own suggestions would be:

(1) That the worker should not panic. Many clients are already afraid of aspects of their deep-seated feelings, especially when these involve hostility and destructiveness. The worker's panic would only confirm for them the destructiveness and uncontrollability of such feelings, making their problems even more acute—if only by adding to their despair that anything can be done about them. For the worker to be able to contain them, may be enough to enable the client to contain them, for him to recognise even if unconsciously, that they are not as destructive as he feared, to accommodate them, come to terms with them and for them to subside within our relationship with them and within his relations with others.

(2) To go back to the diagnosis and re-evaluate the need to deal with this material in terms of the problems, the client's capacity (and the worker's own); to look for guidelines as to whether transference should be contained in the relationship or brought out into the discussion. Even if discussion is decided upon, there may be two ways of handling this: by focussing on the impact of transference elements in the client's relations with others, or focussing on the transference elements in the client/worker relationship itself. Looking at the worker/client relationship, though, could tend to increase the transference and needs to be considered extremely carefully, since we are now bordering on analysis which is not within our sphere of professional competence.

(3) In all situations, we should hold up the reality of the situation before the client. This is not just to safeguard ourselves, but to most effectively help the client. It does nothing for them if we do not assist them to distinguish fantasy from reality, and this applies whether we actually discuss what is happening or not. If we are containing without discussion, our firm grip on reality will assist theirs; if we are discussing, our own clarity will assist clients to identify, talk about and hopefully, deal with their distortions.

(4) Discussion of transference should never be pursued for its own sake, but always brought into the context of the problems of current functioning. We are not analysts who may have concern with the transference *per se*: we are social workers whose prime focus is the here and now.

In all work in which we become really significant, what the worker *is* rather than what he does is of primary significance. This is not to suggest that we always discuss dynamics or aetiology with our clients, but such elements become, through the relationship, part of the situation. If this happens, then it is the relationship which is carrying the work since in itself it is becoming a corrective experience, with a potential re-learning taking place if we can handle it well. While all relationships are a learning experience, either adding to or diminishing a client, this sort of relationship is clearly of particular significance in this re-learning respect. If our goals include attempts to deal with attitudes and feelings which derive irrationally from other (mainly earlier) relationships, then becoming a 'significant other', with the degree of relationship this implies, in which such irrational elements are likely to be stirred and can be dealt with in the new, social work relationship, then clearly this becomes a most significant part of our work.

If we cannot develop such a relationship, this sort of work is not possible and our goals will need to be modified or we may consider say a residential placement where such a relationship might emerge. Similarly, if a transference develops spontaneously which is not part of our treatment plan at all, the transference will need to be controlled—for example, by cutting down on visits, interviewing in the office rather than at home, by turning attention to matters other than the relationship itself, or underlining the reality of our role and function. But transference can sometimes be stimulated, where this is what we want to happen given our goals, by reversing some of the 'cooling' processes—though the occasions on which we would even attempt this will be very rare, and demand a thorough justification for even the attempt.

However, given these limitations, we can sometimes offer the client, where the diagnosis justifies it, a new relationship learning experience and where other relationships have produced difficulty (such as an excessive super-ego) because of their severity, we may offer greater permissiveness; where indulgence has been the problem in the past (producing narcissistic gratification, perhaps) we might offer more firmness; where inconsistency has led to inadequately internalised ego-controls, we might offer a greater consistency.

Obviously, relationships will never be static, and clearly they need to be worked at if objectives are to be achieved. They will develop over time, change with the client's capacity to relate, and change with the client's needs—for example, with setbacks, crises, illness, clients may become temporarily more dependent; while as a problem is resolved, their need of us and the relationship will diminish.

Clearly, too, we must be on the watch for the way our attitudes, responses and counter-transference are effecting the relationship and therefore our work.

As social workers we may desperately want to be successful, and this could colour our diagnosis (we evaluate optimistically), our pacing (we try to push the client at our speed rather than his), our goals (set unrealistically high) or our methods (we may over-use the direct and under-use the indirect, for example). We may relish being the parent, sibling, spouse or lover, stimulate an unwarrantable transference, distort the reality and exacerbate problems because of our needs rather than the clients. We may enjoy dependence and keep clients in a state of helplessness. We may want to be liked and strive to please at all costs. We may fear dependency and avoid involvement in cases where this may be needed. We may have problems of our own around sexuality and avoid discussion even though clients may need to talk about problems in this area. We may have fears around aggression and strive to keep all our relationships full of 'sweetness and light', smothering feelings that need to be ventilated and examined, avoiding action that may arouse anger in ourselves or anger in others—even if such action is needed to protect others. Situations that really need an admission, for example, will be evaded with consequential damage to someone mentally ill who needs to be in hospital, or a child who needs to be away from battering parents. Older social workers, with children of their own, might find themselves siding with parents in situations of inter-generational conflict; younger social workers may find themselves siding with the children. In both instances their identifications (if not their conflicts) will be showing, perhaps to the detriment of their objectivity; almost certainly to the detriment of their ability to work with all the people involved.

A sufficient degree of self-awareness is an essential to good social work practice, whatever the method; and an on-going availability of consultation. Awareness is not a matter that is learned once-for-all during training.

But perhaps we need to realise above all, that if 'in-coming' clients do not come to a relationship new-born, but bring previous relationships with them, then as 'out-going' clients they will take with them what they have derived from their relationship with us into their existing and subsequent relationships. This fact is both the opportunity and the responsibility of social work.

In this chapter, I have not attempted to illustrate the treatment methods by examples. If the two illustrations I used at the beginning of the chapter are examined, most of the methods subsequently discussed will identifiably have been used—at least by implication.

References

1. Gordon Hamilton, *Theory and Practice of Social Casework* (Columbia University Press), 1951.
2. Gordon Hamilton, *ibid*.
3. Helen Perlman, *Social Casework—a Problem-solving Process* (Chicago University Press), 1957.
4. Florence Hollis, *Casework: a Psycho-social Therapy* (Random House), 1972.
5. Florence Hollis, *ibid*.
6. Gordon Hamilton, *ibid*.
7. Nina Toren, *Social Work—the Case of a Semi-profession* (Sage), 1972.
8. Florence Hollis, *ibid*.
9. Florence Hollis, *ibid*.
10. Gordon Hamilton, *ibid*.

Further Reading

Again, most of the standard casework texts contain sections on treatment, though as this chapter implies, I find Florence Hollis's approach the most useful. One specific book on this topic is Jonathan Moffatt's *Concepts in Casework Treatment* (Routledge & Kegan Paul).

With regard to goals, two interesting articles have appeared in *Social Work Today*: Joan Hutten's 'Short-term contracts' (7.2.74) and David Macarov's 'Client-worker agreement' (7.3.74).

The use of financial help is examined very pertinently in *Financial Help in Social Work* by Jean S. Heywood and Barbara K. Allen (Manchester University Press). The 'welfare rights' approach and its relations with social work practice has been extensively explored, beginning with Barbara Wootton's strictures in *Social Science and Social Pathology* (George Allen & Unwin). Other examples are Adrian Sinfield's *Which Way for Social Work?*, one of the contributions to *The Fifth Social Service* (Fabian Society); 'The case for radical casework' by Nicholas Bond (*Social Work Today*, 29.9.71); and Robert Holman's 'Poverty, welfare rights and social work (*Social Work Today*, 6.9.73).

Two articles which have a bearing on part of what I was trying to say about environmental management are 'On disabling the normal' by John Hilbourne (*British Journal of Social Work*, Winter 1973) and 'The mentally handicapped and their professional helpers' by Michael Bayley (*British Journal of Social Work*, Autumn 1973).

As regards relationship, I have previously mentioned Ferard and Honeybun's *The Caseworker's Use of Relationship*; but I would specifically refer students to Elizabeth Irvine's two chapters in *New Developments in Casework*, edited by Eileen Younghusband (George Allen & Unwin), entitled 'The function and use of relationship' and 'Transference and reality'.

Social workers' responses in interaction with their clients are considered in 'Mirrors, masks and social workers' by E. T. Ashton (*Social Work Today*, 27.7.72) and 'Games social workers play' by Michael E. Holtby (*Social Work Today* 7.3.74).

If social work students would like to take a very salutary look at themselves, they might like to read Geoffrey Pearson's 'Social work as the privatised solution of public ills' (*British Journal of Social Work*, Spring 1973).

A behaviourist approach to treatment has very different implications of course, though most behaviourists would acknowledge the validity of sustaining techniques, ventilation, some direct influence, and indirect methods generally as appropriate accompaniments to the programme of say, de-conditioning they would institute. Most would also acknowledge the part relationship plays in the programme. For those students, interested in this approach I would refer them again to Jehu's *Learning Theory in Social Work*.

Discussion

Discussion of treatment can sometimes get a little hard going for a student group. Treatment as a term again has overtones of being rather presumptuous though an alternative word is not easy to find, even though students with a healthy egalitarian, functionalist approach would prefer to find one.

Talking about treatment has certain intellectual and emotive difficulties. To begin with, identifying the separate strands of treatment methods when in practice they are so interwoven is not altogether easy and may initially seem to some students just a little pointless, though acknowledging the validity typically comes reasonably readily. But treatment in the past has quite often been for them an intuitive matter and it is never easy to intellectually identify the intuitive, while in the process the spontaneity and flow of it seem to become arid, calculated, academic and stilted—alien to their whole feeling of the way the task should be: full of warmth and responsiveness. It takes time for some students to recover their natural spontaneity and let it flow through their (now) directed practice.

Treatment almost inevitably sparks students' frustrations about time, skill, resources, bureaucracies, social attitudes and the 'system' as a whole (even clients), which stand in the way of what they would like to achieve. They can get angry, too, with teaching which appears to them idealised, when they know the realities (especially heavy caseloads) which face their colleagues and will face them when they return to practice after training. I would not have students feel otherwise: how would we get the changes we all want to see if new recruits to the profession did not feel impatient? Nor would I have us slant our training to accommodate current realities. The students' problems are not new: they have been experienced by generations of students and by generations of social workers. What we can do, perhaps, is to help students to channel their feelings into constructive action, bear the frustration of what appears to be slow progress, and encourage them by pointing up what has been accomplished in recent years.

'Idealised' teaching is defensible in that unless we know what could (and should) be, we will not know what in the current situation ought to be changed or in which direction. Given that situation is not likely to change very rapidly, at least sound teaching should enable practitioners to make the best use of what time, resources, etc., they have got.

It is discussion of relationship that often seems to produce the most difficulty—understandably, since clothing the subtleties, nuances and feelings of relationships with words, which are at best cumbrous instruments (unless we are poets) is a daunting task even for the fluent. Even as we speak, we seem to be bludgeoning what may have been a profound experience into something which even we can hardly recognise, let alone convey to others. At least in discussion we can recapitulate, re-phrase, elaborate, correct impressions: writing does not give us this opportunity, demanding even greater precision of expression, and becoming even more difficult (as perhaps this book demonstrates). Inevitably, too, we get extremely close to talking about our own feelings—never easy for clients or social workers (we get so little practice at it in our ordinary social lives)—and particularly so in a situation which students may see to be evaluative of themselves and their performance. (This becomes more acute when their own case material forms the basis for discussion.) There are clear implications here for the quality of the relationships between teacher and students and between students themselves. For the educational task, too, relationships are vital factors, with analo-gies to be drawn from what we are trying to teach or learn, about social work practice.

Transference may be an especially emotive area—partly because of a refreshing scepticism on the part of some students about the whole concept; partly because of what it produces in the way of feeling in us. But I feel this particular nettle should be grasped with the student group. It is not that transference occurs very often in field practice, but the impact of it when it does can be enormous. Not to help equip students to handle it would be letting them down.

But transference apart, some students in discussion will back away from the idea that they have become a significant person for their clients (which implies a degree of dependency on the client's part). To be significant can be frightening and to back away is an understandable reaction. I would certainly not think the reaction 'defensive' unless it happened persistently. But acknowledging one's significance can also appear 'big-headed' in discussion and so rather *infra dig* (though not to acknowledge what exists is also unrealistic). Being significant troubles a number of students not because they are necessarily afraid of the degree of involvement this implies, but because they know their practical work placements are limited in time and they hesitate to 'stir something up' in the relationship when they are afraid termination will occur perhaps before they can complete the work they have begun. This is a realistic problem—though probably a matter that can be determined only in discussion with their fieldwork teacher and in terms of specific cases. However, the very realism of the problem also means it could be an effective defensive ploy and not easy to identify as such.

Much of this chapter has been about the sheer necessity, though, of the relationship to treatment and the willingness of the worker to get constructively 'entangled' with his client. Acknowledging this necessity is not likely to be anything but a sobering challenge to any social worker. Yet it is, perhaps, the real reward of the job.

CHAPTER VI

The Casework Process

Some of the following material may seem a little familiar from earlier chapters though I now use it in a new context. I have identified four phases in the casework process: intake and orientation, exploration and testing, the problem solving work and termination. The first three at least may well overlap in practice, or be extant concurrently. The degree to which each phase appears will depend on the problem (a straightforward matter would involve very little in the way of exploration and testing), the client (who might block off access to underlying problems, should they exist, and so reduce matters to the straightforward in effect), the agency (if the difficulty really belongs elsewhere, a matter might be referred with little more than intake occurring) and the worker (his skill, the resources of time, etc. available to him).

(I) Intake and Orientation

This is Perlman's[1] 'beginning phase', which may well last for more than one interview, being largely that phase prior to the establishment of the 'contract'. It is suggested that this is the 'beginning of an experience that is expected to have continuity and produce change'; but I have hesitations about the expectation of continuity since studies of client expectations have indicated that some clients expect the contact to be short and advisory, and the expectation of continuity has been more that of the 'middle class' social worker. (We shall be looking again at this question of the duration of intervention when we examine crisis intervention later.) But I feel it is reasonable to suggest, whatever the duration, that from the start

Casework in Context

the experience should contain those elements and operations that
characterise its nature if the client is to know what he is 'letting
himself in for' (and can, therefore, exercise some self-determination
about it) and is to organise himself for the task appropriately.

The start, then, is not just a matter of the worker giving himself
(through sympathy, reassurance, etc., allowing ventilation, providing
material aid, defining the problem and providing a solution), but
also one of involving the client, as far as he is able, in perceiving,
thinking about, and acting on his difficulties—a microcosm of the
whole process. We endeavour to realistically engage the client to
the point at which the contract is made (and the beginning phase
ends) through the establishment of the relationship, exploring with
him what the problem is, indicating how the agency might help,
demonstrating the worker's competence to assist, and getting the
client's thinking and acting going.

Perlman[2] discusses this beginning phase in terms of content and
method.

This is aimed at eliciting the material for at least a preliminary
diagnosis. She suggests five headings:

(1) The nature of the presenting problem. As we have said, problems are a compound of fact and feeling (objective and subjective
elements). To get the facts may not be easy: the client may not
see the relevance of some; he may be embarrassed and reticent about
others. The worker may miss some if his concentration is elsewhere
and if he is not alert to the significance of others.

There have been fashions in social work about fact-gathering, especially from sources other than the client: from always getting cor-
roboration from elsewhere ('how are we to help if we do not have
the reality?') to never doing so ('it is the client's reality we are dealing
with and facts from others are therefore irrelevant and impertinent').
'Outside' facts are always a supplement to, and never a substitute
for the client's. Perhaps the balanced view now is to get facts (with
the client's permission if at all possible) where we need them to help
effectively: but never in a spirit of 'checking' or curiosity.

Feelings may be of two kinds: about bringing the problem at all (which we have looked at elsewhere) as well as about the problem itself. It is obviously important that we deal with the first before we can really reach the second. Contacting feelings in the problem area is clearly important—they inevitably exist and feelings may be the problem or the only modifiable part. Perlman suggests that contact with feelings assists the client to distinguish fact and fantasy, assists the relationship (the communication of feeling) and eases the tensions (by the use of acceptance, ventilation, etc.). At the beginning phase, the emphasis is on accepting and allowing feeling rather than exploring it, though.

We have also looked at some of the difficulties around presenting problems ('kite-flying', problems shaped to fit clients' expectations of the agency); but we begin there—always remembering that what the client brings is *today's* problem (not yesterday's or tomorrow's) which is always a compound of circumstance, mood, etc. It may well not be the 'same' problem next time because of changes in the interim—not least his coming to the agency anyway (generally an adaptive attempt on his part for which he should be credited), his contact with you and your intervention.

Whether fact or feeling, though, the focus in this phase is essentially on the 'here and now'. To explore with a newly referred client their childhood relationship with parents when they are facing eviction is clearly likely to be unproductive! The 'here and now' is not only the obvious starting point, relevant for client and worker, but also the area most readily accessible (and therefore most readily shared) and most easily available for modification (beginning the work).

(2) The significance of the problem. The significance of the problem is one of the prime determinants of the solution sought. It is possible that significance will be seen differently by the client and worker. The client may see no problem and seek no solution; see it as 'bad luck' (at getting caught) for which there is no social work remedy; see the problem as disciplinary (a 'good talking to' for truancy); or only financial (where emotional problems underlie); they may be overwhelmed since they do not see a solution—perhaps due to ignorance which the worker can help resolve fairly quickly. Clearly, until this question of significance is explored at least to a sufficient degree

to enable a realistically adequate intermediate solution to be agreed and worked at (using perhaps, the first phase or two of the method of reflective discussion), the intake phase can hardly be said to have been concluded. It would be quite unjustified, however, for any worker to assume that the client does not know what he is talking about, and firm evidence is required before concluding that the significance of the problem is anything other than what the client says it is.

(3) The causes of the problem. While the underlying causes (if any) will probably not begin to emerge until a rather later stage, at least some exploration is warranted of the factors which immediately precipitated the referral. While this exploration may yield important diagnostic material and (only where this is warranted) provide a point of entry for subsequent reflective discussion or dynamic consideration, it also begins the process of getting the client thinking about things—which they may well wish to do, anyway.

(4) The client's problem-solving efforts and means. Again, these have been considered elsewhere and we have recognised their significance for the diagnosis—and their significance for the client, too. But at least discussing ways he has tried to deal with matters will lead into discussion of other ways of dealing with them—involving the client's thinking and, perhaps, their subsequent acting. This also gives the worker an entry into explaining the exploring with the client the agency's and the worker's functions, and means of assisting.

(5) What the client seeks in the way of solution and their relations to the help the agency and worker can offer. Perlman suggests it is essential to bring discussion of solutions into the open, even if at this stage they have to be tentative, or of the 'intermediate goal' type. She suggests three reasons for this:

(i) We cannot send a client away in a 'limbo' of uncertainty about what he is to do, what the worker is to do, or how the next contact (if any) is to be initiated. Studies of client reactions where this has happened have highlighted their frustration, anxiety, resentment, distrust or false hopes (opening the way to bitterness and recrimination when they do not materialise), all to the detriment of the client, his situation, the work and the reputation of the agency.

(ii) Without discussion of solutions, the client can have no self-determination.

(iii) It will be impossible to focus client's problem-solving efforts or engage their motivation realistically.

Of course, what solutions the client is seeking will depend on their situations and their definition of it: in a crisis, immediate emergency remedies will be sought, not remedies for any underlying factors (where these exist and are recognised): in a chronic, on-going situation, we may have more time to explore before solutions are determined. Perlman suggests, too that we explore solutions in four stages:

(a) What the client wants—which may vary from being realistic/unrealistic/doesn't know/doesn't care/doesn't want.

(b) Explain what the agency/worker can offer in response to the client's solutions (in specific, not general terms), outlining the conditions and limitations (if these apply) and why—relating them to the more immediate rather than long term objectives. Do not discuss conditions as though they were 'good conduct' hurdles (which sounds controlling and punitive); nor in a 'routine' way—they may be to you, but are not to the client.

(c) Help the client with their *reactions* to the offer—whether positive, negative, submissive, resigned, or ambivalent.

(d) Help the client with his almost inevitable *conflict* of feelings about possible solutions—if only the frustration of delay. Negative feelings may or may not be expressed, but if you do not at least acknowledge and indicate your acceptance of their possible existence, further work may be blocked. We have all been puzzled at times by the enthusiastic client who subsequently disappears—perhaps because the negatives went unacknowledged.

This is not to suggest that solutions will always be considered in the first interview. In a case which begins to suggest there are complex intra-psychic problems or difficulties of family dynamics, the worker may well feel that he needs to know much more before solutions become apparent. If this is so, I feel it is best for the worker to be honest about this and I think the great majority of clients would feel it to be reasonable. When a complex situation may have been developing over years, they will acknowledge that it cannot all be told in the space of an hour or so; and they would be right to be suspicious of a judgment by the social worker on such a limited acquaintance with them and their situation. In the circumstances, an explanation by the worker and a definite arrangement about the next contact would be sufficient. In the interim, the client would know that further exploration would be the task for the next appointment and could be gearing themselves for this by further thinking or perhaps, also engaging other members of the family say, in it too, by the way of preparation.

(B) METHOD

Perlman suggests four methods are primarily operating in the beginning phase:

(1) Relating to the client. The essence here is to convey our understanding (attention, respect, acceptance, concern, sensitivity) and our competence (steadiness, objectivity, knowledge, skill), with the aim of establishing a *working* relationship: the client relating to a real worker (humane and able) not a fantasy.

(2) Helping a client to tell his troubles. We have examined this in listening earlier.

(3) Focussing and partialising. Telling, while often a help in itself, is not enough and focus is needed through clarification and exploring solutions with the client. We assist this through our questions and observations, directed to sorting out the immediate nub of the matter. We need this focus or we may lose track—confusing ourselves and our clients and leading the client to doubt our competence. At this beginning stage the criteria for selection of focus will be:

(a) The problem or aspect of it the client feels is important;
(b) The immediate problem (often the same thing);
(c) That part which falls within agency function;
(d) That problem or aspect which is representative (i.e. related to the larger problem, if any);
(e) The problem (or part) which the worker feels needs help most;
(f) That part which is manageable and most likely to yield to help.

Thus focus will also assist us in partialising the problem, and indicate a portion of it that might be tackled first, structuring and making the situation manageable. This is typical of ego functioning anyway, so we shall be working with and reinforcing the client's own adaptive processes. This is particularly important when the client is overwhelmed or the problem diffuse and his normal ego-functioning is near paralysis. Such partialising will give the client encouragement to tackle matters and motivation to begin. If he succeeds with this beginning it can add to his competence, sense of achievement and motivation to tackle the rest.

(4) Helping the client engage with the agency. Some of this method has been covered under Content (4); but also relevant here is some of the material in Chapter III where we looked at 'typologies' of clients and their presentation of themselves initially and suggested ways of assisting their engagement.

Demonstrably, both content and method in this beginning phase assists all the processes discussed earlier about the microcosmic nature of this phase.

(II) Exploration and Testing

This is the stage in which typically 'public' behaviour evident in earlier contacts is gradually dropped and the 'real' self is revealed, with the contact between client and worker assuming significance and the relationship developing.

It most typically happens in those cases where there are feelings which need (if problems are to be resolved) to be admitted at least, or explored (involving some degree possibly, of insight). We typically hide from ourselves what we do not like about ourselves and revelation is going to involve some degree of pain. But before committing themselves further, clients may go through a period of testing the worker and exploring the boundaries of the situation (a phenomenon which may recur at subsequent stages of the work, when intermediate goals are attained and further objectives embarked upon). Not infrequently this involves talking about their 'bad' feelings or behaviour, or acting them out in the relationship (for example by breaking appointments, flouting advice)—testing our acceptance, and various aspects of our authority, confidentiality, and caring; trying, perhaps, to provoke our judgmentalism. Difficult though some of this behaviour may be, it can be a sign of progress in the work and relationship, and if handled well can lead on to developments in both.

But not all clients find the increasing 'nearness' of the worker, or the problems, if these involve aspects of themselves, easy to tolerate and we encounter resistance. Now it is the worker's turn to explore: to identify and try to deal with possible reasons for it. His skill will certainly be tested. Until resistance is out of the way little progress can be made (given always, the validity of attempting this). Resistance may manifest itself in a number of ways: breaking or avoiding appointments, seeking to terminate ('it's all right now'), more overt expressions of hostility; interviews may be kept superficial, revealing little. Even where the contact continues (which implies the client is getting or seeking something from the contact at least), the problem-solving may be resisted by attempts to socialise or manipulate; or 'invitations' to collude or connive. It is important not to hastily interpret behaviour as resistant, though: bus delays do happen to negate appointments, while transient moods, being 'off colour', tired or appropriately preoccupied elsewhere will affect a client's contribution.

Resistance can be rational. Irritation with procedures, delays, doubts about confidentiality, etc. may be justified; while clients may have many practical difficulties maintaining contact—getting babysitters, taking time off work, costs of fares, getting back for children coming home from school. Pushed into a social work contact by circumstances, events or other people, it is understandable (and probably healthy) that with this immediate pressure removed, clients should wish to pull out and manage their own affairs. A few clients, after contacting an agency, meet with hostility from family or neighbours for having done so. If this hostility becomes translated into supportive action on their part, the problem may thus be dealt with or contained without further social work intervention. Even if it is not, a client may decide bearing with the problem is easier than bearing with the hostility and rationally withdraw. Other forms of resistance are understandable, too: clients see the problem, but 'smell' the cost of solving it coming and settle for what they have; none of us find growing self-awareness comfortable; the pain apart, the more we know the more we become responsible for. None of us embark on a new enterprise (and contact with a social caseworker is just this) without some apprehension.

Some resistance is not so rational though. Clients seeking 'magical' solutions which barely involve them, will break off to seek elsewhere if we do not come up with an adequate 'wand'; others with little motivation or capacity may also give up quickly; while others begin to waver at the point where they will have to start admitting something is the matter with *them* (not others, circumstances, etc.); or they start to realise (perhaps barely consciously) that they will have to give up behaviour that meets a need in them or from which they derive a secondary gain. Very occasionally, a client may withdraw because of the spontaneous emergence of transference—whether hostile, or a positive one of which they become afraid.

Rational resistance can usually be handled by rational discussion appropriate revisions of say, the practical side; or the plentiful use of sustaining techniques on the emotive.

As regards irrational resistance, those with little motivation may respond if we can, with real justification, raise anxiety levels—if school refusal is not dealt with, a care order could ensue; if problems are not dealt with on probation, it might be Borstal next time; if rent arrears are not met somehow, it might mean eviction. With waverers, sustaining techniques might be more productive than anxiety arousing: there is enough anxiety there already, probably. But with the 'magic wanders' or those deriving a secondary gain, the chances of success on a voluntary basis are likely to be small—at any rate with direct methods. We shall have to go back to diagnosis, goals and methods to see if there are other ways of dealing with situations. They may well have to be handled by indirect methods and even here, the chances of success may be limited. Distressing as it may be, we shall have to admit that some clients cannot be helped—or that situations will have to be allowed to deteriorate until a point has been reached to justify say, statutory intervention.

But whenever we encounter resistance our first task is to examine whether we have provoked it: have we been insensitive or lax about administrative matters; not recognised the practical difficulties; not offered a warm enough response for the client to use; misdiagnosed and been working at cross purposes; paced things badly—either 'crowding' the client along too fast, or irritating him by working too slowly; not allowed for negative feelings; or has a counter-transference been showing.

(III) The Problem-solving Work

Many social problems are solved (or have to be 'solved') before getting to this stage, which involves the dynamics of a situation and (in terms of treatment methods) the 'deeper' stages of reflective discussion or consideration of dynamics or aetiology. Typically only a small proportion of a usual caseload reach (or need) this stage. Here we are involved with derivatives of unconscious material and especially defence mechanisms. Remember this sort of work is only warranted if the problem-solving requires it and motivation and capacity allow. We do not deal with all defences (only those which are relevant, i.e. those which are contributing to the difficulties); nor do we attack them (rather thaw them—make them unnecessary) since defences are functional; and we interpret very sparingly.

Some of the defences we may be dealing with are:

Projection: wishes attributed to another since they are too dangerous or threatening to admit and they are then seen as emanating from the other.

Sublimation: drives unconsciously transmuted into socially acceptable forms and activities (Winnicott has suggested that art is a sublimated form of homosexuality for example).

Reaction formation: an over-reaction to stimuli (which may be obscure and not perceived by others).

The over-reaction may not manifest itself directly, but in an obverse form; for example, turning hostility into a rather exaggerated politeness or 'cool'.

Repression: inadmissable wishes or drives pushed into the unconscious but still influencing behaviour.

Inhibition: wishes and drives (more probably at the pre-conscious level) not acted upon for fear of the consequences.

Compensation: behaviour (directly or indirectly expressed) which makes up for (at various levels of consciousness) felt inadequacies.

Adler, for example, attributed a good deal of human behaviour to compensation: the asthmatic turns athlete, the stutterer becomes an orator, the short of stature a Napoleon.

Regression: temporary or permanent behaviour (and again at various levels of consciousness) typical of earlier stages of development to secure needs or avoid demands.

Manic defence: over-activity, sometimes accompanied by ebullience, humour and 'good fun', characterised as extrovert behaviour, but masking depressive, inadequate feelings.

Avoidance: wriggling out of problem situations in various ways, by refusing to face them—though aware of them at a conscious or pre-conscious level.

Denial: refusing to acknowledge a problem exists at all, or exists only at a very superficial level with easy solutions.

Displacement: which puts the problem somewhere else (we get angry with the children, not the boss); or transmutes it into a psycho-somatic problem; or we turn someone into a scapegoat. (The first at conscious or preconscious level: the latter two at unconscious level.)

Rationalisation: in which logical reasons are advanced for behaviour, occasionally amounting to pseudo-insights, tantamount to an intellectual defence—understanding or explanation at a mental level but leading to no change at an emotional level.

Fixation: in analytical terms this means being locked in a developmental stage, unable to progress further to adult maturity: chain smoking, over-eating (oral fixation); obsessional-compulsive rituals (anal fixation), homosexuality, promiscuity, pornography (sexual fixation), etc. Perhaps the 'idea fixe' might also be included here: the rigid adherence to only one interpretation of a situation despite evidence for other interpretations.

In general terms our methods of assistance here may be to act as or reinforce ego-functioning, involving reality testing, self control, etc.; using support techniques liberally as we try to reach and/or help the client to identify (and hopefully deal with) underlying emotive factors; or by providing a 'corrective' relationship in which defences are not needed and so enable (with transfer out to other relationships) a more positive spiral of experience in which defences may relax; or encourage a similar spiral through environmental management—relieving the practical, social and/or emotional factors exacerbating defensive reactions.

At this stage (or any other, for that matter) it is important to identify *movement* (or lack of it), whether in general terms or in particular areas. Movement (or its lack) may call for a revision of diagnosis, goals, methods or plans; help us to see where we are succeeding or not; or indicate whether or not we can begin to move to more 'ultimate' objectives; or give us clues as to whether termination is now approaching.

Movement may be examined in three areas: the situation, the client or the relationship, but they are obviously closely related. Movement in one area may well assist developments in others (or inhibit, if movement is adverse or static); or it may be that we can only identify movement in one area by looking at movement in others (for example movement in the relationship may not be obvious, but is manifested in improvement in the situation or client).

Movement in the situation will often be fairly apparent and will not need elaborating here; but personal movement might be indicated by a reduction in anxiety (or occasionally, an increase in it), greater tolerance (of others and of stress), control of emotional expression and behaviour, a greater appreciation of others' views, developing realism in appraisal of situations, increasing insight or self-awareness, more persistence and a greater willingness and capacity to cope with practical, social or emotive situations. Movement in the relationship might be indicated by a greater willingness and capacity to discuss significant material, the emergence of the 'bad', seeing the worker and his function more clearly and using them appropriately, a greater relaxation in interviews, more welcoming.

To identify progress can give the worker some justified (and sometimes much needed) encouragement, too.

(IV) Termination

Termination is little considered in the texts. It is something many workers find difficult since we, too, have our separation anxieties and needs to be needed. Few of our clients will need permanent support, though, and many of these will be terminal conditions where part of our function will be to help them face death. So with the bulk, termination is implied from the beginning.

Our intervention is accepted on the basis that problems exist with which we might help, and the understanding (even if it is not spelled out) is that when problems have been dealt with we will withdraw. Occasionally the period of our intervention is spelled out from the beginning specifically, by a probation order or the period of a hospital stay, to which we shall have to gear our goals and methods. But in more usual circumstances, termination comes as we move towards goals set up in the original request or its subsequent reformulations. Often enough it is the client who begins to drop the hints, indicating readiness to finish, and provided we feel that this is not resistance and adequate goals have been achieved, we can respond by beginning the terminating process— perhaps by spacing out our contacts, or engaging in a review of the problem-solving process as a form of consolidation of the experience.

Even if we are not altogether happy about closing at this stage, but the client persists in wanting to, it may be wise to respond: attempts to cling to the case may be interpreted by the client as a 'vote of no confidence' and/or provoke anger which will militate against current work and any renewed contacts in the future. Premature withdrawals, even if they mean a subsequent renewal, can be a learning experience for the client and not necessarily damaging. (Withdrawals we label 'premature' which do not become renewals are perhaps learning situations for us!)

There will be the occasional client, perhaps experiencing the social worker's leaving as a rejection, who decides to get in first and reject the worker, breaking off contact before being left. But letting people go can be agonising, especially if after all, we have to bend to 'picking up the pieces' with a client when further damage has occurred—while restraining the impulse to say 'I told you so'. Some clients, though, can/will only deal with practical matters, not the difficulties we can clearly see underlying them and likely to cause more difficulties in the future. With them we can only 'leave the door open' by ending the contact in as positive a way as possible. Referral for other parts of a problem does not happen now quite so often, thankfully (from Welfare to Children's Department for example); and happens even less now hospital social work is part of a Social Services Department's responsibilities: so we are spared this kind of termination. It does mean heavier demands on workers, though, for generic knowledge and skills.

While we have focussed till now on instances where termination is at the client's instigation more, circumstances can arise where the initiative is more with the worker. Examples might be where the worker's involvement merely exacerbates problems—for example in a marital conflict from which both parties are deriving a secondary gratification and both using the worker as a stick to beat the other with. Another possibility might be where we feel we can do no more, but the client still clings. Some degree of cling at termination is natural enough, but occasionally it becomes inordinate. Since this must signify something, it behoves us to check very carefully our diagnosis to see whether we have missed something and our goals, methods and the relationship—perhaps, too, our motivation. We may rationalise our task as complete when we are really trying to be rid of a client. Cling might be an expression of loneliness and isolation with little to do with personality factors: needs which may be far better met anyway, by neighbourly or voluntary visitors or a group, rather than us.

Although this is hardly termination, not all our long-term cases need a constant involvement and we may take them off our active list provided we are sure (in terms of our relationship with the client or the capability of others closely involved) that should the need arise, contact would be re-established. The occasional letter, a brief contact at, say, the physically handicapped centre, or at the time of the annual holiday or Christmas party, can keep lines open for the client to pick up as necessary.

We all leave jobs, get promoted, change to other areas at times, which means we have to terminate cases whatever stage we have reached. If we know well in advance we can complete some cases naturally; but in others we will need to discuss our leaving with clients and handle the matter of transfer, perhaps. Some clients will show little upset, others will be very distressed when we break the news—and we may be surprised by which turn out to be which in our caseload! At least we will know what we meant to clients—seriously. With the distressed we will need to work through with them some of their feelings of bereavement, loss, rejection and the anger or depression deriving from them—as well as their not unrealistic uncertainty about a replacement (if a replacement has been agreed upon) and the depressing thought of having to 'start all over again'. Perhaps one of the most difficult (but necessary) situations to work with is the client who acknowledges what we tell, but then blocks on it, carrying on as though we were staying. But if whoever comes next is not to be rejected in turn, given a very angry reception, have an inordinate amount of grief to work through, or be subjected to constant comparisons with the worker who has left (all of which hold up the work), feelings will need to be dealt with as far as possible before we go. We should arrange to introduce the new worker, if at all possible, an interview or two before the last we have (i.e. give the opportunity to explore the final feelings on our own).

Whenever we terminate a case, in whatever way, with or without a handover, we should let anyone else in the situation (the G.P. for example) know—with a summary of the situation (respecting any confidentiality issues). This is not only courtesy, but reinforces the idea of co-operative teamwork, is good public relations and a useful way of educating others about social work.

Finally, Hamilton[3] suggests three ways in which we should NOT terminate:

(1) Aggressively—saying, in effect, 'I don't want you, you're a nuisance, you won't do what I want'. This is a damaging rejection, hardly likely to enamour the client of us, the agency or social work.

(2) As a challenge—'prove to me or yourself you can do it'. The anxiety this provokes reduces the chance of success and the result of failure can be very damaging. It also makes future contacts (as in the first instance) extremely difficult for all concerned.

(3) As an arbitrary act—i.e. as a result of our own feelings, or an administrative decision, rather than a considered decision rooted in diagnosis and goals.

References

1. Helen Perlman, *Social Casework: a Problem-solving Process* (Chicago University Press), 1957.
2. Helen Perlman, *ibid.*
3. Gordon Hamilton, *The Theory and Practice of Social Casework* (Columbia University Press), 1951.

Further Reading

Casework process gets coverage in the standard texts, but I have found Perlman's discussion the most useful. The case illustrations used in a range of texts illustrate the process at work, or at any rate stages of it; though perhaps for reasons of length not all that number take the process from start to finish or discuss it in this way. The only text which is entirely devoted to process is Jean Nursten's *Process of Casework* (Pitman) and well worth study for this reason alone.

Termination is considered by Denise Mumford in 'Transfer of cases' (*Social Work Today*, 8.3.73) and by Paul Bywaters in his articles 'Ending casework relationships' appearing in *Social Work Today*, 21.8.75 and 4.9.75.

Again, though, material in this chapter—particularly resistance and defences—is dependent on reading elsewhere, especially psychology: but there is an interesting chapter by S. Wasserman in F. J. Turner's book *Differential Diagnosis in Social Work* (Free Press), in which he discusses ego psychology, and social work process and termination.

Discussion

The casework process is typically a matter of very considerable interest to students. The how and why of progress or lack of it is fascinating in itself; but given that as students they are keen to be able to demonstrate success, it is understandable that they welcome material which enables them to assist and identify progress in their cases and examine those elements which appear to be inhibiting it. Blocks to progress can produce a near despair, and it can be very helpful for this to be shared with the group. No student is likely to be alone in feeling like this (which can be some comfort); other students may make suggestions about how matters might be handled (which could bring some encouragement); or the assurance might emerge that in the circumstances little can be expected.

Intake and orientation does not usually present much difficulty, but exploration and testing worries some students who need a little help to see this as a positive development. Resistance troubles students, too; they experience it as thwarting what they would like to achieve, tend to blame their own mishandling for it; yet feel reluctant to push themselves on a resistant client for perfectly sound reasons of respect for a client's right to self-determination.

Defences are understood but some students tend to see them negatively and occasionally discuss them as something to be 'broken down'. They may need reminding of their functional necessity; that an attack on them risks their being strengthened and that the 'thawing' approach, even if it takes time, is more likely to be productive unless a confrontation is justified (as it sometimes is).

Movement is worth exploring since it is not always recognised for what it is by students who are, perhaps, expecting something a little more dramatic and do not initially see the significance of what they consider are only small gains.

Termination is a matter which students can acknowledge intellectually but which some still find hard emotionally. Like most of us, they like to feel needed and may be inclined to be over-protective of clients and anxious about how they will get on on their own. (This despite complaints elsewhere about over-large caseloads.) The idea that termination is implied from the beginning can be a reassurance.

Perhaps the hardest thing for students is to acknowledge that it can be right to give up a case with problems only half resolved or with virtually nothing accomplished at all. As caring people this borders on the unforgiveable, and I am glad that students should feel this way. But the reality is that we have no magic wands, either; there are limitations to what we can do, that clients are free agents, even if they express this freedom in a way which means that a cared-for probationer ends up with a custodial sentence. We know that sentence may do more harm than good, yet in our report we have to admit that probation is not being effective and by implication (if not by a specific recommendation), make that sentence inevitable.

Termination is also very much part of student life, in the sense that it happens to them as many times as they have placements— which is much more frequently than in ordinary practice. They are concerned not only to terminate well (a reflection, perhaps, of the guilt they often feel about using people to 'learn on'), but also about what they are handing over to. This is not meant as a reflection of the quality of work of their colleagues, but what they are likely to be able to accomplish given their existing caseloads. Students know that even though they may not be as skilled as a qualified, experienced worker, they have frequently given their clients time and detailed attention which they are most unlikely to get in future. Reassurance that what happens after they leave a placement is not their responsibility is of small comfort.

CHAPTER VII

Recording

Records include files, reports and letters.

(A) Files

The functions of files have been categorised as for:
(1) social work practice;
(2) administrative purposes;
(3) teaching and supervision;
(4) research.
The emphasis on each aspect has changed over time, given developments in social work practice and aims; and still varies with the focus of the agency (for example whether casework or material aid is the primary method of meeting clients needs). The categories will overlap at points, or entries can serve more than one function.

(1) RECORDING FOR PRACTICE

For good practice, records will need to contain a number of elements:
Facts—to assist the worker's memory, or provide a source of reference. Facts may be incorporated in a front sheet (giving names, ages, or dates of birth, address, name of doctor, names and addresses of relatives, source of referral, category of presenting request, occupation, income, illness or handicap, etc.) or gathered into an initial history. Either way they should be readily accessible. Clearly, the facts which need to be recorded will vary with the nature of the agency and the case: the selection will differ if the focus is a grant

or material aid, psychological problems (child guidance work for example), a fostering or adoption case, or medical social work.

It may be helpful, too, to keep a log of 'facts'—dates of telephone calls, letters, practical steps taken, major events, etc.—as a kind of case abstract for quick reference.

But I feel strongly that facts should not be collected or recorded unless they are relevant or likely to be so. Too often it is what is in the front sheet which pre-determines what facts we ask for. Relevant or irrelevant, we have to fill all the spaces provided. This sort of fact gathering is quite properly resented by clients as bureaucratic nosiness.

Diagnostic material. The worker will need to record what he is told, what he observes and his impressions, clearly distinguishing between each, adding as he goes his analysis and interpretation, to provide the data for his initial social diagnosis—the basis for his determination of treatment goals, plans and methods to be used.

Process material. This will record the events (practical, social and emotional) over time which will assist the identification of movement and the refinement of diagnosis, goals, treatment plans and methods. It will help to clarify what is happening in the relationship, adding to the worker's awareness (including self-awareness) and providing material for the development and/or application of his skill.

Typically, process material is recorded in narrative form, but will be selected for its relevance, and may be grouped under appropriate headings or paragraphed rather than written up just as it happened in the course of the contact. The occasional process recording (i.e. a record of just how it happened) might help, though, in cases where the going is getting 'sticky'.

This process material could, in time, become bulky—not easily grasped in terms of its significance by the worker or any colleague involved, so in a case that is lengthy, or likely to be so,

Summaries are extremely useful. An initial summary could be completed at around the time the initial social diagnosis is made, outlining the presenting situation and the worker's ideas on where the difficulties lie, and what might be done about them; but subsequent summaries (at perhaps, three monthly intervals) would incorporate what has been happening in the case process, re-evaluate the situation and outline how the worker sees he is to proceed now and why. Re-reading his process records and writing up summaries should clarify the worker's thinking, help him to identify what is happening, enable him to 'see the wood for the trees', renew his grip of the case and confirm his confidence in what he is doing and plans to achieve. When a case is closed, a terminal summary should be completed, outlining the initial situation, the closing situation, and what took place in between.

What I think all this amounts to is that good recording for practice should add up to a protection of the client—a way of ensuring that he gets a service as good as we can make it.

We have looked at aspects of records in connection with confidentiality, including speculating about whether clients should have access to files about themselves. Whether this happens or not I think it is not a bad idea to record as though they did have. This should make us think about what we put down and only include what we can justify. Even if we are being a little speculative this should be supported by some evidence. If we have no evidence for our speculations, they belong more to the realm of fantasy and have no place in records.

It is useful to remember that in particular situations, records may have a specific function: for example, where a child is in long term care, they may represent that child's 'memory' and be the only record he has access to of what has happened to him—especially significant for any worker, too, who subsequently assumes responsibility.

Recording does involve problems of accuracy (since our recall is never complete) and objectivity (since the worker may have selective biases and/or misinterpret—though recording should help him, perhaps with supervision, to identify these). But these problems may mean some difficulties when another worker is involved, takes over, or when records are used for research purposes.

It is for reasons of almost inevitable bias that some workers when taking over from another, prefer not to read the records first but obtain their own impressions and then go to the records. They would argue that however one tries to guard against it, reading others' opinions slips a pair of selective perceptive glasses over one's eyes.

Recording in casework is neither a luxury nor a chore—but essen- •
tial for good practice and part of it.

(2) RECORDING FOR ADMINISTRATION

Administration requires records for a number of functions;

(a) *To determine eligibility*: for services—whether grants, aids,
admissions to care, etc.: or for appointments—say as foster parents,
or for acceptance as adoptive parents. Typically, this material is both
factual (the facts required shaped by the type of service or appointment) and coupled with the worker's professional opinion. While
this sort of information is typically abstracted for a formal submission, the information will need to be in the files in the first place,
and copies of the abstract and the decision made about it, should
go in them, too.

(b) *To ensure continuity of service* so that clients do not get
'dropped' or services they need fail to materialise because of malad-
ministration. The social workers records are vital where there is a
handover of worker, or a closed case is subsequently re-opened; so
the new worker knows what he is doing and the client spared the
distress of repeating everything. The front sheet, history, log and
summaries are especially important, enabling the new worker to
quickly get the gist of the material without hours of wading through
process records.

(c) *To assist communication*: (i) Internally, as between groups within
the agency—administrators, social workers, home helps, occupational
therapists, day and residential staff. Where more than one of these
groups is involved in a particular case, they will need to know what
other groups are doing and planning to co-ordinate their part in
the situation. They therefore have to contribute to and have access
to records. (ii) Externally, with other agencies from whom the agency
is asking for information or service, or who are asking it for information and service—courts, housing departments, health services, social
security, trusts, voluntary bodies, etc. Such communications may be
about specific cases, general policy, or co-ordinated planning, and
while case files will very rarely be exchanged, the material for a
letter or report needs to be readily accessible in the records.

(d) *To identify what the agency is doing.* This may involve knowing workers caseloads, types of cases, numbers of residents and categories; whether the budget is being under or over spent (in toto or under various heads); etc. While this information may require special files kept by the various groups, or require special returns at particular times, much of it will depend initially on the case records. This material may be especially significant in justifying the agency's work and/or its future plans to its committee, financial supporters, and the general public (via annual reports for example).

(e) *To identify what the agency should be doing.* Areas of expansion/contraction in the agency's work, priorities, finance, staffing, policy—all forward planning, in fact—even though, again, it will call for specialised records and returns—will basically depend on the case records.

(f) *To protect the client.* Records will be a fundamental tool in the administrative task of ensuring that (whether clients protest or not) they are getting the services—in material terms or in terms of the quality of professional services—they are entitled to expect. Given that what social workers do is 'hidden', their records are crucial in this sort of protective supervision of their activity.

(g) *To protect the agency.* Should the agency be criticised, whether in terms of the amount or quality of service, its policy or its application; in general or in a specific instance; then the agency must be in a position to evaluate the criticism, rebut it or admit it. This can only be done from its records. Recent cases of child deaths should be a warning to us all: but in all cases where legal requirements are involved records should be kept meticulously—if only to keep us aware of our obligations and see that we live up to them. The requirements were designed to protect the client after all.

(3) TEACHING AND SUPERVISION

Records may be used in two ways:

(a) Existing records may be read by a student or new member of staff to acquaint him, as an introduction, to the agency's services, policies and procedures.

(b) The staff member's or student's own records are used as a basis for his development as a professional and as an administrator. (We examine the difficulties of supervision combining these two aspects in Chapter XI.) As far as development of his professional skill is concerned, records will be utilised in much the same ways as for practice.

The compilation of front sheets, histories, etc. will assist the student's ability to collect comprehensive, accurate data.

Diagnostic material compilation will serve to sharpen his observation, perception, analysis and interpretation; while formulating the social diagnosis will assist him to think purposefully, objectively and selectively about material for the establishing of goals, plans and the selection of methods.

Process material (perhaps using a full or modified process recording) will help students to identify their own involvement, add to their awareness, to see what is happening in the relationship and use it, identify movement, modify diagnosis plans, goals and methods, further their objectivity and strengthen their ability to help.

Summaries will clarify thinking, assist direction, facilitate handing over or termination.

While the use of records in developing a student's skill is rarely questioned and always practised, their subsequent use, post-qualification, to continue the development of skill is tacitly ignored. Timms[1] suggests we explore the use of audio-visual aids (tapes and video-tapes) as more effective teaching methods than records, but obviously a vital pre-requisite here would be the client's co-operation.

I sometimes suspect that clients are rarely asked for that co-operation for fear they would be more ready to co-operate than we might like: records can be 'filtered' in a way that may suit us; tapes and video tapes expose us with uncompromising ruthlessness.

(4) RESEARCH

In the design of records, their possible use for research purposes is very seldom considered. While specific research projects might call for the design of special records, much more could be done to improve design anyway, which would make records of much more use for research purposes even where not specifically planned in advance.

Internally, research may assist the administrative tasks of shaping policy, determining priorities, or allocating resources; or it may assist in identifying why existing targets are not being achieved—the blocks in, or unexpected by-products of, existing methods, administrative procedures, and communication processes.

Externally, research may be providing data which will assist others' policy and resource planning and development (Architect's or Treasurer's Departments for example), or provide 'ammunition' to get others' policies and provisions changed (to assist social reform, in effect). Research results may help to gain the support of others for what the agency (singly or in combination) is trying to do; or educate the public about its work. Research may be part of an investigation in a number of agencies or areas which will assist the development of say, social work practice, or assist towards a more effective utilisation of facilities the agencies already possess.

While record systems for internal research are often inadequate, the disparity between agency recording systems makes research involving a number of agencies even more difficult. Some degree of standardisation of records would seem to be essential if multi-agency research is not to be inordinately time consuming, costly—and thus, rare—to the detriment of clients and workers.

It will clearly be no easy matter to establish a recording system which will adequately cater for all the functions outlined above. I feel the probation service has much to teach us, though, in devising a recording system that reinforces good practice; while the best hospital practice has much to offer about the management of multi-disciplinary files—subsectioned, tagged, with standardised colour identifications for each, and centrally indexed. It would seem likely that apart from the centralised files, different groups within say, a Social Services Department, would also keep some records of their own—and this might be particularly important for social workers, given the highly confidential material some of their records contain.

Computers and data banks are being used increasingly in Social Services Departments. This development troubles me rather—partly because one wonders who else within the local authority (or even outside it, if the authority is hiring time on someone else's computer) has access to Social Services Department material; partly because once a computer exists, it has to be used to justify it economically. I can envisage recording systems being devised to keep the computer occupied or slanted throughout in terms of its suitability for computerising: not my choice of priorities.

It is hardly necessary to stress that any records should be flexible, bear in mind who will use them and what for, be visible, readable, accessible, comprehensive, accurate, up-to-date, written in straightforward language, typed and well set out with margins, headings and paragraphs. The material should be selected and as brief as possible. Too often our records are rambling, pointless, inaccurate, out of date, a mass of omissions, largely written up as a matter of habit, the format rarely revised, and utilised more as proofs of how busy we are than anything else. In such circumstances it is no wonder they are so little *used*.

Clients are wary of what we record about them—and rightly. The sheer permanence of records means we have to be conscious of the way they can label people and stigmatise them—perhaps for years afterwards. Basically, records are an infringement of privacy and only justifiable if they are used in the client's interests (directly or indirectly such as through research and teaching)—though in some circumstances they may have to be used to protect others' interests (which could include legal proceedings). It might help to dispel some of the wariness if at least front sheets or application forms for aids, etc. could be completed by the client, with the worker's assistance. Some records (for example social enquiry reports for courts), clients will have the right to see, and these could be a valuable learning exercise—as students who have discussed their fieldwork reports with their supervisors, will appreciate. There is always the problem of whether to include material which might be damaging rather than helpful, at that point in time. The involvement of the client in this record based learning is built into at least one system of helping clients—Eugene Heimler's[2] social assessment scales—which the client completes (sometimes with the therapists help) but which form the basis of subsequent work. The scales are completed at a number of stages which assists the client to identify his progress or lack of it.

(B) Reports

These are one of the primary means of communication within and between agencies. The material for them should be selected, bearing in mind the purpose, the people who will be reading them and their purpose. They should be brief, jargon free, and clear, accurate and precise. Remember, nuances may be read into them which were never intended, with no opportunity for discussion, clarification or amplification of what was 'really meant'.

The fact that they are reports and therefore to a variable extent formal documents only adds to their significance, weights each word, and ensures their filing for safe keeping (i.e. their permanence).

The ability to write a good report is not an optional extra for any social worker, but an essential skill. A poorly written report could deprive a client of badly needed resources, effective help from others or, just conceivably, of his liberty.

(C) Letters

Again, a primary means of communication. Letters to clients may vary from the straightforward (appointments, information, confirmation of arrangements made, etc.—useful where clients are anxious and not really taking things in, or are forgetful) to, in effect, substitutes for interviews. While in general the work that may be done by a 'substitute interview' letter may be limited, letters can be very significant. They may help to keep a relationship alive: for example, where a contact is only occasional or where time and distance—as with a child in care in an establishment a long way away—make contacts infrequent. But either way, letters can be re-read and deeply considered. What is written needs to be carefully considered, therefore, bearing in mind the knowledge of the client and his likely responses. Remember, too, the circumstances which may surround the receipt of a letter—the time lag, that it will probably arrive at breakfast time, that the client may not wish others to know where letters come from (so use plain envelopes).

Letters to other agencies may again be straightforward or complex—brief reports in effect. When giving information (as with
reports) bear in mind the purpose and the recipients', and the permanence and consequence of writing—as well as confidentiality.
When asking for information or a service, the idea is to motivate
a positive response. This is achieved in part by getting 'blocks' out
of the way—don't write unnecessarily, be brief and clear, quote references or identifying data, be courteous, don't 'issue instructions' but
write as one professional to another respecting their expertise, don't
ape their jargon and avoid using our own. It may also help to personalise the letter—addressing the individual concerned or marking
it for his attention—and making sure his style and titles are right,
the address correct and names spelled properly.

The other part is to demonstrate clearly why the request for information or service is being made: the function it will serve within
an overall purpose. This will help the receiving agency to evaluate
the request (bearing in mind they will be faced with priority choices,
probably) and, on the assumption they accede, to bring in information or service in an effective, co-operative way. A social worker
should be able to sign most of his letters himself since they will
come within his professional sphere and degree of responsibility; but
sometimes his letters will involve agency matters (matters of policy
for example) and these should be signed by the person with responsibility for them—even if the social worker drafts the letter in the
first place for his signature.

I deplore the practice in some Social Services Departments of
nearly every letter going out under the signature of the Area Officer
if not the Director himself. What must a client think of a letter
they receive from a person they have never heard of but who sounds
important, yet they know has probably not seen the letter since his
signature has been rubber stamped on the bottom, telling them that
'his' (the Director's) social worker, Mr. Soandso will be coming to
see them at 2 p.m. next Wednesday. Apart from generating fantasies
of an omniscient Director (or omniscient bureaucracy), it hardly does
a great deal to engender respect for the professional autonomy or
responsibility of the worker. He must arrive with an aura of the
office boy about him.

References

1. Noel Timms, *Recording in Social Work* (Routledge & Kegan Paul), 1972.
2. Eugene Heimler, *Survival in Society* (Weidenfeld & Nicolson), 1975.

Further Reading

The standard texts give scant attention to recording, while books about it are few. The two I would recommend are *Social Case Recording* by Gordon Hamilton (Columbia University Press) even though this was written some years ago; and *Recording in Social Work* by Noel Timms (Routledge & Kegan Paul).

Discussion

Recording is not a matter to inspire much enthusiasm among students. It is a chore or worse—though they tend to be anxious about it at the beginning of a placement until they have got the measure of what that agency wants of them.

It is not long before they recognise the value of records for teaching purposes—though the thought of process recording scares them a little until they have tried it and come to appreciate its value (though still wrestling with problems of trying to remember everything that was said and the sequence of it). Most students also see the administrative reasons for records, though some are surprised by the range of administrative functions involved which they had not thought of before. This tends to make them a little more sympathetic to recording than before.

The idea of using records for research purposes is for many students at best a nebulous idea—a sad reflection, I feel, on the general state of research in most social work agencies.

Getting reports right bothers some students but reflects almost all students' awareness of the significance of them for their clients.

Letter writing is something quite a number of students do rather badly and sometimes there does not appear to be much experience in the agency to assist them. Students with some decent commercial experience before coming into social work have an advantage here. The importance of correspondence is sometimes under-rated; but if only half the stories one hears about the ineptitude or non-existence of the correspondence of social work agencies are true, the importance should need no underlining.

PART III

The Differential Uses of Casework

CHAPTER VIII

Crisis Intervention and Long-term Work

Crises have been categorised under three headings:

(1) The impact of an external calamity—such as unemployment, illness, death, enforced re-housing.

(2) The impact of role re-distribution—either as a result of dismemberment (the loss of a family member) or accession (the gaining of a family member).

(3) The impact of role transition—starting school, leaving school; adolescence, marriage, parenthood; job change, promotion, disrating; menopause, grandparenthood, retirement, etc.

Clearly, in social work there are many circumstances in which these criteria might apply: admissions to care, hospital or old people's home; in many family and marital situations; in work with people in areas of slum clearance or new housing estates; in work with parents who have given birth (especially where a child is premature or handicapped); in work with adolescents; in adoption work, and so on.

I would like to stress that crises can be triggered by opportunity as well as disaster; creating tensions for the person with the chance or resulting in others in the family facing problems of dismemberment, loss or re-housing for example.

Crises are not necessarily negative experiences, either. They can be positive growth opportunities in which families develop new skills, resources and relationships; and while they can be dangerous, they may also present opportunities for very valuable social work intervention. In crisis situations the problems are typically acute and demonstrable; and as a consequence, accessible. The feeling level is often high and feelings are being expressed, too. The motivation to do something about the problems is frequently strong. Crises are

typically of short duration with an inbuilt tendency to right themselves in one way or another, so worker and family are usually pull-
ing together in the situation.

Crises occur even in the most normal families and while it is true
that most normal individuals and families cope without aid from
social workers, many families are vulnerable if only because in many
respects these days we are not well prepared for crises: death is
rarer and a taboo subject anyway—as are physical handicap and
mental disorder which get 'hidden away'; children rarely get the
chance to explore work situations before they are pitched into them;
adolescence is culturally an awkward time; advertising's use of sexual
prowess and fulfilment may not help realistic marital adjustment;
easy credit masks income realities, etc. Even though well prepared,
the actual impact of a crisis may hit us hard and produce reactions
that were 'normally' unanticipated since it activated aspects of ourselves previously unrecognised because circumstances did not touch
them—for example aspects of marital interaction. But it probably
remains true that many of the families social workers see in crises,
even though previously functioning within the broad definition of
normal, have some degree of handicap:

The poor, for whom even a 'small' event may precipitate a major
   crisis;
The rich, with much to lose, for whom an event such as redundancy
   may be very threatening;
The isolated family, with little kin or neighbour support;
Families where tension already exists, but is contained, may have
   little to spare to deal with a crisis;
Crises may renew old conflicts, ordinarily dormant or coped with;
Crises may disrupt the distribution of needs and satisfactions.

As the categories suggest, crises can be due to threats which are
'external' or 'internal' to the family. While an external threat can
lead to disintegration, it may also present as a challenge to which
the family responds with greater cohesion: it is the internal threat
which always tests cohesion and may be the more serious.

But it is always important to realise that crises are not just a
product of circumstances, but will also depend on the family's defini-

tion that a crisis exists (about which, there may not be a unanimous view, of course). Cases can present as crises when to the outside observer the precipitating factor is so small that it would 'normally' never be defined as such. It is up to the worker then to try to understand why the situation has been presented this way: why a small event is seen so significantly; whether it masks an underlying problem, for example. Even major crises can be defensively reduced to little significance by denial, avoidance, need resignation, or 'looking on the bright side'.

The typical crisis pattern may be diagrammatically represented thus:

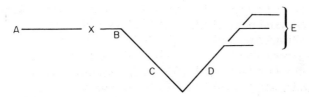

A is the pre-crisis 'normal' life-style or equilibrium;

X is the crisis;

B is the typical period of numbness, in which the life-style is maintained for a while before the crisis impact is felt;

C is the period of disintegration, which may itself contain three stages:

(a) Initial tension, in which the family strives to maintain equilibrium and meet the crisis impact by their previous problem-solving methods and adaptations. Given that the crisis is a new experience, these methods may prove inadequate or inappropriate; demanding as yet undeveloped techniques. The failure of the usual methods would lead to

(b) Further tension, and a resort to a variety of 'emergency' techniques—rather desperate measures, including perhaps, the defensive reductions mentioned above. If these failed, the stage of

(c) Disintegration might be reached: tension high, outbursts of emotion; resignation, despair or helplessness—being carried along by events; obsessive planning but little action; disorganised, unconstructive behaviour geared to internal stress rather than outer reality

—magical thinking, self-preoccupation rather than co-operative action, with family members involved in complaining, recriminations, blaming others, scapegoating, etc.

Typically, it is not until this third stage is reached that the social worker gets called in to assist:

D the restoration;

E the establishment of a new equilibrium which may provide rather less (but enough) satisfaction, much the same as before, or possibly greater satisfaction then hitherto.

Before discussing crisis intervention work, it must be stressed that certain pre-requisites have to exist: i.e. that the individual or family functions within 'normality' ordinarily—specifically that there exists a sufficient minimum of:

(a) positive family ties;

(b) ego strengths;

(c) ability to relate to others (including the worker);

(d) motivation.

A good social history would greatly assist in establishing whether this pre-existing 'normality' was there or not. Where problems are demonstrably of long standing, a crisis approach would not be sufficient in itself; but where there was normality, there is no need, *a priori*, to delve into the 'pre-crisis' time as such.

Assuming a situation can be handled as a crisis, the aims would be:

(1) to relieve anxiety;

(2) to mobilise internal and external resources;

(3) to promote the healthiest recovery—to stimulate growth and prevent further events becoming crises.

These aims may be seen as sequential, but in practice they will inter-mingle, or earlier stages may recur.

Relieving anxiety will involve the worker getting information about the problems; allowing ventilation of feelings; and offering accept-ance, sympathy, and understanding; giving information, advice and practical help. This will provide client and/or family with some imme-diate relief, begin the process of clarification (for clients and for the worker's diagnosis), give the clients some direction and assist morale by bringing at least some aspects of the situation under a degree of control. It should give them the feeling of being supported—enabling them, with anxiety reduced, to begin co-operating with each other again and releasing resources for them to work more effectively on the problems. In a badly disintegrated situation, the worker will probably need to act with some firmness as well as efficiency and speed: not only to demonstrate his concern and ability to help but also to provide a framework and the supportive control that the family have lost. It is vital that he is not seen to be overwhelmed too.

Mobilising internal and external resources. Mobilising internal resources will involve the extensive use of supportive techniques (concern, encouragement, realistic expressions of confidence) as well as the on-going use of advice, information and the beginnings of reflective discussion. External support will involve the introduction of material aid, the use of referral to bring in those people or services needed to help meet aspects of the difficulties; the mobilisation of kin, neighbours, and/or significant others. It is important that clients should experience enough success and satisfaction at this stage to maintain motivation.

Promoting the healthiest recovery. Among the tasks the client and/or family will be undertaking here are working at new perceptions (of themselves, others, interactions and situations), rehearsing for the new realities, acquiring new models for identification, developing new skills for new tasks and roles, learning new ways of handling situations. Among the techniques the worker may be using to assist might be reflective discussion, offering himself for a model or engaging others who could be, and perhaps utilising a wide range of group situations which might help—evening classes, rehabilitation centres, youth clubs, community centres, groups concerned with particular issues (from Claimants Unions to the Spina Bifida & Hydrocephalus Association), day centres, psychiatric clubs, adoptive parent groups, young mothers clubs, etc.

Care must be taken at this stage to see that the new patterns emerging are likely to be lasting and satisfying to all those involved—for example, that a new equilibrium is not established at the expense of, or by overloading, one family member. Should they 'crack', another crisis will occur.

Crisis intervention involves particular skills and emphases:

(1) A quick and accurate diagnosis of the crisis factors through an analysis of

(a) the previous life-style/equilibrium;

(b) the present problem solving methods being used (crucial in identifying how best internal and external resources can be mobilised, introduced and applied);

(c) the need/satisfaction/response patterns (to identify a potential new equilibrium).

Such a diagnosis is necessary when it is an individual in crisis; but vital in family situations. In crises, the clients' network and the worker's relation to it, are critical.

(2) A focus on the crisis—for example, on the interaction in family situations rather than the problems of individual members; and on current feelings rather than an inordinate concern with their aetiology. There is an excellent case for the use of joint interviews or conjoint family therapy.

(3) Limited, crisis-resolving goals. Goals should be:

(a) Clear cut and demonstrably crisis related. This will give the work focus, engage motivation, and give a clear indication of roles and tasks to the client/family, to the worker or team, and the distribution between them; assisting purposeful communication and distribution of function;

(b) Manageable and achievable for both 'sides', with the plentiful use of intermediate goals in the early stages to bring increasing areas under control until the whole situation becomes manageable and equilibrium is restored;

(c) Limited—the aim being to get the inhibiting, crisis-induced factors out of the way and set up a 'positive spiral' of experience. There is no attempt at a radical restructuring of personality or functioning.

Where the problem is one of role transition, do not forget that successful transition requires three elements:

(i) Role readiness—learning in advance (though we have already seen the difficulties here of insufficient learning opportunities and unanticipated impact effects).

(ii) Disengagement from existing networks (with the problems of separation anxiety and insecurity, but the advantage of the typical drive towards the new and maturity).

(iii) Accommodation in the new roles ensuring previous gratifications are adequately provided for in the new roles to 'cement' people into them and avoid subsequent regressions.

The crisis concept is particularly applicable in cases of grief/loss/ bereavement.

Crisis work has the advantage of being both effective (as Reid and Shyne[1] indicated) and economic. The authorities suggest that between 5–10 sessions should be sufficient, but even one good interview can achieve a tremendous amount. This economic and effective use of our time can leave us freer to deal with those cases which are not crises but require more protracted work on 'clinical' and 'aetiological' or long term supportive problems. Even in cases of this nature, crises do occur which may require us to temporarily set aside long term objectives and employ some of the crisis techniques.

But because of the particular circumstances of crisis work, the social worker can quickly establish himself as an important, influential, 'significant other'. He may have to *do* little, but may *be* much—a source of information, advice, strength or resource (material and emotional); be the recipient or the target for much strong feeling; or be an identification model. The sometimes apparently inordinate gratitude we receive for *doing* little is perhaps an indicator that we have *been* much.

The tragedy is that so little crisis intervention work is done at the right time. Too frequently we get called in too late and situations are complicated by long-standing, post-crisis events and feelings (for example, the 'work' problems of a handicapped adolescent produced by years of parental rejection because nothing was done when he was born). To get into situations at a sufficiently early stage seems to require two elements:

(1) Sufficient resources to cope with not only 'tertiary prevention' (in Caplan[3] terms)—rescuing the casualties, with which Departments are currently overwhelmed; but to reach out (as Seebohm[2] envisaged) into those 'secondary prevention' crisis situations (birth, death, starting school, leaving school, marriage, parenthood, etc.) which happen to all of us—even at the risk of a degree of stigma attaching

to those we see at these stages (a risk Seebohm felt was justified). There would be little stigma if

(2) Social work agencies had an acceptable image and their intervention was 'natural', even sought in such circumstances—as say, education is or preventive medicine. In other words, social work has to become a service all people use (or may)—a Seebohm ideal again—and lose its stigmatising association with failure.

Tom Higgins, at 42, was made redundant by his employers, a small firm of toolmakers where Tom had worked as a fitter for the previous six years. Initially he was not bothered even though the unemployment level in the small industrial town where he lived was quite high, due to an economic recession. Unemployment was something that happened to others (often layabouts in Tom's estimation) and with his work record, qualifications and determination to get something else, he did not envisage being out of work for long. He had his redundancy pay, so there were no financial worries and he and his family continued to live in their accustomed style. He quite enjoyed the first few weeks at home, regarding it as a holiday, and he spent his time catching up on the gardening, household repair jobs and re-decorating that he had long planned to do 'when he had time'. After two months, though, he began to get a little fed up: the jobs were done and he began to feel 'spare'. He was also beginning to get a bit more worried about job prospects. Despite his efforts, nothing had come up in his line. The one or two jobs he had been offered were unskilled jobs which he considered beneath him and the wages that went with them were only fractionally more than he was getting on unemployment benefit plus earnings related supplement. He started to get moody and irritable, found himself snapping at his wife, who promptly snapped back. Mrs. Higgins was inclined to be a bit houseproud and much preferred an ordered routine. Having her husband at home all day where he got under her feet and disrupted her ordered way of life as well as scattering his cigarette ash and 'clobber' all over the place, were an increasing irritant. After reading the morning paper for vacancies and the rest of it for the sake of something to do, Mr. Higgins got into the habit of grouchily taking himself out, wandering the streets rather aimlessly, dropping in on one or two of his former workmates in a similar plight, winding up at the pub at lunchtime, sometimes having a little too much to drink, arriving home late for lunch and more quarrelling with his wife. He would have a sleep in the afternoon until tea, go through the evening paper, then slump for the night in front of the TV.

After six months, his earnings related supplement finished and he was reduced to flat rate benefits. The significance of this did not dawn until a hefty electricity bill arrived which what was left of his savings did not cover. Financial retrenchment was clearly called for: Mrs. Higgins' housekeeping money was cut and the pocket money of the Higgins' children (Pamela, aged 15 and Paul, aged 14) was halved. All three grumbled, but accepted the situation. As time went by, however, they began to realise that the annual holiday would have to go, that a school trip to the Lake District for Paul was out of the question now and that Pamela could not have the pair of new-fashion shoes she had set her heart on—since all her school contemporaries had them. The children's mutterings grew. The first major row blew up, though, when Mr. Higgins discovered that his wife had run up a debt at the local corner shop and the owner was refusing her any more credit until the debt was settled. The stigma of being branded as uncreditworthy stung him deeply and he was furious with Mrs. Higgins. She was equally angry with him, demanding to know how he would manage on the money he gave her. Why didn't he get up off his backside and find himself a job. The implied slur of being a layabout was more than he could tolerate and he took a wild swing at her. He missed, fortunately, and immediately realised the enormity of what had happened and guiltily apologised. Mrs. Higgins also calmed down, but decided that the time had come for action.

The debt was settled by cashing in an insurance policy, but Mrs. Higgins decided to get a job herself. Vacancies for women existed in the area and she started work as an orderly at the local hospital. Though the wages were not good, and Mr. Higgin's benefit was reduced, the family were marginally better off; and besides, as Mrs. Higgins rather bitterly explained, she would be away from her husband's moods and the work she did at the hospital would at least be appreciated.

With the house empty all day, Mr. Higgins found time hanging even more heavily on his hands and though it gave him something to do, he found that getting his own cups of tea and cooking his own lunch irked him. He had been brought up to regard this as women's work. He had to avoid the pub at lunchtime even, since he could no longer afford to 'stand his round' and he saw next to nothing now of his former workmates. With Mrs. Higgins at work during the day, he seemed to see even less of her in the evenings and at weekends since she was busy with the household chores. She began to be increasingly resentful of what she saw as a double burden (house and job) and started to complain that Mr. Higgins, with nothing else to do all day, could easily make the beds, put a duster round and get the shopping in. Swinging between anger, resentment, guilt, frustration and despair, his self esteem eroding, Mr. Higgins became increasingly intolerable to live with. His authority as head of the house seemed to be slipping from him. Mrs. Higgins was increasingly 'calling the tune' since she saw herself as 'paying the piper' through her earnings; while the children more and more referred to her when they wanted permission to stay out late for a special occasion or something similar. Mr. Higgins felt he had become a cypher. When he angrily tried to assert his authority the others merely patronised him.

The final straw came when the Employment Exchange told him that he only had two more weeks of benefit: after that he would have to apply for Supplementary Benefit. It seemed to him the final confirmation of his uselessness. That evening he arrived home the worse for drink. He was greeted by a disparaging sneer from his daughter which triggered a furious row, ending with her packing some clothes and taking herself off to her aunt's, swearing she had finished with her father for good. Later, when Mrs. Higgins and Paul got home, they gradually wormed out of Mr. Higgins what had transpired with Pamela and another row developed. Mrs. Higgins threatened to throw him out: he was breaking up the family, they were sick of him, he was worse than useless and they would be better off without him. Incensed, Mr. Higgins struck out, connected this time, and a physical fight ensued. Frightened for his mother, Paul raced round to the neighbours who promptly telephoned for the police. The police stopped the fight and cooled the immediate situation down from boiling to simmering point. They gave Mrs. Higgins the option of bringing charges, but she could not bring herself to do this quite, even now. The police were, however, anxious about the situation, including just exactly where Pamela was, so referred the matter to the Social Services Department the following morning.

Arriving, the social worker found the Higgins very subdued. They had been badly shaken by the events of the previous evening and were quietly moving around the house avoiding one another. They were reluctant to talk about what had happened, perhaps because they were feeling rather ashamed; but at the same time the social worker felt their hostility towards each other was still very much there but bottled up for fear of the consequences should they express it again. He went off to see Pamela, who had also been re-appraising matters, and it did not need much persuasion to get her to return home with him.

With Pamela there, the social worker gathered the family together to try to get them to examine what had been happening. With him there as a safety factor, the hostility began to bubble up again. The social worker allowed this to go on for a while, but at the point where they were all shouting at each other with no-one listening to anything anyone else said, he intervened. He got them to agree to a 'one-at-a-time' presentation of their views, but asked them to say what they saw as the problem in the family. He felt that having ventilated their feelings, they might now be prepared to take a rather more constructive look at their difficulties. With one or two flashes of anger obtruding, the four of them managed to hold their focus on the problems rather than their own feelings. Mrs. Higgins and the children saw Tom as their problem: he was a boor, impossible to live with, showing no understanding of what they had to put up with from him and the situation his unemployment had created for them. Tom saw them as the problem: they had no idea what it was like to be unemployed, to be bored, fed up and useless. What he wanted was their help, not their nagging. Though still defining the problem in radically different ways, the social worker felt that at least the two 'sides' were understanding the other a little better;

and one or two bridges were being built between them. (Mrs. Higgins said, for example, 'We want to help, but you won't let us!') The worker thought he might further the bridge building by asking them what the family was like before Tom lost his job. All four began to say that it was, in effect, a good family to belong to. Beginning with Mrs. Higgins, they began to wonder how it was that it had all gone so wrong to have landed them in last night's mess.

The social worker ventured that the nub of the problem seemed to be a job for Tom and he began to explore with Tom what he had done in the way of a job, what he would like to do and what avenues he had tried to get himself a job. Tom admitted that in the last few weeks he had got so dispirited he had really given up trying to find a job. He said he really must have another go—and sounded as if he meant it. The social worker explained that he had a few contacts and would explore matters if Tom wished him to. Tom said he might as well, though he felt possibly, he 'knew his way around' better than the social worker. The rest of the family promised their support to Tom in his new efforts.

Getting a job was not easy and there were times when Tom was despondent again, the family support grew thin and the social worker needed to encourage and sustain their respective efforts. Tom eventually found work—not quite up to his expectations but reasonably well paid. Getting on their feet financially took time, though: holidays and shoes had to wait a while which strained patiences occasionally. Mrs. Higgins kept her job since she found she enjoyed it and both she and Tom had some work to do before they finally accommodated the more permanent role re-distribution between them that her working represented.

When the social worker finally withdrew, his offer of further help in the future should it ever be needed was met by Mrs. Higgins saying that she did not think they would need to take up his offer. They had learned a lot and would manage better themselves should there be a 'next time'.

I have indicated earlier that cases which involve intra-psychic problems or long term support cannot be handled as crises *per se* but need a different focus. To these instances I would like to add those cases in which there is a pre-determined time span for the social worker's intervention; for example probation, supervision and statutory periods of prison after-care or parole. May I reiterate that in long term cases crises will occur. Frequently it will be some sort of crisis that precipitates the long term intervention in the first place and crises may often crop up during the course of a lengthy contact. But they will need to be seen and handled as only part of the situation rather than its totality.

Long term supportive work is, of course, far from homogeneous. In general terms it may be grouped as work with difficulties associated with:

(a) Ego deficiency. Even here we are generalising, since difficulty may be due to impulsive acting out with little thought for the consequences; or behaviour may involve other aspects of ego-functioning—a lack of persistence, a lack of 'know how', or a distortion of perception. A wide range of cases could be involved under this heading from the so-called psychopath to the so-called problem family. Ego deficiency is not the prerogative of individuals either, since whole families may share say, a distorted view; or groups (from adolescent or criminal gangs, to football 'hooligans' and 'terrorist' groups) may be deemed by others as, in effect, ego-deficient and social workers asked to 'do' something about them.

(b) Prolonged dependency, generally involving some degree of diminished capacity. The client groups to which this might apply could include some (though by no means all) of the mentally handicapped, the mentally ill (or at least those with a residual handicap), some of the elderly, the chronic sick and disabled, and children.

(c) Problems whose resolution is inevitably going to take time. I have in mind here problems such as that of a family suffering financially where father is unlikely to be in anything but low paid work, or where to really remedy matters involves changing aspects of the Social Security system. Or it may be a housing problem which, given the contraints of time and resources involved, could take years to resolve. Again, if problems arise through lack of say, play facilities, poor school facilities, etc. these too, are going to take time and involve on-going work in the interim very possibly, with the individuals and families concerned.

In grouping problems in this way, I do not wish to suggest that they are discrete entities; they overlap and in any one situation there may well be elements from more than one grouping—for example, a 'problem' family in poor housing in an area deficient in any amenities.

Supportive work is sometimes a euphemism used by social workers when really they do not know what they are doing. The crucial question here to ask ourselves is what we are supporting. Quite apart from the question of whether we are supporting social structures which ought to be changed, we can be supporting ourselves: by unnecessarily supporting the problems and thereby perpetuating or even creating dependency since we enjoy it; we can be supporting large caseloads to demonstrate to others how busy and therefore, indispensable we are; or we could be supporting the agency—assisting it through its policies to demonstrate its own busy-ness and indispensability, whether the objectives of this ploy are to get more resources or to empire-build.

But I think there are certain identifiable features common to all long term work and I would like to examine the implications of these in terms of the groups I have mentioned above. These features may be grouped as:

(1) problems of maintaining motivation;
(2) problems of maintaining focus;
(3) problems of maintaining the worker's objectivity.

Again may I stress that these features are not discrete but interrelated.

(1) Problems of Maintaining Motivation

We have seen earlier that motivation tends to ebb when crisis pressures are eased or when the cost of change begins to be appreciated. I feel sure that this is true of work with intra-psychic problems, where the cost may be the pain of insight, and may be just as true with the range of ego-deficiency problems. The pain may be the foregoing of the pleasure of immediate gratification and the cost, that of self-control. The pain may be the giving up of a distorted view which originally had some functionality and the cost that of accommodating new perspectives. There is pain and cost in persisting when other parts of the self are crying out to give up. Even new 'know-hows' involve the cost of new learning and the pain of one's first, inept attempts to use new skills.

With the dependent, the pain and cost take different forms, since within this group we can identify those who are dependent now but with the prospect of becoming independent later (children being the most obvious example, but including at least some of the chronic sick, the mentally ill, the handicapped and the elderly); while others are dependent now to a degree but with the prospect of becoming more so later (multiple sclerosis sufferers would be an example and some of the elderly). For those with a prospect of independence, the pain might be the giving up of a dependency they might find gratifying and the cost that of assuming a greater responsibility for themselves. For others, the pain might be the delays which frustrate their drives towards independence and the cost the effort required of them to attain independence; for example, waiting for a possum machine which, when it comes, may demand much of them to operate. For those whose dependency is likely to become progressive, the pain would be their increasing loss of independence; the cost, their growing dependency on others.

In those problems which involve delay, there is the cost of grinding on day by day with nothing appearing to change and the pain of knowing that by the time anything is achieved it may be too late for you: by the time the playgroup comes, your children will be at school; by the time anything is done about the school, your children will be at work; by the time the youth club opens, you will be too old for it. The damage will have happened before any remedy arrives.

With the pre-determined time span, the motivational problems may be the same, should the problems be those of say, ego deficiency. Indeed, the statutory hold on the situation could be a help here in the sense that the worker has a little extra leverage to maintain the contact when motivation ebbs. Where the contact is voluntary it is often at this point that it is broken off. Not all those clients who are the subjects of a pre-determined span of intervention are reluctant: some welcome the intervention from the beginning, others come to welcome it when they see its helpfulness; but there are some whose involvement with social work was calculative at the beginning (for example, they saw probation as a means of possibly avoiding a prison sentence, or saw parole as inevitable if they were to get out of prison sooner), and it remains so throughout. Here the motivation is such that contacts, however frequent, are likely to remain distanced and about the only 'contract' negotiable is that of staying out of further trouble with the law during the period of supervision. This is still something worth while, though.

Rather different in character are those cases where the behaviour that precipitated the worker's intervention on a pre-determined time span basis was a product of a true crisis situation. If we accept that crises have the potential for fairly rapid resolution (and assuming this is achieved) it could leave us with a time span that the social work problems no longer warranted. The situation is complicated by the fact that the 'severity' of the behaviour may be the determinant of the time-span, where this is flexible, on the basis of a 'tariff' system; but the severity of the offence may have little to do with the social work 'severity' of the problems which precipitated the behaviour.

Should this occur, it seems to me that the supervising officer has three possible choices: to 'invent' problems to justify the time-span of involvement, to reduce his contacts to the nominal just for the record, or to go back to court to ask for the order to be discharged. To do the third too often could conceivably have repercussions on his relations with the 'significant others' involved; to do it too soon is likely to bring a refusal. The first is unethical and the second has tinges of it, but may be the only practical answer if the third choice is not available.

To sustain motivation in genuinely long term contacts is often hard going. It seems to me to have four elements:

(A) To understand and communicate that we understand the pain and the cost and allow our clients to ventilate about them. This is not easy for the worker. It is not just a matter of empathy or communication skill, but also involves a willingness on our part to expose ourselves to clients' pains and burdens when we may feel we have enough of both ourselves—consciously or unconsciously.

(B) To try to temper the amount of pain and cost to what the client can bear at any one time. This may involve careful pacing: whether of insight in the intra-psychic problems or of demands as a worker one makes on say, the ego-deficient. It will almost certainly involve an appropriate measure of sustaining techniques (encouragement, expressions of confidence, sympathy, etc.); and in some cases (whether of physical handicap, finance, or poor housing) the use of material aid—whether this is directly given or indirectly obtained by say, a 'welfare rights' approach to the Social Security system or the landlord.

(C) By the measured use of those stimulators of motivation— anxiety and hope. In looking at some of the client groups involved in long term work, the validity of using these stimulators is evident enough—whether the emphasis is on the anxiety or the hope. But I wonder how far we can use them with say, a client who is dying by inches with multiple sclerosis, or a client whose desperate housing plight is unlikely to be remedied before years have passed. In such cases I feel it is only the use of elements (A) and (B) that can really stave off the apathy and despair. There is enough anxiety already and so little hope; while our own anger may do little but increase our feelings of helplessness. It is possible to live without hope and the dying sometimes achieve a serenity once they have abandoned their hope for a cure. It is conceivable that the social work task is to help them abandon hope to achieve a degree of peace and so deal with the pain, cost and anxiety produced by an impossible hope: to enable them to relax and utilise to the full what they have left. The focus of our work with relatives and staff (if the client is in an institution) could be very similar. Both relatives and staff can react to the loss of hope with apathy and despair—though often enough they will mask their feelings by forms of denial or avoidance, even rejection; but these defensive reactions do nothing to help the dying. But the fact that they do react defensively only highlights how difficult it may be for the worker too, to abandon hope, face with those concerned the pain of abandoning it and learn to live without hope himself in these cases.

There are analogies here for work in other cases, not involving physical death but the 'death' of expectations—for example, in the work with the parents of handicapped children, with adults and their families facing the sudden impact of disablement, etc. where they are mourning the loss of 'what might have been'.

For the worker to abandon hope and help others to is, of course, only justified in those cases where this is realistic. (If the client unrealistically abandons hope and achieves serenity, the worker is probably obliged to accept this.) Those suffering from protracted difficulty which is remediable or ought to be, such as poor housing, need their hope sustaining. This brings me to the fourth element:

(D) Reward. For hope to be sustained, it is important for clients to be able to identify positive movement, experience some achievement. In Chapter III we have already seen the significance of the identification of movement for the worker and the achievement of intermediate goals for the client and for the worker, including motivation. May I reiterate it here. The hope in a case of protracted problem may be very dependent on feedback from the worker since he may well be more in touch with the movement than the client—for example, what pressure is being brought to bear on the Housing Committee and any change in plans the pressure has achieved.

(2) The Problem of Maintaining Focus

Long term cases tend to be diffuse, but perhaps in rather different ways: in a long term case in which little appears to be happening the purpose of the continuing contact may become lost for both client and worker and meetings become more of a social chat, and so become diffuse in this way and awkward for both. But a number of long term cases have repercussions over a wide life area and so become diffuse in this way. An intra-psychic problem, for example, may have ramifications that are not only personal but marital, familial, involve both work and leisure and lead to the client engaging with a wide range of agencies. A husband and father suffering from agoraphobia could be a case in point. A similar diffuseness may occur where the difficulties are acting out or dependency which may also affect wide life areas. A 'problem' family will have widespread difficulties typically, involving them with housing, Social Security,

Department of Employment, gas, electricity and rating officials, Education Welfare Officers, Health Visitors, doctors, W.V.S., etc.—quite apart from other facilities—play groups, home helps, youth clubs, mothers groups—which the social worker may bring in to try to assist. Protracted problems of housing or amenity while they may be fairly specific in themselves could, in attempting remedies, involve residents associations or other kinds of pressure groups, service groups, local councillors, landlords, a whole range of officials (planners, building departments, architects, public health inspectors) at local level—even national officials such as M.P.'s; or if it came to a public enquiry, a range of experts, legal representatives, etc. Local pressure groups might try to involve other groups with similar concerns; or national groups to back their efforts; press and TV publicity, fund raising activities and a plethora of others. The problem resolution then involves diffuseness.

The problems for the worker then become:

(a) Establishing a focus where the purpose of the work has become diffuse;

(b) Determining priorities where the life area involved is wide and diffuse, to focus what client and worker are to tackle now. Here the discussion in Chapter IV regarding the focus of the intake phase may offer some useful guidelines even for on-going work.

(c) Holding the diffuse together into some sort of cohesive picture so that he can keep the inter-relatedness of what is happening in the different areas well in mind.

The idea of focus is akin in some ways to the concept of contract and we have already seen how important contract is to focus and the process of engagement. But the implications of focus are rather wider than this. I feel it is important for the worker to hold the diffuseness in focus not only for his own benefit but for the client, too. I can envisage a situation in which a client becomes pre-occupied with one area to the neglect of others and his pre-occupation becoming disproportionate to the whole. It would also be possible for him to be caught up with some processes to the point where these become ends in themselves rather than means to an end—for example, the pressure groups becomes an end in itself rather than a means of getting better housing. To help the client hold the focus could be important if problems are to be dealt with effectively and he is not to experience other life areas crumbling while he is busy elsewhere; or to get sidetracked by a form of goal-substitution: the intermediate goal replacing the ultimate.

(3) Problems of Maintaining Objectives

In long term work, there is a real risk that the worker will lose sight of his objectives with some of his cases—more usually those where there is little apparent activity or there is considerable diffuseness. In the first instance he wonders 'what he is at'; in the second, he may not be seeing the 'wood for the trees'.

To begin with, there is every justification sometimes for continued contact, even without apparent activity, where the relationship is significant and needs to be maintained. In other words, maintaining the relationship validly becomes the objective. There are a number of possible examples here.

Elsewhere, I have mentioned the 'life-line' type of case, where a person can function given the security of knowing there is someone around to whom he can turn should occasion arise (and so prevent such occasions ever arising, perhaps). May I stress that the 'life-line' here may not be connected to the client direct, but to those who have the prime care of the client—the parents of a handicapped child; a landlady; perhaps even hostel and homes staff. As long as the worker knows what his objective is, he can relax in even 'social chat' situations, and enable clients and others to do so.

For all children, and maybe other dependent clients, the relationship itself may be significant since a contact broken off by the worker may be experienced as a rejection and one more example of the unreliability of 'adults' in general. (This may be important whether or not there is much 'Stage II' work—see Chapter X—where the client is in residential care.)

A relationship may be important to sustain not so much for its significance now, but because it may well become so in the future. I have in mind here children in care who are isolated from their families but who will be facing leaving care virtually alone in a year or two's time; the handicapped client being cared for by say, elderly parents who will not be there to care (whether by death or diminished capacity to manage) eventually; the client suffering from a degenerative disease who will eventually need residential or hospital care.

Even in those cases where, with a pre-determined time span, the social work task is accomplished but the only option is to let the contact run on, as long as both worker and client know what is happening, they can accept and feel comfortable in the situation.

In those cases involving diffusion, where there may be considerable activity on the part of client and worker, it is important for the worker to refresh himself regularly by going back to the diagnosis and process (in effect, his records) to reappraise matters, with a particular look at the capacity/workability of the situation (including movement or the lack of it and the potential for movement). This should assist him to re-establish his goals, an appropriate level of expectation (at least in the medium term) and so his objectivity. At a very generalised level he may determine that his expectations are:

(i) *Protection.* Some of our long term clients are very vulnerable and need to be protected against potential exploitation: the mentally handicapped. the disabled, the single parent. the neglected child. In many such instances, protection may well be only part of our work; but even if it is virtually the whole of it, it is still very worth doing.

Vulnerability can arise too, because of mismanagement and we may need to protect clients from the consequences of their mismanagement. How we do this may vary: It may involve sorting out with a mentally handicapped wage-earner each week how he is to allocate his money; putting each separate amount away in different coloured boxes, with strict instructions that if any one box becomes empty during the week, he is not to borrow from any other box but to come back to the social worker. Or it may mean continuing to pump resources into a 'problem' family despite a mismanagement which is not likely to improve because this is the only way to protect the children from the trauma of an admission to care—given always that family relations are good, that their preservation is well worth protecting and that the physical care of the children (with the resources put in) is not giving rise to concern.

Some clients—the impulsive, the apathetic or the psychopathic—will need protecting from the consequences of their own actions. How we can do this, again will vary: perhaps by putting our foot down in anticipation of behaviour that will have destructive consequences; perhaps by persuading people when they feel they are going to 'blow their top' to contact us and discuss it first; or perhaps by doing what we can to clear up the mess afterwards. While work of this kind can hardly be described as progress, it is at least minimising the damage. Even if it is all we can do, it is still worth doing.

(ii) *Containment.* In general terms, this means setting our sights on the social survival of the individual, family, group or community concerned, so that even if they still do not particularly like the situation they are in, they are at least getting a sufficient degree of satisfaction from life, with the aid of the social worker, to avoid the individuals or groups falling apart. Picking up the pieces can be a painful and costly business for client and worker.

> Adolescent Billy and his father are never going to like each other but if we can get some agreement about what time he is to be in at night and who is to be responsible for keeping his room tidy, it may make the situation sufficiently tolerable for both so that Billy doesn't leave home or his father throw him out, with all the additional problems that Billy (and maybe father) would have to face.
>
> While the house will never be adequate, some financial help for mother to get a washing machine and some 'leaning' on the landlord to get the roof repaired may ease things enough to prevent mother attempting suicide, the children coming into care, or the whole family ending up in bed and breakfast temporary accommodation.

I realise that the objective of containment may have ethical implications as well as practical, that will trouble many workers; but it can be justifiable in some cases and whatever the conflict of ethics in others, the balance may come down on the side of containment.

(iii) *Progress.* Diffuse problems are often remediable, but with an embracing focus, it still could be advantageous for the worker not to try to tackle the whole 'wood', but to select the really significant 'trees' and to concentrate his efforts: working at identifiable objectives around these, using either compensating opportunities, building on strengths, or clearing away blocks. Hopefully an upward spiral of experience in one significant area will have its pay-off in others, reducing the size of the 'wood' even without specific social work intervention with those other 'trees'.

Phillip was a miserable twelve year old, constantly denigrated by his stepmother, failing at school, and eventually ending up in court for petty vandalism. He was put on a supervision order. Work on the home situation got nowhere.

Eventually Phillip was included in an intermediate treatment group almost in desperation. His one interest was first aid. Within the group this was capitalised upon; his expertise was acknowledged and he became the one who attended to cuts, bruises and headaches, etc. and occasionally showed the others how to bandage, deal with fainting and so on. The boost to his self-esteem and status were such that he became a good deal more cheerful, relaxed and outgoing. Even at home they noticed the difference and relations with his parents became less tense and much more positive, while his school performance also picked up considerably.

References

1. W. J. Reid and A. W. Shyne, *Brief and Extended Casework* (Columbia University Press), 1967.
2. Report of the Committee on Local Authority and Allied Personal Social Services, CMND 3703, H.M.S.O., 1968.
3. Gerald Caplan, *Principles of Preventive Psychiatry* (Tavistock), 1964.

Further Reading

Essential reading is *Crisis Intervention* edited by Howard J. Parad (Family Service Association of America) and a book with the same title by Gerald A. Spector and William L. Claiborn (Behavioural Publications). For the rest, it is a matter of articles such as 'Custodial remand as a point of crisis intervention' by R. J. Harris (*Social Work Today* 31.5.73) or 'Crisis intervention: the climacteric man' by Martin Stickler

(*Social Casework*, Feb. 1975); or exploring situations, such as bereavement and loss, where crisis work could be appropriate.

Little has been written on long term work *per se*, though a number of the standard social work texts have material and case illustrations which are relevant—though typically about cases where movement occurred and the social work task was clear. One article which illustrates long term work in a situation where many of us would have felt unclear is M. L. Shepherd's 'Casework as friendship' in the *British Journal of Psychiatric Social Work*, Autumn, 1964.

Discussion

Crisis intervention usually means work where the crisis itself forms the focus entirely. Some students find it conceptually difficult to distinguish this work from cases where a crisis forms part of the totality to be dealt with; but I feel it is important for students to identify the distinction. Quite why this block occurs is not always clear, but it may have something to do with the implicit assumption in some casework texts that the contact will be on-going. However, once the concept is grasped there seem to be few other difficulties.

As regards long term work, a number of students before they come on a course have undertaken this rather unquestioningly: it was either part of the traditional way of using untrained workers in their agencies or part of a tradition anyway, surviving from the routine visiting of the mentally and physically handicapped and the elderly. Under the pressure of work in recent years, this traditional work has been severely curtailed often but left some students feeling rather guilty that it isn't being done properly, others pleased that it left them free to do 'real' casework, however they define it (though with overtones that it is somehow dramatic). Yet other students will admit that though they were involved in long term work they were never really clear about the point of it. None of these three viewpoints are particularly healthy.

From the point of view of both effectiveness and economy, it is important that students should focus their work whether short or long term (and learn to distinguish one from the other). They need to be able to distinguish which of their long term clients still need them and which can do without them. I have found some of the ideas I have discussed in this chapter useful for students working towards these ends, producing no particular teaching problems.

Reinforcing teaching in this area from practical work placement experience is not altogether easy. Block placements lasting typically one term of 10/12 weeks give little opportunity for experience of long term work; while concurrent placements, though they may last for two terms, mean the absence of the student for part of each week and may thus restrict their experience of crisis work. The format of the practical work may indicate where the emphasis of compensatory teaching should go.

CHAPTER IX

Family Group Therapy

Family group therapy has been defined as a treatment approach designed to modify or change those elements of the family relationship system that are interfering with the management of the life tasks of the family and its members.

The justifications for family group therapy are numerous. It grew out of experience of individual treatment: other family members were found to be interfering with, even blocking, the treatment of an individual member; or through contacts with the therapist were asking if they could help, or be helped themselves.

The family is the critical unit between the individual and society: it is the unit of deepest significance for the individual and even in individual treatment can never be ignored, while society is also crucially concerned with it.

We have become aware that the family is more than the sum of the individual members; it is an interactional system of its own, struggling to maintain a homeostasis. The family is faced with developmental tasks of its own: it has constantly to face problems of joining and leaving, and needs to adapt and grow if the growth of individual members is to be successfully achieved. There is trouble for both the family and for individuals if these tasks are not accomplished.

The family system meshes so closely with individual systems that (particularly in the case of children) they are barely separable. Conflict in the individual produces conflict in the family and exacerbates the individual conflict: conflict within the family produces conflict in the individual and further conflict in the family. Even when not directly involved in family conflict, all members are affected by what is going on—negatively where there are problems—positively, as problems are resolved.

As a method, much more diagnostic material is produced: problems are demonstrated in interviews rather than reported (with the opportunity of blocking or filtering problem related material). It engages the 'healers' in the family as well as the 'sick' and so extends the resources available to work on problems. The 'healers' too, are sometimes those family members who are prepared to identify collusive elements within the family, or give information kept hidden by those deeply involved.

There are no problems of confidentiality as sometimes arise when family members are seen individually.

Changes as and when they occur are accepted by all the family members, so the blocking of change within one individual which sometimes happens in individual therapy, is avoided.

As a method, some writers consider it of particular value with adolescents.

In practice it has been found to be an economical, effective and speedy way of helping—perhaps because of the 'homework' which goes on in between even quite widely spaced interview sessions.

As a method it seems natural and acceptable in those families who see problems in family terms and want to 'get down to it'.

Family group therapy can be used in situations with a wide variety of symptoms or conditions: where children are showing signs of disturbance (acting out, delinquent, school phobic, etc.); in some cases of mental illness; where there are physical or mental handicaps; with psychosomatic symptoms; or where dealings with an elderly parent is resurrecting problems in their (now adult) 'children'.

The aim of family group therapy in general terms is to assist maturation and growth through the relief or resolution of conflict or pressure. These aims are achieved through:

(1) Improvement of communication. Communication is both verbal and non-verbal, and each may be at three levels: the overt, covert (pre-conscious) and unconscious. In these six ways, the communicator may express himself clearly and consistently—or the opposite. Unclearness and inconsistency are typical of disturbed families.

Unclear communication is said to contain three elements:

(a) Over-generalisation: from one incident generalising about another's behaviour—verbally and/or non-verbally indicating "He's always telling lies" when there has been only the rare occasion when this has happened. Or over-generalising from one expressed opinion or act of indulgence; indicating "she's always soft with the children".

Such over-generalisations are, in effect, stereotypes indicating the communicator's need to treat the other as such for reasons of his own. They will be experienced as stereotypes by the receiver, felt to be unrealistic and unfair and produce anger/or hurt in the receiver.

(b) Incompletenesses: which do not amount to complete omissions, but by hints or by leaving things half expressed (whether verbally, by a grimace, or a gesture) creating uncertainty or anxiety in the receivers about the totality of the message and confusion about how to respond.

(c) Disconnections: which may occur in two ways, though these are not dissimilar:

(i) Where the thread of a communication has some sort of 'logic' for the communicator, if only by an internal association of ideas or feelings (whether the communicator recognises the 'logic' or whether it is unconscious) but the 'logic' is not apparent to, or understood by the receiver.

A husband gets home after a hard day. His wife, as an expression of her sympathy and caring, makes a fuss of him. He rejects the fuss and asks to be left alone. His 'logic' is "my mother always smothered me, reduced me to a feeling of angry helplessness and now you are doing the same". His wife, not understanding his logic, feels hurt: the husband does not know why she is upset. Such uncommunicated and therefore disconnected 'logics' make for very confused communication.

(ii) Where the communicator is pre-occupied elsewhere (perhaps with a communication which has previously occurred or one that is shortly to occur) and he brings elements of these pre-occupations into the current communication, where they may be realistically quite inappropriate. The receiver may 'over-include' and attribute the total communication to the current inter-play; or recognise that part of the communication belongs elsewhere but remain unsure about which part or where it belongs. In either circumstance communication will become confused.

The wife, having had her fussing rejected thinks her husband must have had a bad day at work, and makes some allowance for this in her response. But she is not sure, and not sure what the 'badness' was about, so remains uncertain how to help until her husband communicates further about it.

Inconsistent communication Inconsistencies may exist between verbal and non-verbal communication or within each. An apparently warm greeting is accompanied by a slightly forced smile. Affectionate words have a vaguely hostile inflection, a 'wise crack' or sting in the tail; fairly aggressive banter be wrapped in an envelope of good humour; threats contain a hint of amusement, collusion or indulgence—an 'I don't really mean it though I feel I have to say it' overtone. If challenged, the speaker might be prepared to admit the mixed feelings in the message, but could be quite unconscious of the mixed element and 'honestly' deny that he meant anything other than what he said.

Non-verbally, we can also convey mixed messages: 'affectionate' teasing; or 'funny' practical jokes. A baby may be cuddled warmly, or cuddled with an edge of roughness indicating a tinge of hostility somewhere. Or the child may be 'accidentally' dropped or injured—again very suggestive of hostility but at the quite unconscious level. Accused, the injurer might again, honestly and vehemently deny anything but affection for the child.

Inconsistent messages always present the receiver with difficulty. He has to determine what weight to give each element in the mixture in order to shape his response and then calculate the risks for himself in choosing which part of the mixture to respond to. Perhaps he will compromise and send a mixed message back, further tangling the communication.

But the most difficult element to respond to is the unconscious, where this is not consistent with other elements of the message. The unconscious element is not always perceived, of course, but frequently is—and experienced as powerful. Yet it seems almost pointless for the receiver to attempt to communicate back about it with clarity, since it is unconscious and would be denied by the communicator.

When the messages at the different levels of conscious and unconscious are flatly contradictory, the receiver is in a 'non-win' situation—a 'double bind'. Whatever he does is going to upset the communicator at one level or the other. This double bind situation is said by some analysts to be at the bottom of much mental illness. It forces receivers to retreat to a stage of personality organisation they can tolerate, even if this is labelled 'schizophrenic'. They withdraw from attempting to realistically communicate with others (and how can they realistically communicate in a 'non-win' situation?) and communicate largely with themselves, their inner reality, which has a consistency.

'Hearing' a communication may also add to the complications especially where the receiver may have needs or fears which means he selectively attends and responds to communications anyway. His responses, then, are to part of the communication only and may leave the communicator puzzled by those responses or angry that only part of what he tried to convey was heard. The response, either way, has twisted his communication out of shape, as he sees it. At best we probably only 'hear' half of what is communicated. For much of the time we are self-preoccupied, awaiting the opportunity to get what *we* want to say across to others rather than really hearing what they are saying. I suspect, too, that some of our responses surprise ourselves a little on reflection, since we cannot consciously account for them—the 'trigger' is unrecognised. It may be that our own unconscious is at work in our response; or it may be that we only subliminally appreciated some aspect of the other's communication and we cannot subsequently identify it.

Communication can be slanted in a way which tries to elicit the response the communicator wants rather than the response the receiver might prefer to give, again giving rise to resentments and non-communication in effect.

Families may develop their own particular codes or 'language' of communication, within an overall style: for example, action-orientated rather than verbal.

Touch, gesture or grimace may be used to 'speak volumes', with expression through speech only minimally used. A gift, slamming the door, a turn away of the head, an eye contact—these can tell more, more tellingly, than half a dozen speeches.

Communication improvement will assist the family in:

(a) The identification of the real problems in the family (rather than what family members say they are);

(b) Develop awareness of the patterns of dysfunctional interaction in the family and each members' contribution to them;

(c) Assist members to see themselves and other family members with greater clarity and to abandon any stereotypes.

Each of these developments are necessary before effective change can occur; while developing skills in clear and consistent communication will equip the family more adequately to deal with any future difficulties.

(2) To diminish inhibitions regarding expression of feelings. Until feelings are in the open, there is little prospect of being able to deal with them more appropriately, either by those who experience them or other members of the family.

(3) Assist the development of role play appropriate to family position and chronological age. An older child or a grandparent may be in effect playing the mother's part: one spouse may be relating to the other as a parent or child rather than as an adult. One member may be cast in the role of scapegoat—and remember that the scapegoat may carry the 'goodness' and hopes and aspirations of the family as well as the 'badness'—and find that role just as much of a burden. Other members may be carrying the guilt or the pain, or be used as the carrier of 'messages' from one member to another which they may be afraid to send directly. Another member may be playing the 'sick' role in order to obtain some secondary gain. Until roles are carried more appropriately not only will the family be unable to carry out its developmental task, but the development of individual members may be arrested and/or distorted.

(4) To foster an appropriate interdependence by identifying the effects on interaction of unmet needs and aspirations and defensive ploys such as projection, displacement, denial, avoidance, emotional distancing, etc. The needs, aspirations and defences may appertain to an individual, sub-group or indeed the whole family; but they are commonly at the bottom of the splitting, warring, scapegoating or collusion which threatens the interdependence. I would stress that the interdependence should be appropriate. It is appropriate, for

example, that a late adolescent should be striving for independence from his family of origin and problems may have arisen because the family were unable to let him go. Also, each member of the family must have a sufficient degree of individuation (independence) and not regarded or used as an extension of the 'self' of other members (as quite often happens in disturbed families).

Broadly, then, through the focus on family interaction, family members will develop new ways of thinking, feeling and acting which will relieve family pressures, with a consequential relief for individual members of it, leading to a greater satisfaction of valid emotional needs.

Given these aims, the means (methods) of achieving them have a great deal in common with casework. Clearly a relationship is vital. The therapist must be trusted by all members of the family before any working alliance involving all of them can be established. To do this he needs to convince them of his goodwill, concern, competence and confidence and his impartiality as a participant observer. He has to establish the climate in which members can express themselves increasingly freely.

Sustaining techniques (empathy, support, encouragement, realistic reassurance, etc.) will be used throughout: particularly, perhaps at the beginning and when the going gets rough—and for the same reasons as in casework with individuals.

Direct influence Information, suggestion, advice, will play their part similarly, and so will the use of authority (whether of expertise, position or relationship). The therapist may at times use his 'ego support' to assist the family's efforts to control, especially at times where the feeling levels are high and tending to be destructive—either by 'cooling it' or by defending a family member under particularly heavy attack from the others.

Ventilation will clearly be used very considerably, valuably, and for the same reasons as in casework.

Reflective discussion is perhaps the most extensively used method—the level (family/situation configuration, dynamics or aetiology) depending on the goals (see below) or the stage in the process. The therapist's contributions to reflective discussion may be thoughts on what is happening in the 'here and now', making connections between what is happening now and previous events (whether during the treatment or the family's history), attempting to reconstruct feelings around other events, or normative reflections (for example, what happens in other families or at this stage of development).

As part of reflective discussion, it seems considerably more use is made in family group therapy of interpretation than might be expected in casework. Therapists justify this by suggesting that many people can 'take' more interpretation than we give them credit for usually; and given that the focus is the family interaction rather than the individual, interpretation is less threatening and can therefore be used more extensively. Even if the focus happens to be on an individual at any one point, it is the interactional aspects that are of concern, not the individual as such.

Bearing in mind the aims, interpretation would focus around:

(1) The communication in the family: pinning down the generalisations, incompletenesses and disconnections: pointing up the inconsistencies between verbal and nonverbal communication, overt and covert messages (even if the unconscious might only rarely be touched upon) and 'double binds'.

The implications here are that the therapists needs to 'tune in' to the codes used, perhaps adapt his methods to suit the family communication style; but above all to be a model communicator himself—demonstrated by his checking on the communication flow. He tries to identify the content of messages sent, checking where necessary with the communicator; and examines whether the messages sent have been appropriately received. He subjects his own communication and reception to the same process. He must obviously be prepared to be questioned about his own communication; clearly must not monopolise talk himself, nor allow others to. At the other extreme, he cannot opt out of communication or allow other members to. All this adds up to a real involvement in the process: there is no place in family group therapy for the 'sounding board' role of traditional analysis.

(2) The roles being played—including an awareness of his own, and attempts being made by various family members to push him into inappropriate roles—the parent, the 'expert' who does the work and provides the solutions for the 'helpless', or the arbitrator. There

may be a particular risk when working with one parent families of being drawn into the family functioning in the role of the missing parent.

(3) Assisting appropriate interdependence, which implies:

(a) Identifying the defences that are being used by individuals, sub-groups or the family as a whole in terms of their effects on interaction;

(b) Putting the problems back where they belong by gently refusing to accept the family's identification of, for example, the scapegoat by emphasising the reciprocity of the interaction.

(c) Assisting realistic perceptions by identifying stereotypes, projections, displacements, fantasies, or fears;

(d) Emphasising the shared responsibility for what happens in the family interaction;

(e) Where the inter-dependence has reached such extremes as to be inappropriate, to assist towards a clearer delineation of self and others, to allow of sufficient individuation, tolerance of different-ness, and permission for members to leave the family where they need to do this if their growth and maturation is not to be stunted.

(4) Assisting expression of feeling by being prepared to comment on family members and their behaviour both good and bad (though never in a judgmental way), not being afraid at times to indicate disapproval. He should clearly be prepared to accept the family's comments about him.

In general while avoiding attacking defences via interpretation, it is possible to use confrontation to a greater degree than might be usual in individual casework.

The above are the direct methods (most commonly used), but do not forget the place of the indirect—referral, material aid and environmental management. They can be vital.

While the methods of family group therapy are very akin to casework, there are certain aspects that may present additional difficulty:

(a) Maintaining the family interaction focus may be hard for a caseworker, especially resisting the temptation to drop into the individual focus he is more used to;

(b) Avoiding over-identification with one member of the family;

(c) Containing a transference from one family member in the interest of the relationships and work with the family as a whole;

(d) Containing the counter-transferences likely to be stirred by the emotive content of the interactional material and his own deep-rooted pre-conceptions (often culturally influenced) of how families should behave towards each other;

(e) To recognise that many aspects of the process are not his responsibility alone but since family group therapy has aspects of group process about it, his task is to assist others' contributions often. This applies not only to the identification and resolution of problems but also to the use of available resources—for example, to support the sustaining efforts of the 'healer' at any point in time (a role that is likely to shift, depending on who happens to be the 'punisher' and the 'victim' at the time—also shifting roles);

(f) Establishing his fairness in relation to all members of the family. This does not mean that at any particular time he will not be taking sides: he may need to come to the aid of the current 'victim'. But by rotating his support, avoiding blaming individuals, concentrating on interaction and reciprocity and demonstrating his understanding of, and concern for all members over time (especially those he may have criticised), he should be able to establish his fairness.

There are two particular areas of threat for the beginning practitioner in family group therapy. He may have doubts about his capacity to 'keep tabs on' a much more complex interaction situation—but this should come with experience and good supervision. He may be afraid of opening the 'floodgates' of feelings extant in the family situation and losing control of, especially, the destructive, angry feelings. As I have indicated, he may need to step in with controls at times, but practice has clearly shown that however strong the feelings expressed, families rarely ventilate more than they themselves can cope with and even the bitterest sessions have subsequently proved productive in problem resolution. In handling anger, it may be useful to deal with this as an expression of hurt (which it frequently is).

Given these aims and methods, it would seem clear that family group therapy would be the method of choice where:

(a) The family wanted to stay together;

(b) Was prepared to acknowledge this was a family problem and was motivated to work on it (even if the stimulus was a particular crisis);

(c) Where the problem is one of interaction rather than individual pathology (where disturbance in the children is involved for example);

(d) Where the disturbance is interlocking and where change in one member cannot be tolerated (via say, individual treatment) because of the needs of other members—for example, where one member (the 'identified patient') is carrying symptoms of a family disturbance.

Contra-indications would amount to, in general terms, a lack of sufficient 'workability'. More specifically these might be:

(a) Where the problems of key individual(s) are such that they are unlikely to yield to an interactional focus. Paranoia, psychopathy, perversion, excessive narcissism or masochism, are examples sometimes given.

(b) Where key individual(s) are facing demands that may leave them little to spare to cope with further tasks (severe illness, severe loss of self-esteem, a pre-existing commitment to individual therapy, etc.).

(c) Where defences are particularly rigid (for example, where dominance is a marked feature) and interpretation might result in their collapse and the risk of mental illness (depression with potential suicide for example), psychosomatic illness or violence.

(d) Where the family is already breaking up—whether through divorce, or the appropriate disengagement of say, late adolescents—and motivation is low.

(e) Where the family's energy is primarily devoted to extra-familial affairs, cohesion is low, but individual satisfaction levels may be reasonably high, so reducing motivation.

(f) Where the family pattern is that of emotional distancing (perhaps to the point where key figures refuse to engage in therapy) and so no real basis for the family group method exists.

(g) Where the family is so pathologically dishonest in its communicating that again, no adequate basis for family group therapy exists.

(h) Where validly certain family members wish to retain certain 'secrets'; but where family group therapy might force these private matters into the open.

(i) Where the problem is essentially a symbiotic interaction of a subgroup (for example, a seductive relationship between parent and child).

(j) Where cultural or religious objections exist to this form of therapy (for example, where the role of the wife, or relations between parents and children are defined in authoritarian terms and the sharing implied by family group therapy would be unacceptable).

In such circumstances, rather than family group therapy, other methods of working would be used—casework with individuals, or involving individuals in group therapy. These alternatives do not rule out the valid and valuable use of family sessions at stages of individual treatment for example; nor do they rule out the possibility of validly using family group therapy once certain, say, individual problems have been overcome. Obviously, ascertaining whether family group therapy might be used could involve quite some exploration before deciding.

In family group therapy the therapist (as in casework) would seek to formulate a diagnosis as the basis for working out with the family mutually acceptable goals (i.e. establish the contract) and choose methods by which to attain them.

The content of the diagnosis would be geared to the focus of the work—family interaction. In addition to the mainly factual data (ages, date of marriage, parentage, significant events, health, income, housing, the referring complaint, attitudes to it, etc.) much of the content will be concerned with the communication patterns, role playing, expression of feelings, and the interlock of needs, fears, aspirations and defences; to identify what the problems are, the conflicts, splits, collusive alliances, or scapegoating they were producing, and the factors around which the difficulties gather (control, obedience, sexuality, money, cleanliness, feeding, intelligence may be among them). Of considerable significance would be the way the family handled its sameness and different-ness, the joining and leaving, the distribution of authority and whether it is so tight individualism and growth are stultified, or so loose that the family is in chaos; how decisions were arrived at, who made the decisions, how they were implemented and the effects of them (cohesion, fragmentation, collapse, collusion, scapegoating, or withdrawal); how stress was handled, the sort of controls used to deal with aggression, sexuality, anxiety, etc.; the degree of intimacy/distance in relationships.

The cultural influences on patterns of relationships, roles, and communication must be assessed: the work of Bott[1], Dennis[2], Bell[3], Willmott and Young[4], Bernstein[5], Goldberg[6] and many others is of crucial importance here.

The diagnosis would help to establish goals. In very broad terms it could indicate whether this was a family functioning well in the past but which has got 'stuck' in a current task or phase of adaptation, suggesting a goal-limited 'crisis intervention' approach: whether disturbed relationships have existed for a considerable time, but only now has something triggered a referral and the dynamic level of intervention will be needed; or whether the problem is that relations of any sort have never really existed at all and work may be at the aetiological level.

What may realistically be achieved, of course, will also depend on estimates of capacity, resource and motivation—and what the family is prepared to acknowledge and agree to in terms of the contract. They may be content to settle merely for the relief of currently distressing symptoms (enuresis, stealing, etc.) and not be prepared to work at more than this.

The diagnosis and goals will help to establish not just methods but also provide guides to where to begin the therapeutic process in indicating which problems are salient and what are accessible in terms of the family's and the worker's views of the problems, where motivation, capacity and resource currently exist and can be engaged.

In the American literature the treatment process often begins by a mother phoning the agency complaining of a child's behaviour. The contact has frequently been precipitated by a particular event; but given that the child and his behaviour is often functional in terms of family disturbance, contact can be the result of pressure from a significant outsider (such as the school) who have been concerned about the disturbed behaviour, while the family have not.

Over the phone the mother is told a little of what the agency can offer and how it operates and an appointment is offered to both parents. Many agencies insist on both parents coming as a condition for any further help. The rationale for this seems to be:

(1) That family group therapy is impossible without the engagement of both parents.

(2) That it acknowledges the greater degree of seniority, authority and responsibility of the parents within the family.

(3) That experience has shown that disturbance in the family is typically an indicator of disturbance in the marriage relationship in which the children have been caught up and of which they are displaying the symptoms.

In the preliminary phase a number of decisions have to be made—the first being whether family group therapy is seen as the method of choice or alternatives determined (see earlier). The number of therapists to be involved must also be decided. It is not uncommon for there to be two—often one male and one female, reproducing a quasi-parental team with extended opportunities for diagnostic interactions and therapeutic interventions. Two views of what happens can be of great value; while two therapists may reduce the chances of transference and counter-transference obtruding. But it is obvious they must work in close collaboration for consistency of approach, to resist being played off against the other; and be prepared to face the rivalry that could possibly develop.

After the parents have been seen together, even if it is decided to offer family group therapy, there may be tactical decisions to be made as to whether other family members should be seen as individuals, pairs or subgroups—coloured by what has already been gleaned about the salient problems, those directly involved, current capacities, resources and motivations. (Similar considerations would also recur at stages subsequent to the meeting of the whole family, when determining how best to handle the problems emerging given their saliency, those involved with them and their capacities.) Opinions seem to differ, though, as to the advisability or otherwise of seeing family members individually, as pairs or subgroups. Some therapists insist there should be no contacts other than with the whole family since this exacerbates problems of trust, fairness, confidentiality and transference, and could side-track the interaction focus; but others are more flexible in approach—though most of them would usually insist that such other contacts should focus on interaction, and the right to bring material back to the whole family from such other contacts made explicit.

Almost all writers would suggest that a meeting of the whole family should be held as soon as possible in these early stages if only to avoid individual transferences developing, and to provide the diagnostic material required for further progress. This still leaves the determination of who constitutes the family. Basically this means including those among whom the mutual reverberations are felt. Grandparent(s), the lodger, perhaps even foster children, could be included.

There is sometimes felt to be a problem about the inclusion of very young children. Most of the therapists would suggest including them in the early stages, if only for diagnostic purposes; some would then prefer them left out as being too distractable and distracting; a few would still include them, providing play material for them. Most would, in any event, include those able to make a verbal contribution—but again there seems to be little agreement at what age this can happen—some suggest including the 4+, others only the 8+. The inclusion of younger children can be a source of embarrassment to parents regarding their control and distractability: the books suggest that control is primarily a matter for the parents, but can be reinforced by the therapist via 'rules' about what is or is not permitted during 'his' sessions. Experience shows children frequently quickly respond—especially if early on they are deliberately involved by such means as asking them about themselves, getting their ideas about what they are there for, where they got these ideas from, getting their opinion as to what the problems are, their reactions to them, how they feel about others and what they are saying.

Parents are anxious often, too, about saying things (about their sexual relations for example) in front of the children, or displaying their anger and frustration with each other. Again experience suggests little harm is done and often a great deal of good by verbalising and ventilating in this way. Even young children know full well there is trouble, their fantasies about it are often much worse than the reality, and they gain reassurance from seeing problems out in the open and being tackled in a much more constructive way.

How much structure the therapists should try to erect in the early phases is another area of disagreement. Some therapists prefer an almost completely unstructured situation, while others prefer to establish certain rules: that the focus is on interaction, one person only speaks at a time, with no interruptions, etc. Some prefer to take a family history, covering the parents' background, how they came to meet, get married, what their expectations of each other and marriage were, their early days together, how they reacted to parenthood, the history of the family as the children came and grew, what they see as the problems, how they feel about them and each other, how they have tried to tackle difficulties, what prompted the referral, and what sort of daily routine they have. It would be important in the history-taking to point up the positive things they were saying when most of what they relate might be negative. Others mainly let the history emerge as the family sees aspects of it which are relevant and meaningful and struggle to take some responsibility for it. All therapists see it as vital to establish the alliance relationship early and to establish the climate in which communication can develop—though again, some therapists would see this as mainly a verbal matter, while others (especially when working with families that typically act out rather than talk) would see value in such activities as drama, dance, movement, games simulation, etc. Practically all the American agencies seem to use television and/or tape recording and to use playbacks to further family insight.

The period and timing of family sessions also provides no unanimity of view. Skynner[7] prefers $1\frac{1}{2}$ hours every three weeks: in America some agencies' initial diagnostic sessions last a whole weekend in residence. Other sessions seem to be longer than the $1\frac{1}{2}$ hours, too. The venue for the sessions may be in home or office; but there seems general agreement that the atmosphere should be informal. The period of intervention is seen variably as from six months to two years.

Bell[8] goes further than other therapists in suggesting that after the initial meeting with the parents, the subsequent interviews with the whole family should be structured to allow the children to have their say, with subsequent emphasis on the parent/child interaction, the mother/father interaction, and sibling interaction, before returning to the family focus. This sort of sequential pattern frequently emerged in his experience and he now feels it is warranted to try to steer matters this way.

Structured or not, either way should provide an adequate entrée to current and underlying difficulties, complete the intake and orientation phases, establish the alliance and the contract. In the 'hard work' phase which follows, feelings may run high, the family feel threatened, fearing loss of control. Defences and anxiety levels may also be high and there may be attempts at diversions, such as bringing in extra-familial material. Such developments are signs of progress, however, but will mean the therapist using the full range of methods of treatment available to him as circumstances and objectives dictate.

The termination stage will be indicated by improvements in communication, greater realism, more appropriate role play, a greater degree of delineation between self and others, a greater tolerance of disagreements and different-ness, a developing ability to learn, make effective choices, growing openness, relaxation and good humour, greater satisfaction reported and symptoms disappearing. In effect, the family will be indicating their readiness to try to manage on their own. It is useful in termination for the therapist to summarise what has developed, to express his on-going interest and support, and offer the reassurance of further assistance should this be required.

Jordan[9] is rather sceptical of the applicability of family group therapy on the 'classical' American model outlined above: suggesting there are few occasions on which it might be used in the British social worker's usual caseload. The families we deal with are more likely to be 'centrifugal'—seeking safety from angry feelings by separation: pushing members out or turning out themselves, or fighting demands experienced as unacceptable. Many families might prefer one member to act out rather than disturb the equilibrium the other members experience. In such families the social worker may be seen as a threat, culturally alien, and be used as the family members want rather than how the social worker would prefer to be used. Given their centrifugal tendencies, coupled with a cultural pattern that develops external controls rather than internalised, the family may seek to involve the social worker as a 'big stick' or demand his help, not in terms of interpretation but in terms of removing a troublesome child into care. Stalling on this usage or help is likely to be interpreted as another negative aspect of 'them' with the consequent reactions. It takes a great deal of courage on the part of the social worker to resist demands of these sorts and bear the reactions; but resisted they have to be, perhaps, if the problems are to be really dealt with where they belong—in the family. We can at least, share the pain and disappointment and anger as demonstrating our concern—especially if we are on the spot when these feelings erupt, which means being readily accessible.

Jordan also makes a plea for understanding the social situation of such families. While society may see their centrifugal behaviour as dysfunctional and ask social workers to 'put it right', it may be functional for the family in the sense that it is the only adaptation they can make to say, gross overcrowding. He also stresses how important the external networks are for such families in terms of social, emotional and practical help. The trouble is that 'authority' and social workers, see such networks as negatively reinforcing the families' difficulties (perhaps in 'sub-cultural' terms) rather than their value.

Even centrifugal families are still a unit, however, and should be seen and worked with as such—with a family focus, even if this means work with individuals has to be sacrificed to some degree. To see individuals only, reinforces the splitting. To work with large families especially, as a group has the merit of adapting method to experience, since the members will have little experience of 1:1 relationships. Centrifugal families, too, have their feelings about the family and other members of it; and it is no accident that they play their roles as they do. Nor are any entirely without resources.

Helping such families may require a much greater appreciation of the functions of the external network and considerably more work with it and through it. Networks can be usefully provided through nurseries, play groups, child minders, youth clubs, etc. though these tend to be formal, may not be as useable as the families' informal ones, and cannot be imposed. Even when using the 'classical' model of family group therapy, Skynner suggests that work needs to be done with the 'minimum sufficient network'—involving the schools for example. The ethos of many Social Services Departments, which tends to see cases in individual terms, may inhibit work along this network dimension—perhaps through fears of stirring up demands from other families for services in short supply and involving the department in problems of allocation and disputes over fairness.

While family group therapy has been extant for a number of years, now, there is still a wide variety of approaches and no real agreement about a holistic base for it. Approaches are rooted in analysis, group theory, social psychological interaction theory, phenomenological sociology, etc.; or use medical pathological or even moralistic normative frameworks. With this diversity it is understandable there is little unanimity—which may be no bad thing, anyway, as long as troubled families benefit.

References

1. Elizabeth Bott, *Family and Social Network* (Tavistock), 1971.
2. Norman Dennis, *Coal is our life* (Tavistock), 1969.
3. Colin R. Bell, *Middle Class Families* (Routledge & Kegan Paul), 1969.
4. Peter Willmott and Michael Young, *Family and Kinship in East London* (Penguin), 1969.
   Family and Class in a London Suburb (Routledge & Kegan Paul), 1960.
   The Symmetrical Family (Routledge & Kegan Paul), 1973.
5. Basil Bernstein, *Class, Codes and Control* (Routledge & Kegan Paul), 1971.
6. E. M. Goldberg, 'The Normal Family: myth and reality' in *Social Work with Families*, edited by Eileen Younghusband (George Allen & Unwin), 1971.
7. A. R. C. Skynner, 'A group analytic approach to conjoint family therapy' (*Social Work Today* 15.7.71).
8. John Elderin Bell, *Family Group Therapy* (Bookstall Publications), 1971.
9. William Jordan, *The Social Worker in Family Situations* (Routledge & Kegan Paul), 1972.

Further Reading

Apart from the books by J. E. Bell and William Jordan mentioned in the references, I would suggest students read *Treating the Troubled Family* by Nathan W. Ackerman (Basic Books) and Virginia Satir *Conjoint Family Therapy* (Science & Behaviour Books). There is also a very good chapter on 'Family therapy' by Frances H. Scherz in *Theories of Social Casework* edited by Robert W. Roberts and Robert H. Nee (University of Chicago Press). These texts represent a range of approaches to family group therapy.

Interest in family group therapy is growing in Britain. The Family Welfare Association have published a collection of papers under the title *Family Therapy in Social Work*; but much British writing is still in article form. The article mentioned in the references by A. R. C. Skynner is one of a 'set' of three published in *Social Work Today* in July, 1971—the titles of the other two being 'Indicators for and against conjoint family therapy' and 'The minimum sufficient network'. Dr. Skynner's later article 'Boundaries' published in *Social Work Today* 22.8.73. is also of relevance. Among other valuable articles appearing in *Social Work Today* are Anne Needham's 'Working with the family as a group' (4.5.72) and Gill Gorrell Barnes' 'Working with the family group' (3.5.73).

Discussion

Family group therapy is rarely practised as yet in this country outside certain specialised centres or by individual workers. I have rarely met a student who has any first hand (or even good second hand) experience of working in this way. In these circumstances discussion tends to be unrealistic, though I am sure it helps students to think about a method that tends to be not only rather abstract but also rather threatening. If at least intellectually they can discount some of their fantasies and recognise the advantages of it as a way of working, they might pluck up courage to risk using it (even if it is after they have established themselves in practice subsequent to the course). It is only ultimately through use that conviction about the validity of the method will develop.

Rather than discuss this matter, I have found it far more profitable to use one of the number of films that are now available. To see the method in use more effectively dispels the fantasy, reassures regarding the threats, and demonstrates that the skills involved are ones that they know something about already.

CHAPTER X

Fieldwork and Institutions

In this chapter, we shall be examining relations between the case-worker and those institutions which require that their clientele live in—whether homes, hostels, hospitals or penal establishments. While in practice there is probably some difference of emphasis depending on whether the caseworker is field or institution based (the field-worker is more concerned with pre-admission and after-care; the institution-based worker is more concerned with the 'during admission' phase), I am convinced there is a conceptual common ground that it is extremely important all workers should share if the needs of the client and his family are to be adequately met throughout what is for them an ongoing experience.

The basic position of the worker involved with institutions may be diagrammatically represented as under:

 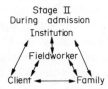 

i.e. at each of three stages, the worker is at the hub of a triangular interaction between client/family/institution. Ideally, the worker should be engaged in all three stages, but may be called in at, say, Stage II or Stage III only, in which case there may be problems 'overhanging' from earlier stages: or he may not be involved in sub-sequent stages, which would mean possible problems to be passed on to whoever was dealing with such stages.

Stage I: Pre-admission

(A) In assisting the *client* regarding his admission, a number of problems may need to be dealt with, centering around:

(i) Dependency fears—typically expressed as a fear of losing independence—being helpless, at the mercy of others, having little self-determination, losing control over what happens to him. Many of us have fantasies about the all embracing potential for 24 hour control of institutions; while some of our clients will have experienced institutions before, experienced them very negatively and will be realistically aware of what they are going into and what they are losing (or at least, that will be *their* reality).

(ii) Insecurity—arising from fears of the unknown, often: of institutional procedures and/or treatment methods; the new people to be faced and lived with in a situation where little escape from engagement with them is possible; of self-reactions to the situation (for example, 'Will I make a fool of myself?!'); of how the family will manage while the client is away.

(iii) Guilt—either self-blame for the causes of the admission, or self-blame for the consequence of the admission on the family (hardship, stigma, etc.). Such guilt feelings may not be overtly admitted, but be disguised in not untypical ways—displacement, denial, or aggression.

(iv) Authority—since institutions are seen (often realistically) as having a very pervasive and inescapable authority system, clients may be experiencing anticipatory reactions to this. Such reactions will be coloured by the type of institution to which they are going, and the reasons for it: but more general attitudes and feelings around authority may be activated, and the patterns for handling such feelings evident: overt or covert antagonism, overt or covert submission (prompted by a wide range of personality factors)—or a mature appraisal.

(v) Anticipatory bereavement—the loss of familiar and cared for people, places, objects, routines—and sometimes the anticipatory loss of personal functions, positions, status—whether from disablement or stigma.

(vi) Fears of loss of love—'What will people think of me?', 'Will they think of me?', 'Will my place in the family close up behind me?'

(vii) Fears which may be specific to certain situations: of surgery, anaesthetics, etc. in a hospital admission, for example.

Here I have stressed the problems, since the worker is more likely to be involved where these exist. This is not to suggest, though, that clients will not also welcome an admission as a relief from pain, uncertainty, or responsibilities they are finding harder and harder to discharge; or as a welcome regression during which they can recoup to tackle anew situations that have got beyond them. Too hearty a welcome for admission, though, I would see as a rather unhealthy wish for dependency: a healthy approach to admission would, to my mind, always contain a degree of ambivalence about it.

(B) In assisting the *family* in an admission, the worker may be dealing with a situation in which the family is keen to eject the member, reluctant to let him go, or have very mixed feelings. Some of the problematic feeling areas may be:

(i) Understanding and bearing with the client's reactions to admission.

(ii) Dealing with their own guilt feelings: about the reasons for admission, or about not doing enough to assist the client. Again, this guilt may be displaced, denied, etc. They may connive or collude with the client's own expressions of guilt, see things differently, but still support him; or get irritated by his view.

(iii) Dealing with their feelings of relief that an intolerable situation is ending, or anxious waiting is over. This relief may be difficult to admit—even produce guilt, then or later. The relief may be hard for the client to bear, experiencing it as rejection.

(iv) Insecurity. The family may share the apprehensions of the client through their identification with him. They may have fears for themselves as to how they will cope when he is away—the financial hardships, keeping in touch with him, reallocating his roles and functions. A mother may anticipate reactions from the children if say, father is being admitted, and wonder how she is to respond. They may be under pressure to keep these feelings from the client.

(v) Anticipatory bereavement. Even if a family can accept the necessity for an admission, they may still fiercely resist the loss of one of their members, whether the significance of that member is as a source of love, support, or strength; or as an outlet for dependency needs, hostility, or dominance. Reactions to anticipated loss may be good indicators of family dynamics.

(vi) Anticipatory jealousy—that others will be doing things for the client that they cannot; underlining feelings of incompetence or precipitating fears that the client will transfer gratitude or affection to others.

With both client and family in this stage, the concentration is on the admission crisis. It is unlikely that any work can be undertaken on pre-existing problems at this stage where these exist and whether or not they are related to the admission. This would obtain whether the worker had just come into the situation, or whether he had been working on pre-existing problems for some time.

While in admissions we tend to work with the adults involved (whether one of them or a child is involved), it is essential that the impact of an admission on the children is just as fully dealt with (whether a parent or a sibling is to be admitted or the child himself).

(C) As regards the *institution* at this stage three elements concern the worker:

(i) The choice of an appropriate institution if there should be any discretion (be this hospital, children's home, foster home, old people's home, or probation hostel).

(ii) The preparation of the institution for the reception of the client: agreeing the date, time or manner of admission; the supplying (preferably in writing) of an appropriate report/history (to include an account of the family situations, attitudes to admission and institution, etc.); and full discussions beforehand if at all possible, with the institution's staff about the objectives of the admission and allocation of roles and tasks in the light of these among the parties concerned: client, family, institution and worker.

At this stage, the overall aim of the worker is to make the client/family/institution receptive to each other, so that the objectives of the admission can be met (or at least, any damage arising can be minimised). The worker's main methods will be to disseminate knowl-

edge between the parties (including a preliminary visit to the institution by client and family if possible); and to handle any emotional
blocks. Failure will involve misunderstanding and resistance and
prejudice the whole operation.

There is hardly need to emphasise that the actual admission needs
to be handled with great care. At such an emotive juncture, all parties
will be hypersensitive to what is said and done and expressed—for
good or ill, assisting or inhibiting the entire programme.

(iii) The worker has to deal with his own feelings about his involvement in the admission. It is not often that all the parties concerned
welcome the admission whole-heartedly; ambivalence if not downright hostility is likely to exist somewhere in the 'triangle' of parties.
In other words, the worker has to face his own reactions to the
pain of others—pain the worker may feel he has in some measure
contributed to if not actually created. He will be able to face himself
if he is confident that on the basis of his assessment he is taking
the right course of action and the institution concerned is appropriate, competent and caring. But this is something of an ideal situation. His decision may be based (and have to be based) on the
balance of evidence (for example, in the case of an application for
a Place of Safety Order in a suspected baby-battering case) and complicated by the variable support he gets regarding his decision from
the parties concerned. Support may come from only one party
(whether client, family or the institution—the institution in this instance, including its 'community based' representatives: general practitioners or the police for example); or from any two against the
third (client and institutions versus the family; family and institution
versus the client; or client and family versus the institution—which
can mean not just that client and family are against the institution,
but that the institution can resist an admission where both client
and family want this. Not all institutions welcome people they see
as potentially difficult or inappropriately placed with them.)

Even if all the parties do come to some sort of agreement, the
worker may still have reservations about the institution (and therefore, admission) if he feels that institution is incompetent, inappropriate and uncaring. Many probation officers, for example, have fairly
strong and negative feelings about prisons. While accepting that there

comes a point in the balance where society has to be protected against the behaviour of the individual, they see a prison sentence as only contributing further to the difficulties of that individual. Yet given the range of options available to the courts (in themselves often constrained by the range of facilities available), they may have little alternative but to shape their social enquiry report recommendations in a way that leaves a prison sentence as inevitable. Fortunately, our range of options (community service orders for example) have been and still are, steadily growing, but the dilemma will probably always remain.

A worker's uncertainty about a decision whether to admit or not, may well be picked up by one or more of the parties concerned and played upon (whether with the objective of persuading him to admit or not to admit). Should this occur, it will only add to the worker's uncertainty. His decision should either be a firm one, or he should make it firmly clear to all parties that he has yet to make his decision and why. Even when a worker has made his decision, he may still wonder (especially in an emergency situation) whether he has colluded or connived with one or more parties, whether his decision was to admit or not to admit; or whether his own feelings about institutions have coloured his actions to the detriment of his objectivity. The matter will only clarify, perhaps, as the consequences of his decision emerge in the pattern of subsequent events—convincing him he was right or wrong at that time.

Obviously no social worker would contemplate an admission, or work on this premise, unless he were satisfied that any conditions attached to a statutory admission were in fact, fulfilled.

Stage II: During Admission

(A) There is a continuing function for the worker in direct work with the Client, based on the worker's position as an 'outsider' to a degree from the institutional hierarchy, and as the person who is in contact with the family situation. The areas of work might be grouped as:

(1) Assisting the client's relations with the institution. Experience of the institution may be:

(i) Enriching: providing the client with new opportunities to develop practical skills (occupational therapy, games, debates, etc.); develop his specific industrial training; relieve him of pain; assist his education (classes, visits, etc.), provide experience of new and satisfying relationships with staff and peers, or help him to come to a new self-awareness and realisation (via group or individual therapy). The worker's objective would be to support this enrichment by encouragement, praise, bringing it to the client's awareness, and so on.

(ii) Produce regression: clients may become dependent and childish, self-centred and complaining, adolescent and irresponsible, boisterous, flirtatious, or rebellious. Such reactions are diagnostic, but the worker's task might be to provide a place where such reactions can be explored and discussed reflectively, or to provide a relationship which the client finds supportive and therefore has less need to resort to regressive behaviour.

(iii) Be damaging: the client feeling isolated, cramped, frustrated, bewildered by the institutional processes or treatment, humiliated, misunderstood, or experiencing relations that serve to reinforce his problems or negate the objectives of the programme—even create new problems. Again, the worker can provide a place where such feelings can be discussed reflectively, ventilated, or he can feed in information which will lead to modifications.

(2) Assisting the client's relations with his home situation.

(i) In current terms. Even if the family are visiting, such visits may be formalised and stilted, geared to assuring the client that everything at home is 'all right'. The client is likely to feel that he really does not know what is happening, leading to fantasies (including, perhaps, fantasies about a spouse's fidelity); he may, be anxious if he thinks things are not 'all right', yet threatened, too, if he thinks the family are coping without him. If the family are not visiting, then clearly there may be a multitude of problems (both practical and emotional) for the worker to tackle with client and family. It is here that the worker, with his knowledge of the family situation, can assist by keeping the reality before the client besides offering practical services: but he may be in a very difficult position if the situation is not 'all right' and some fantasies have a basis in reality.

(ii) In future terms. The worker and client can begin to look at the range of problems the client may face on his return home: re-establishing his life during convalescence; facing disablement and a profound life change; facing stigma; taking up family roles and relationships after, perhaps a long absence with problems around accession rather than dismemberment now, but still involving role re-distribution; dealing with his guilt about what is happening to the family in his absence; how sex relations with a spouse will fare; and a general anxiety about how he will cope. Much may need to be done in this respect.

(3) Assisting the client to examine any pre-existing problems. The crisis of admission itself may have raised the client's motivation to examine these, while the distancing effect of institutionalisation may produce a greater objectivity and provide a real chance for the worker to explore and modify problems. But distance can also make them more inaccessible: the client may see them as hopeless and have little motivation—though he is more likely to see them more rosily and deny their significance. With the admission crisis over, defences may come into play—rationalising the reasons for his admission and pre-existing problems, projecting or displacing blame, etc. Such defences may be reinforced if his experience of the institution is negative. Here, perhaps, the worker's main task may be to keep the reality of pre-existing problems before the client.

(B) Work with families during admission. This may be grouped under three headings:

(1) Problems created by the admission. All families are faced with problems of the maintenance of routines involving role-redistribution (dismemberment effects). There are problems (practical and emotional) of maintaining contact with the institutionalised member; and problems of utilising external support where this is needed. Kin and neighbour help may not be easy to accept (because of feelings of inadequacy, or shame for example), especially if it is ambivalently given (on certain conditions). Much will depend on previous relationships coupled with attitudes of the parties to the reasons for the admission. Help, where available, from the social services may be time consuming to obtain, inconvenient, involve payments, or be grudgingly given, reinforcing humiliation and stigma.

The created problems may be particularly acute where one of the parents is admitted and the family becomes one-parent—though the degree to which problems will be felt will depend on a number of factors, including the factors around the admission but more particularly, its length. Morris[1] and Marsden[2] highlight the problems of prisoners' wives and mothers alone in the areas of poverty, care and control of the children and the dual role with them, housing, debt, work, sex, and the difficulties of finding and utilising support. Stress symptoms, tiredness, depression are understandably common. George[3] examines the problems of a lone father: deciding in the first place whether to give up work or try to run both job and home, similar problems of reduced income and combining the unfamiliar role of mother, his frequent ignorance about social services; isolation, sex, hostile attitudes to the alleged 'workshy', etc. These books should be read by all social workers if only for the salutary comments they contain about the adequacy, and terms of help of social services and comments on the casework help they have or have not received. (Though remember the difficulties and biases likely to come in when a survey by a previously unknown survey worker is being made.)

Morris's book underlines the additional problems of on-going worry about the institutionalised member and the anxiety about the accession problems which may arise on the institutionalised member's return home.

(2) Pre-existing problems. These may be directly related to the admission (of a child to a residential school for the maladjusted for example), indirectly related (prison for shoplifting as a symptom of other problems) or unrelated (hospitalisation after a fortuitous accident). In any event, the admission may (as with the client) tend to raise motivation and to distance the problem which creates an opportunity for effective work to be done: but similar forms of blocking may also make problems more inaccessible and the work hard (especially if immediate problems are also acute). However, it would seem that families—perhaps because they are in the same environment—do remain rather more realistic about pre-existing problems. One of the factors in accessibility of pre-existing problems may be the degree of relationship between the admission and pre-existing

problems, but even where there is no connection really a guilt association between them may provide some motivation; while a contact
with a sympathetic social worker about the admission may provide
the opportunity for the client to bring out pre-existing problems—
especially where pressures have been severe (and the admission a
'last straw', perhaps).

(3) Problems of relating to the institution. Families' attitudes to
the institution may be positive or negative or ambivalent initially,
with the latter more likely—and more likely over time, as the wholly
positive or negative become modified with experience of the institution. Clearly, such feelings should be taken up (not forgetting the
practical issues such as visiting arrangements, or lack of information
which may help to engender irritation) where they are damaging
the family, creating difficulties with institution staff, or impinging
detrimentally on the client's progress (since the family are sure to
communicate feelings about the institution to him). Good Stage I
work will help to mitigate difficulties, but some snags are inevitable:
worries about the client may be displaced, fantasies build up, latent
jealousies emerge, certain expectations not be fulfilled, etc.

As a person in touch with the client and the institution as well
as the family, a worker can be of tremendous help here.

(C) Work with the institution. There are a number of functions
in relation to the institution the field or institution based worker
can exercise in this stage:

(1) To discuss with institution staff the progress the client is making
towards the previously established objectives and his response to
treatment or institutionalisation. With due respect for confidentiality,
the worker may feed in his own information, based on observations
his own direct contacts with the client have provided. Modifications
to the original diagnosis or treatment goals, plans, and methods,
may be made and the worker will bear these in mind when considering his work with client and family.

(2) The worker can similarly feed in his knowledge of the family
situation. This may have a bearing on the client's behaviour or responses in the institution, or require some modification of the institution's objectives or methods. It may be appropriate here to feed in
information about the family's attitudes to the institution since this

will have a bearing on client's attitudes, and also to examine with the staff the interaction they are experiencing with the client's family, since inevitably the family is going to be involved with both worker and staff. This may be the opportunity to re-examine any initial allocation of roles, tasks, etc. as between worker and staff, since it is vital for the whole programme that good, consistent, teamwork exists in this as in any other sphere.

(3) It can happen, though, that a clash between staff and worker remains: perhaps about the aims and objectives in a particular case; or the worker may feel that this institution is not sharing his aims with any of the residents: or that though the institution may share aims, the resources it has at its disposal are quite inadequate to achieve them; a view the staff may share. In such circumstances (and after checking his own aims and methods) the professional responsibility of the worker may be to utilise the range of options he has (inside and outside his agency) to bring about change: in his specific case, as regards the institution generally, or to join forces with the staff to secure the resources that are needed.

Demonstrably, at Stage II, whether working with the client, family or institution, there is a wide range of need to be met and a wide scope for social work intervention. The sad fact is, though, that this work is rarely undertaken. Particularly for the fieldbased worker in the press of other matters an admission is seen as the end of a case—at least until the question of discharge arises. Yet the importance of on-going work, if only in terms of keeping relationships alive and positive, to the success of after-care, is plain. To drop matters not only vitiates much of the institution's work, but may be experienced as a rejection by client and family—and institution staff.

Stage III: After Admission

Stage III work, in terms of rehabilitation and re-adjustment (accession) problems, will have begun in Stage II with both client and family; but now the abstract becomes the reality, and the discrepancies minimal or great. Good Stage II work will make problems less and the task easier for all parties.

We have already seen the difficulties endemic in the convalescent period and these may be exacerbated if say, the client wants to re-assume roles and responsibilities quickly, but the family are uncertain of his capacity to do so (especially if a disability exists—for example, after a schizophrenic episode). Again the client may have enjoyed his dependency in the institution and be reluctant to take on respon-sibilities again; or the family may have enjoyed their new responsibi-lities, or the freedom from tension, and so block the client's attempts to return to the original patterns.

After discharge, too, there is likely to be a 'honeymoon period' in which problems are seen as minimal and motivation to dis-cuss them is low. To see a client and/or family at this period may give a false impression and lead to a premature closing of the case.

An opportunity to get to grips with pre-existing problems may depend on whether they had a bearing (direct or tangential) on the admission or not; whether distancing helped or hindered; or whether the admission added to or diminished motivation and capacity to tackle them. The disparate experiences of client and family and what these did to each, could add to the difficulties especially if the admis-sion involved profound change (amputation for example) or was pro-tracted. Each 'side' will have changed to a degree and perhaps be 'out-of-line' (for good or ill) with the other's expectations—especially, perhaps, the children, growing and changing in the interim.

It is disturbing to read, in Morris' book, how quickly pre-existing problems recurred, however: work, drink, sex, household mismanage-ment, mainly. It is true these were often manifestations of profound disturbance often difficult to treat; but institutionalising did little to assist, it would seem.

The institution also has a place in the discharge period: in actuality or fantasy. The client may still be in contact (Outpatient appoint-ments, Borstal licence or prison parole) with obligations, too, for the social worker to remain in touch with institution staff. It may be part of the social work task to assist the client to maintain con-tact—which may not be easy for him; again for practical or emo-tional reasons. The family's attitude will also be significant here— encouraging or discouraging contact, either in support of, or in contradiction to the client's attitude (and/or the workers). Much patient work may be needed.

The experience of the institution will clearly be a great influence on the client and his family in terms of remaining contacts; but even if the client is no longer in touch, the influence of the institution will still be acutely felt and profoundly affect the worker's task; together with the influence of the reasons for the admission, whether the admission achieved its objectives or not, and other's reactions to the whole process. Feelings about all these aspects will colour the client's and family's views of the worker. If reactions to the experience were negative, the worker may be seen as a spy or informer, a hand reaching out from the institution to snatch them back, etc.; or he may be a reminder of an episode all would rather forget. Resistance in these circumstances is only to be expected: whether overt hostility, a bland 'everything's all right now', or a resigned 'it's done no good: therefore you cannot help'. Co-operation in after-care is more likely if the reactions are at least sufficiently positive—though even some negative reactions can be utilised if they are translated into a determination 'never to go back there' and the worker can get it across that this is his objective, too.

Co-operation between fieldbased and institution based staff is often poor, to the detriment of clients and families. There are perhaps, three reasons for this:

(1) The structural differences of the settings: each organisation has differing personnel, hierarchies, communication systems, procedures, objectives, methods, priorities, loyalties, boundaries, identifications, pressures, constraints of resources, etc. A thorough understanding of the other's setting is a pre-requisite of co-operation.

(2) Communication is often poor. This always tends to go when either 'side' is under pressure, but both experience difficulty when trying to get hold of the right person in the other organisation: even if you know who it is, the social worker may be out, a residential staff member off duty. A number of people in the opposite organisation may need informing (psychiatrist, registrar, charge nurse, occupational therapist, etc./social worker, Home Help organiser, day centre staff, etc.), but telling one may not ensure the others get told too. Communication is not helped sometimes by attitudes about the

other's competence, or feelings that 'they' have an easy time, while 'I' get lumbered with 'their' problems.

(3) Status. Residential staff particularly have good reason to be bitter about lack of status in the past—reflected in lower pay, longer hours, poorer working conditions, shorter training and fewer opportunities to do it. Residential work has been 'anyone's' job: the demands of it and the skill in it have only slowly been acknowledged. Their feelings have been reinforced by the actuality of the power of the fieldworker to make decisions about residents, and the cavalier way in which such decisions have often been made and implemented, with little or no consultation. While this situation is improving, much remains to be done—and even when it is, the memories may still be long. In some circumstances, the boot has been on the other foot and case-workers have been upset by say, 'social work' decisions being made by the medical profession. But if they know how this feels, they should be able to understand how some of their residential colleagues have felt!

References

1. Pauline Morris, *Prisoners and their Families* (George Allen & Unwin), 1965. .
2. Dennis Marsden, *Mothers Alone* (Allen Lane, the Penguin Press), 1969.
3. V. George and P. Wilding, *Motherless Families* (Routledge & Kegan Paul), 1972.

Further Reading

To make sense of work in conjunction with institutions as well as to understand the reactions of individuals and families at the various stages of admission, the field or institutionally based caseworker needs to comprehend the processes of residential care. Three books which, though utilising specific situations, examine processes which have a generalised application are Erving Goffman's *Asylums* (Pelican), Isabel Menzies *The Functioning of Social Systems as a Defence against Anxiety* (Tavistock) and *A Life Apart* by E. J. Miller and G. V. Gwynne (Tavistock). Other texts which examine specific situations though perhaps in a less generalised way are *Residential Life with Children* by Christopher Beedell (Routledge & Kegan Paul); *Patterns of Residential Care for Children* by John Gibbs (National Children's Homes); *Care in a Planned Environment*, an H.M.S.O. publication which mainly looks at child care but draws some interesting analogies between this area and the residential care of the elderly; *The Last Refuge* by Peter Townsend (Routledge & Kegan Paul); *A Place Like Home* by David Wills (National Institute for Social Work Training); *Pentonville* by T. and

P. Morris (Routledge & Kegan Paul); and *Put Away* by Pauline Morris (Routledge & Kegan Paul).

Work with institutions *per se* is rarely pulled together in the way I have attempted here but work appropriate to the stages I had identified remains rather scattered throughout the texts—including the three I make specific reference to in this chapter. There is relevant material in a number of casework texts, such as Noel Timms' *Casework in the Child Care Service* (Butterworth), *Social Work with Children* by Juliet Berry (Routledge & Kegan Paul), *Social Work in Medical Care* by Sophia Butrym (Routledge & Kegan Paul), *Social Work Practice in the Health Field* by Harriett Bartlett (National Association of Social Workers—U.S.), *Casework in After-care* by Mark Monger (Butterworth), *The Work of the Probation and After-care Officer* by Phyllida Parsloe (Routledge & Kegan Paul). Some of the books which examine the client's view, such as Noel Timms' *The Receiving End* (Routledge & Kegan Paul). Enid Mills' *Living with Mental Illness* (Institute of Community Studies) and Diana Dewar's *Orphans of the Living* (Hutchinson) also have much to say that is pertinent: and in terms of working with the institution as well as the client, *On Death and Dying* by E. Kuhbler-Ross (Tavistock) is a very thought-provoking book. There is also a very nice chapter in Goffman's *Asylums* which looks at the way people get processed into institutions by outside agencies and definitions which should make all fieldworkers pause to think.

Discussion

This chapter has been written at a fairly high level of abstraction in an attempt to deal with the wide range of institutions which a generic worker is likely to encounter and the variety of reactions likely to be aroused. The teaching aim then becomes in discussion to help students to identify the abstractions' relevance to specific situations; best achieved, perhaps, by drawing on students' own experience or using case examples.

Discussion is likely to produce anxiety or strong feeling in three areas:

(1) A quite widespread hostility to institutions *per se*, backed by a suitable range of 'horror stories'. The general attitude of fieldwork students seems to be that 'we'll keep our clients out of their clutches at all costs'. While this attitude may have its healthy side, it becomes destructive if it rubs off in practice into fieldworkers' relations with residential staff. I find the hostility tends to diminish once students have completed a residential placement (a must for all fieldwork students, I feel); while its existence may be one of the best arguments for training field and residential social workers together. After a residential placement, too, I find most students have seen their field

performance in a new light and have a good deal more sympathy for the hostility of residential workers towards field workers. But it takes a long time for the 'dustbin' image of residential care to be modified and for the opportunity elements of residential care to be acknowledged.

(2) While field workers seem relatively happy with their functions in the pre-admission and post-admission stages, they often have considerable difficulty in identifying a role and function for themselves at the during admission stage: particularly their involvement with residential staff. They seem afraid of 'treading on toes' (especially where they fear this will have repercussions for their clients in residence or their families' relations with residential staff); uncertain how or at what level to communicate; or how to change things within the institution if they feel this change is needed—a situation that generates feelings of helplessness. Lack of involvement at 'Stage II' is I suspect, just as much due to this uncertainty of role and function at this point as it is to the pressure of caseloads (and the latter may be a rationalisation for the former). Discussion can help; involvement in case reviews in child care practice also assists—and one wishes that such a system could be extended, especially in the sphere of the elderly where admission still tends to be seen as for the rest of life and the 'Stage II' function of the fieldworker is even more unclear. Hospital or other institutionally based placements can often help to clarify 'Stage II' learning if the student can be helped to 'transfer out' this learning.

(3) Students are often looking for clear criteria regarding whether to admit or not, which are difficult to establish in theoretical terms other than at an extremely abstracted level. Students are well aware, though, that in practice the initiative whether to try to admit or not rests with them (even if the final decision about it is not always theirs). Some case material involving borderline situations might be of value here and be the starting point for considering this whole question of relations between field work and institutions. Anxiety tends to be acute in emergency situations where the worker has to handle high levels of anxiety and pressure among all those concerned, yet may have little time in which to really assess the situation. Emergencies do not often happen in a student's fieldwork practice, since

the students tend to be protected from this degree of responsibility. Yet students rehearse what they would do and how they might feel in such situations, which they know will face them once qualified. They worry about how to resist or handle pressure, remain objective, and avoid collusion—especially where pressure is coming from authoritative sources (such as doctors); from influential or charismatic figures (councillors, neighbours); or where the consequences of their decisions may involve repercussions from their own hierarchy. After the recent spate of public enquiries into the deaths of children under the supervision of Social Services Departments' social workers, they feel they will be under Departmental pressure to 'play safe' and admit; yet realise this may be damaging to their client and prejudice their chances of working with them in Stages II and III. Mental health admissions produce similar sorts of anxieties, as does probation work involving (implicitly or explicitly) a recommendation for a custodial sentence.

Yet students are well aware of the necessity for good work in this part of their job—work with institutions—and often feel badly about it when they acknowledge they are not doing it as well as they would like.

PART IV

Outside the Interview

CHAPTER XI

Casework and Administration

Social work and administration may be examined from two angles: the administration of a department and its impact on social work practice, and the social worker as administrator. These aspects are closely inter-related since social workers are part of the administrative system (with a degree of responsibility for it and loyalty to it) and part of the inter-dependency of administration (agency), worker and client.

(I) Administration

Both administrator and social worker are needed if the agency is to attain its objective of meeting client need; but though they share the objective, their methods of achieving it differ and often tension arises. This coincidence of objective but tension occurs whether the setting is primary (that is, where the agency is a social work one) or secondary (where the primary objective is not social work but the agency incorporates some social workers). There may be particularly identifiable difficulties in the secondary setting, but these are frequently illustrative of the tensions in primary settings, too.

Many institutions with other than social work objectives have found it very useful (if not necessary) to incorporate social work skills to enable them to meet their objectives for at least some groups of their 'consumers'; to help incorporate them into the institution's work where practical, personal, social or even administrative factors inhibit clients' engagement with the agency; to deal with 'blocks', whether personal or social, once consumers were engaged; to complete the agency's programme or prevent the work done being vitiated subsequently (via after-care for example); or sometimes, to

273

provide an addition to the range of treatment methods available. Medical and psychiatric social workers attached to hospitals, education welfare officers attached to schools, and youth employment officers are clearly in this sort of situation. Even if workers are in primary settings, much of their work is characteristically secondary—helping their clients to engage with medical services, social security services, residential establishments, etc.

But this incorporation of social work extends the range of function of the institution in a way which creates tension by obliging that institution to look two ways and try to reconcile needs which may be conflicting: for courts to take account of personal as well as societal factors, for hospitals to balance the need for a patient to remain occupying a bed for social reasons when there is a waiting list for admissions on medical grounds; for schools to reconcile the factors behind truancy with educational demands for compulsory attendance. The social worker is frequently at the heart of this tension, perhaps even engenders it and gets blamed for it—or at least has to carry the negative projections of the ambivalence raised in others.

Social work in secondary settings often has to adapt its objectives to the over-riding objectives of the host institution—and quite properly so when that institution is dealing with a salient, immediate need. But there will be times, even within a secondary setting, where the social worker should be able to demonstrate to colleagues the primacy of the personal/social factors which are the social worker's province, assume the team leadership in such cases, and expect colleagues, while that primacy remains, to adapt their objectives in support of the social work task. Again, this way of working often occurs where the setting is primary. If a client is taken ill, the primary worker will adapt what he is doing to support the primary objective of seeing his client gets well. In this sense, the setting is no pre-determiner of whether the social work is carried out in a primary or secondary way. Good team work is implicit either way, which means successfully educating others about social work, and social workers understanding what others' functions are.

Given that administrators are professional colleagues (and as administration becomes more highly specialised this is, in effect, what they are becoming), this concept of teamwork is of increasing relevance. Given, too (as we shall see) that the standpoint of the administrator is not the same as the social worker, the concept of 'looking two ways' has an applicability even in primary settings.

Administration, whether in a primary or secondary setting, carries responsibility for the agency: to get something done by organising resources in relation to objectives. But it does so within certain constraints:

(1) Of *opinion*: that services should be valid, specific, economical, fair (impartial, and therefore with rules, little administrative discretion, and as a consequence, a tendency to the impersonal); nor be 'nosey' in the process (making unnecessary, humiliating and off putting enquiries of clients).

(2) Of *resource*: these are never unlimited and therefore have to be distributed between functions on a basis of priorities which only administration can determine from its over-view position.

(3) Of *accountability*: the administration is responsible to its committee which in turn is responsible to its supporters (whether subscribers, rate or tax payers). Justification is typically by measuring: i.e. a numerical expression of costs, numbers of cases dealt with, categories of cases, success rates, etc.

(4) Of *relations to other structures*: the agency has to mesh with other organisations and therefore has to run similarly, with limits to a 'special case' plea. A Social Services Department cannot be radically different from other local authority Departments with their committee, budget, measuring systems, pay scales, etc.

Social workers tend to see things differently: our concern is for the individual—very frequently individuals who are unpopular, costly, or both. So the potentiality for clash arises at various points.

In terms of *opinion*: we see services as valid when other opinions (given the unpopularity of our clients) do not; we see multiple needs (many of them outside our agency sphere) when we are asked to be specific; we are asked for economy when our clients are costly (even if spending money now would save it later on); we are asked for efficiency when we can see how time-consuming objective attainment needs to be; we are asked to implement fairness by the rules when we see that to be really fair we need to discriminate (however unfair this may look on paper) and want discretionary powers to be able to do this; we object to the impersonality of the 'system' when we are trying to personalise and individualise; we want to bring in a whole range of factors to make a decision, and feel frustrated when decisions are made on a limited number of factors only.

As regards *resources*, we would argue there is never enough, especially for our unpopular or costly clients; and since we experience the needs of *our* clients, we argue about the priorities and distribution of what resources there are.

In terms of *accountability*, we argue you cannot reduce people to numbers and categories or treat them on this basis; and since we often deal in intangibles such as human feelings, we cannot balance costs with demonstrable 'successes' (success being often immeasurable in social work, anyway).

For *relations with other structures*, we would prefer all systems to fit people rather than vice versa. Where other systems do not, we would like to change them: where we cannot change them we would like to insist that at least our system should anyway and others allow that ours is a special case.

So even in primary settings, social workers may still *feel* they are in a secondary. Yet administration and social work still need each other and need to work together with a sufficient degree of co-operation, understanding and tolerance if client need is to be met.

Organisation theory can help us understand administration by analysing organisations in terms of goals, structures and processes—though these are closely inter-related. The ideal is achieved if structure and process effectively meet goals—but the ideal may be rare in practice: one element is often skewed to a degree, with consequences for the others. The following are examples of theories which may assist analysis. Each has elements of truth; each is applicable to social work agencies and the wide variety of organisational settings in which social workers will find themselves operating and engaged with.

(A) Analysis by Goals

(i) ORGANISATIONAL GOAL ANALYSIS

Tasks are said to be organised around the goal of an image of a desired future state; but in practice goals are:

Multiple: they may conflict basically or at least produce tension over resource allocation between them;

Diffuse: therefore problems exist of translating them into effective action to attain them;

Perceived differently: by the occupants of the various levels in the organisation, or the clients;

Changing: priorities change or goals become displaced. Organisations tend to perpetuate themselves—perpetuation becoming a displaced goal. Changes (whether required by external circumstances or as a result of internal policy or priority changes) tend to be resisted since change upsets existing patterns, redistributes power, requires new skills, and cuts across personal motivation.

Social Services Departments goals are certainly now multiple, with consequent resource allocation problems. It has been suggested they may even have basically conflicting goals. Departments have a responsibility now for promoting social change—for example, by employing community workers. These workers may viably assist clients who are endeavouring to solve problems by changing power structures that operate to their disadvantage, including the power structure of the Department itself or other Local Authority Departments—a goal the Department is hardly likely to see as compatible. The multiplicity and diffuseness of goals may well be at the basis of some of the current confusion that exists as to what Social Services Departments are there for—a confusion that blurs social workers' sense of professional identity and purpose, and affects morale.

With Departments now both larger and embracing a far wider range of disciplines (and therefore client groups), the chances of different perceptions existing about goals are much greater; while new legislation, consequent policy changes, organisational change, and surrounding social change have, and still are, creating difficulty. The Chronically Sick and Disabled Persons Act and the Children and Young Persons Act brought new priorities and demanded new skills (intermediate treatment, for example); the 1971 'Seebohm' reorganisation and generic caseloads certainly upset many of the workers from the pre-existing departments; while with Local Government reorganisation and still larger Departments, many fieldworkers feel that the power has shifted from them to the expanded hierarchies. Accusations have been levelled against the Seebohm reorganisation to the effect that it mainly served social workers' career ends rather than the clients' welfare—a distinctly misplaced goal in the accusers' view.

(ii) ANALYSIS BY PRIME BENEFICIARY

Blau and Scott[1] suggest four types of beneficiary, calling for different types of organisation each with a characteristic problem to solve. Where the beneficiaries are the members, a mutual benefit organisation is required and the problem is democracy: where owners are the beneficiaries, a business organisation is required and the problem is efficiency; where clients are beneficiaries, a service organisation is required and the problem becomes the reconciliation of a professional service with administration; where the public are the beneficiaries, a common weal organisation is wanted and the problem democratic public control.

Difficulties arise where the internal, external and recipients' views differ as to the beneficiary and, therefore, the type of organisation required; or where the organisation is in practice used for the benefit of a group other than the 'official' one. Thus the 'common weal' policeman may see himself as part of a 'service' and at cross purposes with the official beneficiaries (the public) and resist attempts at democratic public control of a 'professional' organisation. The probation 'service' may well feel itself under pressure from the public to serve 'common weal' ends by controlling criminals. While mental hospitals may be universally regarded as a 'service', in practice they may be used for 'common weal' purposes as dumps for community problems and asked to wall in patients to the detriment of their service function. A disillusioned client may well see a Social 'Services' Department as a 'mutual benefit' organisation for the social workers; and not without truth, since service professionals can use organisations for mutual benefit ends such as the career opportunities already mentioned, vitiating the service ends. Social workers can be punitive, too—i.e. serve common weal ends rather than service/client ends.

(B) Analysis by Structure

(i) BUREAUCRACY

This is typically a hierarchical structure, pyramid shaped, in which information passes up and decisions are handed down. Within the hierarchy each member has a firm place, occupying a position with a defined role, task, rights and duties and in a clear relationship with other positions. There are rules or precedents to follow, and clear indicators of the authority attached to a position: therefore, not all information goes right to the top and decisions can be made at lower levels—though if the authority to decide a particular issue is doubtful, referral will be made higher up. Relations are typically impersonal internally (for example, promotion is by rules and/or qualifications) and externally (clients are dealt with by rules, too). Employees are almost invariably salaried career officials with security of tenure.

Bureaucracies have qualities of efficiency, stability, predictability and power (that is, not subject to influence)—qualities which can be valuable or a handicap. They are efficient at routine: the normal is rapidly forthcoming, the unorthodox becomes 'grit in the works'; stability and predictability are assets until adaptation is wanted; resistance to influence is protective (of the clients as well as the officials) until change or some injustice to be righted is required.

The problem for professionals in bureaucracies (in addition to the tensions we have already mentioned) is that their position in the hierarchy is often uncertain. While professionals are trained to take decisions and take responsibility for those decisions within their sphere of professional competence, they may have no hierarchical authority and be only in a position to advise the bureaucrat with the positional authority: or they get into a protracted argument as to who has the power to decide what in terms of what is done, what resources allocated, etc. The bureaucrat (identified with and loyal to his organisation) tends to be suspicious of the professional (with his tendency to identify with and be loyal to an organisation outside the bureaucracy). While he is tempted to discount professional opinion, he has to be discrete about this since the professional, through his contacts elsewhere, could get support and make trouble. So his position is not easy either. Even in a bureaucracy, of course, supervision of much the social worker does is virtually impossible, since he is usually alone with his client.

With the tendency in social work agencies for the professionally trained worker to be promoted to administrative, hierarchical positions, this may mean more effective communication and understanding between professionals and administrators and an administrative system more attuned to professional and client need; but there are snags. Few professionals are currently trained in administration, affecting its efficiency; while in the lower levels of administration at least, opportunities exist for acute personal dilemmas to arise, when the person concerned has to decide over a particular issue whether the 'hat' he wears is that of professional or administrator. His identity may face a severe challenge.

While being outside the hierarchy can be frustrating for the professional, it has some advantages: he may be able to 'side-step' some of the internal wrangles, and sometimes clients can use him while still engaged with the organisation, in their dealings with the hierarchy. Mental hospital patients will sometimes use the psychiatric social worker in this way. (This matter is discussed further in the chapter on Fieldwork and institutions.)

(ii) FRONT LINE ORGANISATIONS

This type of organisation exists typically where the executive process is decentralised, with individuals or groups operating at the periphery. The initiative is with the front line groups working largely independently of the centre and each other. Often this is the sort of organisation a social worker calls for: independently, or as a group, he can determine his objectives, sphere of action, method of working, and make his own decisions about resource allocation, admissions, etc. He feels as though he can operate as a professional in the best interests of his clients.

Many Area Offices of Social Service Departments operate in a front line, decentralised way, controlling their own budgets and resources. The risk here is that area offices of the same Local Authority will develop different styles and priorities which effectively mean a variation of service for clients living within the same Local Authority boundaries.

This amount of independence can be isolating for the worker, though; and there are limits anyway to decentralisation. The centre cannot abdicate its broad responsibility for generally determining policy and allocating resources. It will supervise its peripheral workers at least to the degree of ensuring standards by employing trained workers; and retain some communication by sending out information and asking for returns and reports. If it feels the periphery is getting too remote, it may try to re-establish itself by calling in workers to central meetings, sending out its own inspectors, insist on copies of all reports, call letters in for signature or pull certain specialised functions (courtwork, etc.) into the centre. It can control recruitment and only employ the subservient, get front-line staff who 'know the tricks' on centre staff. A front-line organisation depends on trust: so if as social workers we want to retain it we cannot risk exploiting it.

Centralising has certain advantages: it can be protective—of the client against the worker's power of discretion (an 'appeal' system); and of the worker against manipulative pressure from the client by providing some rules. It can support the worker: guidelines to ease the burden of decision making, back-up facilities of many kinds to make his job easier—from clerical help to information and training.

Even in a bureaucracy not all initiative is removed from the worker: he can edge out the area of his work gradually, or change it slowly in such a way that it becomes incorporated.

(iii) TOTAL INSTITUTIONS

These are usually residential and characterised by compulsory attendance (legally enforced) or quasi-compulsion (through lack of alternatives). Typically, there is a lack of separation of the sleep, work, recreation and domestic spheres which are all scheduled by the institution and occur within its domain, and involving the same social groupings. This is quite unlike normal life where these spheres occur in different places and with different people: so institutional life is hardly the best preparation for everyday life. A basic separation exists between staff and residents with no interchange between these roles. New entrants are introduced to the social order of the institution often by a symbolic stripping of their former life (baths, new clothes, etc.) and their indoctrination to the new order is supported by a reward/punishment system which promotes the well accultured. The identity and social processes of the institution are often fostered by rituals and a language peculiar to the institution.

The effects are alleged to be disastrous: inmates are first humiliated and confused, then gradually robbed of any sense of separate identity. If they react (whether with violence or withdrawal) these are cited as a need to be in the institution. Acceptable behaviour is that which assists the staff to run the place smoothly. Discouraged from contact with family or the outside world, inmates become more susceptible to institutional pressures, but as these are atypical in objective, they become increasingly less fitted for discharge.

The black 'literature of dysfunction' about institutions was a stimulus to community care programmes (though no measure of how effective these were existed, nor adequate recourses allocated); but the accusations levelled against institutions may be somewhat exaggerated. No institution is impermeable—TV, papers, letters, staff, visitors, voluntary workers, etc. bring in the outside world and some residents do go out; while memory cannot be obliterated. Even Goffman shows how people can retain identity by living in the 'cracks in the walls'; and prisons survive through a *quid pro quo* between prisoners and warders. The effects of institutional care depend on the stage in the life cycle and may be worst for the young and the elderly. The success rates of Borstal and prisons (which are not high) are arguably an indicator of how little effect they have: while the after effects of public school life are generally deemed to be beneficial rather than harmful: and experience of Service life is similarly sometimes held to be advantageous. Certain total institutions are reckoned to give a service back to the community, too: some orders of nuns, for example—or even Borstal boys undertaking a community project.

Even in social work, certain total institutions are considered as positive, either for those who society finds insupportable (from the elderly frail in one way, to battered children who have adverse supports in their own homes, in another); or for individuals who find their part of society insupportable and need a retreat at least for a time (convalescent holidays for example). For both groups, an institution may give them protection, or provide the physical, social or emotional structures that will meet their particular needs when these do not exist in their society. We need to remember though, that most residents will need to be prepared to return to society. Institutions which contain both 'returners' and 'non-returners' are in a particular difficulty (for example, a hospital which contains both those who will get well and those who will die: a hostel sheltering those who need permanent care and others with only temporary needs).

The processes and structures identified within and ascribed to total institutions should not be regarded as peculiar to them, however. In many ways they only (rather dramatically) identify processes which are extant in non-total institutions. Even fieldworkers may find themselves being 'brainwashed' into the 'way we do things here' on joining a Department: and we are all aware that in many ways we have to 'live with' the people we work with.

Fieldworkers may not be part of total institutions, but need to understand the processes that may exist in them. They will frequently have the responsibility of deciding whether to admit a person to them, work with them while they are there and deal with any consequences after discharge.

(iv) PERMEABLE ORGANISATIONS

These may be typified by voluntary organisations or voluntary activities (clubs, etc.) and a caseworker may be deeply involved with both, whether trying to run them or work with them. Members and staff (i.e. those in official positions) tend to change frequently, and these roles are frequently inter-changeable. Because of this movement, permeable organisations are very susceptible to outside networks and influences. A number of corollaries follow:

Members and 'inter-changeable' staff tend to use the organisation

for their own purposes. The organisation has to tailor its programme to take these purposes into account and individualise
much more. Its plans have to be flexible and are likely to be less
co-ordinated. It has to work with what it has got in terms of
resources, personnel and individual wishes.

It can only use normative controls—no coercion is possible. (For
a discussion of compliance systems, see below.) Even permanent
staff cannot use their positional authority nearly so much and have
to rely on their expertise or relationship authority. If the normative
carries little appeal, apathy becomes a problem (and may be institutionalised through associate membership).

Because of the outside network influence, it is difficult for the organisation to counter the influence of 'significant others' or to build
up members' identification with the organisation. The ideology
then tends to become amorphous, negotiable and possibly changing. Group boundaries are weak and the prestige of the organisation and its work may also tend to be weak.

Doubts exist about the organisation's effectiveness, its ability to sustain its programme, and its continuity, which leads more permanent organisations, such as Social Services Departments, to dis-
parage permeable organisations and not to trust them with responsibilities.

Bureacratic or total institutions suspect them, since they are not con-
trollable, have external loyalties and are repositories of external
influences which may upset smoothly-running operations. For such
reasons, a hospital may keep a wary eye on its League of Friends,
or the school on its Parents Association.

But just because of their flexibility, individualising, etc. they may
be in the best position to recruit, sustain and deploy volunteers.

(For further discussion on relations between professional and
voluntary workers, see Chapter 13.)

(C) Analysis by Process

(i) BY COMPLIANCE SYSTEM

This analysis pre-supposes organisations are composed of élites and lowers (though one person could be in either position in different circumstances). It is suggested that élites may use three ways to gain compliance: coercion (power), material reward (remuneration, etc.) or normative methods (which may involve the use of appeals to symbolism or imagery, if only by reference to loyalty to the Department—or how other families manage). An organisation may typically use one way, guided by the goals of the organisation as the élites see it: if the goal is order, coercive methods; the goal economic, then material reward; the goal cultural, normative methods would be preferred. All are likely to be used in various circumstances, though: but using one may inhibit the use of others—normative methods may be weakened if coercive methods are used elsewhere in the organisation. Or they may be used in sequence. An 'out of line' social worker may be approached initially by normative appeals ('See how you are upsetting people'), followed by offers of material reward ('Get in line and I will recommend your promotion') or ultimately by coercion ('Fall in line or get the sack'). Social workers may well use the same progression with clients: from 'Why cannot you pay the rent like others do', via 'If you will pay regularly in future, I will get some help towards the arrears for you' to 'If you do not pay, I will recommend your eviction'.

Lowers may respond to any of these methods by indifference, approval (implying a concurrence in the system being used); disapproval (whether expressed by revolt, resistance, non-co-operation or alienation—withdrawing from engagement with the organisation: resigning or breaking off contact); or calculative involvement (i.e. playing along for purposes of their own).

For social workers, the question is whether we regard clients as part of the organisation. I have already inferred above we should, but this raises a number of issues. Do social workers regard themselves as élites and clients lowers? What compliance system characterises client/worker interaction? As a cultural organisation, it should be normative—but is it? What compliance system is the client using? What effect does the agency compliance system have on the client/ worker interaction? If the agency uses coercion and the worker responds with calculative involvement, can he then use the normative in working with his client? Will not some influence be there from the agency system?

(ii) BY PERSONAL AND SOCIAL PROCESS

Individual factors cannot be divorced from role performance. Personality (obsessional/careless; anti-authority/submissive, etc.), likes and dislikes for aspects of the job or those we work with, the degree of commitment to the job (involved/only there for the money), ambition (wanting to get on or disliking responsibility)—all will influence the way we perform.

The interaction processes initiated by work processes will lead to group and subgroup formations, influencing individual action. Group norms (about acceptable behaviour or output for example) and group loyalties (influencing behaviour towards and attitudes to other groups) will exist; leaders, isolates, etc. emerge to complicate personality factors in terms of performance.

External influences cannot be excluded (family pressures, non-work groups and significant others, age in relation to other employment opportunities, etc.).

No formal structure, then, operates as theoretically as it should: blocks, short cuts, distortions, informal communications, manipulations and so on, all occur.

That such factors operate in social work agencies is undeniable, and they may well be most intense in residential establishments. As social workers we ought to understand them more clearly and be more skilled in dealing with them—but I sometimes wonder whether we are.

Any social worker should be able to identify from practice material which illustrates these various theories and his place and/or part in them. It is important we understand what is happening and how this influences our practice. It is particularly important that we identify what is happening in our own agency, since we have a degree of responsibility for it. Until we do, we cannot protect our clients' interests where such influences are harmful, nor can we effectively try to change them; nor can we reinforce them where the influences are helpful. When we are senior staff, not to understand could be disastrous for agency, staff and client.

While no administration is easy, administering a social work agency is particularly difficult. Administration may be seen as having four tasks:

(1) To formulate objectives—and by implication, to evaluate progress towards them.
(2) To implement action to achieve objectives—acquiring and deploying resources, both material (buildings and equipment) and staff—in terms of numbers and skills—for present and *future* needs (budgeting and staff development programmes, for example) and seeing these get to the people they are intended for.
(3) To promulgate the values of the organisation: externally, to help secure resources and the understanding and co-operation of related organisations; internally, to foster understanding and co-operation between various groups of staff.
(4) To turn the above into tangible arrangements of organisation, communication, etc. so that the day-to-day working supports rather than vitiates these tasks.

Social work objectives are often a matter of argument among social workers themselves, so the administrator has a hard job presenting agreed objectives to his committee, whose ideas may vary, anyway, and be at variance with 'society's'; let alone attempts to 'sell' his objectives to other organisations. Even with agreed objectives, arguments are likely about cost (the acquiring resources function) or priorities (the deployment function). Objectives are derivatives of values, so promoting values has similar and perhaps more difficult complexities. The methods by which objectives are reached can also be disputed, especially if some staff see a 'softly, softly' approach as the most likely to succeed while others would prefer a more abrasive stance. Evaluation of movement towards objectives is typically hard to measure in social work at the best of times; while the complexities of organisation and communication in large departments, quite apart from between organisations, are only too obvious.

At times, a Director must wonder how many 'bosses' he has with Committee, inspectors, Central Government, professional and union groups and various pressure groups coming at him with various demands. Wider functions, with added specialisms add to the 'who does what' disputes, exacerbating problems already created by geographical distance and unavoidably formalised communication systems. The subsequent feelings of remoteness (reinforced by the sheer numbers of staff employed) make the realisation of the administrative tasks identified above that much more difficult.

(II) Social Workers as Administrators

As social workers, we are part of the administration, share its tasks and, as a consequence, get caught up in a network of rights and privileges and obligations and constraints. To help identify these, I use as a framework, the tasks outlined above.

(1) FORMULATION OF OBJECTIVES

The agency gives us our objectives (focus) and while we may feel this as constraining, nevertheless it is the agency which gives us the rights and privileges of positional authority to carry out the tasks associated with the objectives. A given focus can help if a client (to some degree) sees the objectives as valid, helping to establish the common goals needed for effective work. Identified goals and positional authority also assist our dealings with other agencies. Moreover, administration may rely on us and authorise us, in order to discharge its functions, to individualise objectives in a particular case—given that agency objectives are often diffuse.

We are also part of the evaluation process and ought (in our clients' interests) to accept evaluation of our work and contribute to the agency's evaluation by research, reports, statistics, etc.

(2) IMPLEMENT ACTION TO ACHIEVE OBJECTIVES

We are an essential means by which many agency objectives are attained and we accept obligations to work effectively in return for the right to adequate facilities. Any agency which does not provide the facilities cannot expect its staff to fulfil their obligations. The way we do our job will have a bearing on the agency's ability to acquire resources in that clients and others will evaluate our performance in achieving objectives. We *are* the agency to them, often; its reputation is in our hands—and the reputation may be crucial when it comes to willingness to provide resources. It may be part of our responsibility to add to resources where we can, for example by recruiting voluntary help; and it is certainly part of our job to see that the resources we have are used to the best advantage. We are ourselves, a resource and so part of the deployment; so we should see that we deploy our time effectively and maintain ourselves as a resource by keeping up-to-date and training for the future—with a right to the agency's assistance with this.

(3) PROMULGATE VALUES

We do this chiefly through our work which demonstrates our values and we should see that what we do does not conflict with what we say our values are. Work expression is often informal, inferred by clients, agency colleagues and colleagues from other agencies and disciplines from the way we work with them in specific instances; but formal opportunities (addressing meetings, writing to the press, joining committees, etc.) also exist. Formal and informal expression applies both internally and externally and requires not only our understanding of people, but of people as practitioners, people in groups, people as part of organisations and organisations as such, since we are dealing with them in all of these contexts. It also requires that we have a clear idea of what we are and what we are about and why. Others are not going to understand unless we accept the obligation to tell them; nor can we ask them for the privilege of their understanding of us unless we accept the obligation to understand them.

(4) TANGIBLE ARRANGEMENTS

Many tangible arrangements are mentioned or indicated above. Perhaps more than anything it means communicating: orally and in writing, internally and externally—appointments, staff meetings, projects, research, committees, reports, case conferences, letters, telephone calls, etc.—which are the essence of good teamwork. These are frequently just as important as what goes on in interviews for meeting client needs, and often call for as much skill. But they are time-consuming, and under pressure it is often the communication which goes—to the client's detriment. Communication ought to have an appropriate priority, both among workers, and within the agency to see that its staff have the time and facilities needed for it.

We have seen the incipient tension between social workers and administrators and given we are both (even without any seniority) we are sometimes forced to ask 'whose side am I on?' The degree to which this tension arises will vary: where social work is the only agency activity tension may rarely arise—but at the price of command over few resources. When we add resources, that is when we add a social service or welfare function and become involved with its administration and the accountability that goes with it (from determining who will get the resources through to auditing the accounts afterwards), the problems really begin—though with the advantage of resource-command. Five areas of problem have been identified:

(a) Mountains of time-consuming paperwork, for which social workers are not trained, which 'prevents' them getting on with what they are trained for and for which administration is blamed. Administrators may be culpable (and if so, social workers should tell them so); but we may also need to acknowledge that effective work on behalf of clients involves more than interviewing. If foster parents do not get paid because of our administrative oversights or incompetence, they are not going to be happy about it.

(b) Involvement in a service/welfare function as well as a social work function (if they are separable) raises issues of who does what: that is, becomes a question of deployment. Do trained social workers do both (even though trained staff are in short supply) or do we employ separate welfare workers? The Central Council for Education and Training in Social Work's commitment to two levels of training (a Certificate of Social Service as well as a Certificate of Qualification in Social Work) implies a distinction can be drawn and C.Q.S.W.

trained workers in future will have to learn to make such distinctions. Some have felt bogged down by the welfare function, again feeling they are not doing what they were trained for; but if we employ welfare workers how do we distinguish what is welfare and what is casework? In many cases both are needed: do we then involve two workers, let the social worker undertake the welfare as well, or risk a welfare worker getting 'out of his depth'? A particular case may start off as one but become the other: do we then continue with the same worker or hand over to another? In facing this problem of delegation to ancillary workers (for lack of a better term) we are not alone: medicine and teaching have faced problems of the use of medical and teaching aides, though so far, they have largely decided against them. Ways round are possible: for example, an initial diagnosis by the social worker who decides what is needed and who shall do it, but retains a supervisory function for any welfare work. The implication here is that perhaps straight from training, a social worker may be involved in elements of staff supervision and the deployment of others and we would need to incorporate training for this even in so-called 'basic' professional training courses. It could not be left to any post-professional training courses—though it could become the responsibility of an immediate post-professional in-service course.

(c) The introduction of an administrative function with resource control elements brings in factors which may be inimical to casework. Instead of a normative compliance system, the worker can exploit material reward—which may be tantamount to coercion where needs are desperate. Even where the worker does not, the client may fear he will. The client may respond with disapproval (expressed or hidden for fear of the consequences) or with calculative involvement—playing along. These responses are at variance with what good casework needs—frankness and trust. It is for such reasons that Toren[2] argues for the separation of welfare from social work and suggests that before social work can be effective, clients must have basic necessities secured. Where we have used coercion or material reward, it is difficult subsequently to use normative compliance systems.

(d) Problems arise in staff or student supervision where the supervisor's function of assisting professional skill development are combined with administrative functions of controlling resources, seeing rules, policy and procedures are followed and protecting clients' interests. The professional development function needs to be supportive; but can support be given by someone in a hierarchical position who will have a crucial say in whether a student passes or staff are promoted? One needs a normative compliance system, the other smacks of material reward. Professional development requires a degree of intimacy between supervisor and student or staff member and is bound to contain certain personal elements from the very nature of the material they are examining (aspects of the student's personality as they affect interaction with his client, for example); yet the administrative element in supervision requires a degree of distance and objectivity. Can a student be really frank (as professional development requires) when his career, on the administrative side, may be at risk? It is not easy in supervision anyway, for a student to reveal what really went on in an interview without that student being under yet more pressure to put a gloss on it. Aware of the difficulties, does administration try to insure itself by playing safe in staff/student selection—choosing self-images? Given that younger students and staff tend to be more radical, is any generation gap reinforced by the administration orientation of older supervisors with more to lose?

(e) We are often caught as 'middlemen' between clients and administrative decisions regarding allocation or the rules which govern allocations, and may be tempted to wriggle out of difficulty by blaming 'them' to our clients when we have to say 'no'. This is indefensible: the client is no better off and it may introduce a collusive element into the relationship. We can only tell them 'no', explain why, and try to help clients with their feelings about it. This is not to say that there may not be much that we ought to be doing and can do, outside the interview situation.

If we are administrators in part, then we have the responsibility and opportunity within our organisations to criticise constructively about administrative matters, whether objectives, resources, policies, resource allocation or procedures. Things can be changed. Some are afraid promotion may be jeopardised by criticism; but to do so constructively can also mark one out as one of the 'up and coming'.

I have heard Directors of Social Services, for example, complain that their staff tell them nothing, that they work in a desperately uncomfortable vacuum and would be only too glad to respond to staff approaches and initiatives. It could be that staff prefer not to communicate, merely complain among themselves, since if the administrators did respond positively, and the workers' fantasies and projections were destroyed, they would lose the comfort of a very convenient scapegoat and have to face, at least in part, the responsibility for the implementation and consequences of the changes made at their suggestion.

Finally, remember neither administration nor social work are static: each is developing new techniques and concepts. Social workers will have to learn to cope with computer systems, and administrators with the enormous developments in social work thinking and practice of the last few years. Both have to cope with external change—be it changes in priorities demanded by the Chronically Sick and Disabled Persons Act, or the rising demands for consumer participation—and neither might be happy with such changes.

References

1. P. M. Blau and W. R. Scott, *Formal Organisations* (Routledge & Kegan Paul), 1963.
2. Nina Toren, *Social Work: the Case of a Semi-profession* (Sage Publications), 1972.

Further Reading

For much of the material in this chapter, I am indebted to three books: *Social Work and the Sociology of Organisations* by Gilbert Smith; *An Introduction to Administration for Social Workers* by Joyce Warham (both published by Routledge & Kegan Paul in their Library of Social Work series); and Anthony Forder's *Social Casework and Administration* (published by Faber & Faber). There is also some useful material on this subject in B. J. Heraud's *Sociology and Social Work* (published by Pergamon) and some excellent chapters in Nina Toren's book referred to above, especially those in which she looks at relations between social workers and agency hierarchies and the influence on relations between workers and clients of the resource allocation function. Some of the dangers inherent in this function for practice are explored by Joel Handler in his book *The Coercive Social Worker* (published by the Academic Press) though the gist of his argument is admirably expressed in his article 'The coercive children's officer' published in *New Society*, 3.10.68. How the organisation of social work departments might be geared to concepts of client need is explored in an article by Gilbert Smith and Robert Harris in the Spring, 1972 issue of the *British Journal of Social Work*; and there is an excellent article by Dr. R. W. Rowbottom entitled 'Organising social services: hierarchy or ...?' in the journal *Public Service* (Autumn 1973).

Discussion

This topic often generates a great deal of animated discussion. Students typically express a great deal of hostility towards an unspecified 'them'—the administrators—who are blamed for denying social workers the resources they and their clients need; for enmeshing them in infuriating 'red tape'; and for making decisions about clients over their heads which the social workers regard as their professional prerogative. Students often fail to see the administrative aspects of their own task and hate the thought that in a few years they, too, might be part of 'them' through promotion—asking for career structures that leave them with little or no administrative responsibility as they see it.

Many students are uncomfortable with the 'middleman' role—not so much where they are able to provide material assistance, from which they derive (quite fairly) gratification, but more particularly where they have to tell clients they cannot provide it. In this latter circumstance they are hard pressed not to find someone else to blame for this and to share their anger with their clients. A few students (while elsewhere expressing a deep concern for poverty) still find the welfare function irksome and getting in the way of, or being different from 'real' casework. Others wish they had much more to offer in the way of resources and discretionary powers over its allocation; yet are rather jolted (though they see the validity of them) by suggestions that resource control powers may be inimical to what they need to establish in the way of a relationship with the client for other casework purposes. Sometimes students will rail at the way discretionary powers are used by, say, the Department of Health and Social Security, but do not see that similar valedictions could be directed at them. They are confident their discretion would be used 'properly' (despite the lack of an appeal system) while the Supplementary Benefits Commission's discretion (even with an appeal system) is not.

Effective communication with the upper reaches of the hierarchy are often seen as non-existent: 'they' do not know what it is like, what is going on, at the grass roots level and are not concerned about it. Social workers are expected to care for clients when no-one at the top seems to care about them. Communication, if it goes up the bureaucratic system at all, is filtered in terms that the higher reaches would like to hear rather than informing them of the reality. Channels of communication outside the hierarchical structure are often sought. Students' depression and feelings of being helpless to change anything are often evident.

On another point, I have often been struck by the way in which knowledge, experience and skill available to social workers (whether diagnostic or in relationships) *vis-à-vis* their clients is so seldom applied to the way the organisation of the agency is run or the way the people in it function. One might expect more of social workers, given their training, in handling relations in their own and with other departments.

Given the strength of student feeling, getting discussion going is rarely a problem and there is usually plenty of scope for social work teachers (field or college based) to try to modify views where this is needed or to assist students to think rather more constructively how situations they so rightly see as needing change, might be changed.

CHAPTER XII

Professionalism Re-examined

Professionalism in social work is something of a contentious issue these days, with arguments centering around 'is social work a profession or not and if not, should it be?'

Is it? The texts seem to suggest that new professions emerge

(1) From non occupations;
(2) By claiming a special package of skills;
(3) By claiming specialisation of partial skills of others;
(4) Via new technology.

Social work's emergence has elements of each of these. It has come from being spare time and voluntary to full time, paid. It claims a package of skills (with the implications of a professional body identifying them and formulating them to make them transmissible, and largely controlling and validating the transmission process). It is arguable social work has specialised what used to be the partial functions of a wide range of others from Lady Bountifuls, Dr. Finlay type G.P.'s—perhaps even the extended family itself. The new technology social work derives from could be considered to be the new knowledge emerging from psychology, sociology and social administration, with an acknowledgement to the general technological development of society which has not only created some of the problems, but also provided the wealth which enables us to focus concern on the quality of life and afford paid staff to assist with it.

The stages in becoming a profession (some of which may occur concurrently) are said to be:

Becoming a full-time, paid occupation;
Development of training for it;
Development of a professional organisation;
Emergence of a task definition;
A stage of internal conflict between 'old' and 'new' practitioners;

Competition for recognition from existing professions;
Pressure for legal measures to endorse professional status.

Social work has come through the first three of these stages. It is still wrestling with task definition; and there has certainly been some tension between groups that might loosely be called 'old' and 'new'—though whether the distinction is between the 'old' non-trained and the 'new' trained, or between 'old' trained and 'new' trained is hard to say: perhaps both. Social workers would like to see other professions acknowledge their competence and in this sense competition for recognition has certainly begun and in some respects, been conceded. Pressure for legal endorsement has not seriously begun, if only because the whole issue (as I said at the beginning) is contentious: but at least there is toying with the idea of a register of social workers of some sort, which may be the embryonic stages of such pressure.

But social work still has some way to go before it acquires all the attributes ascribed to a full profession: high income, high status/prestige, influence, high educational requirements, autonomy of practice, professional control of education and recruitment, licensed practice and a monopoly position, a system of ethics and discipline, a cohesive and committed membership of a professional organisation maintained by intensive socialisation, a service ideal, guaranteed standards of performance, and privileged communication. An occupation will not become a full profession, though, unless the activity is valued by society and incompetent practice is regarded as dangerous in a significant area: particularly in crisis situations requiring a wide range of competence.

Professional status infers the existence of a professional organisation of which membership is virtually compulsory, and based on qualification.

The distinctive marks of a full profession have been identified as:

(1) *A body of knowledge*, sufficiently specialised to make it beyond lay comprehension, determined by the profession and communicated (especially to new recruits) by the profession, which will decide standards required.

(2) *A system of ethics*, formulated by the profession, subscribed

to by members who are registered, with a system of punishing and/or disbarring offenders from practice.

(3) *Skills*, determined by the profession, with standards laid down in which recruits are examined.

(4) *Autonomy of action*, whether self employed, employed in a professional organisation, or holding a position within another organisation. Autonomy involves no supervision, or supervision only by a more experienced member of the profession.

(5) *Exclusive right to practice*, usually backed by a statutory form of licensing controlled by the profession, guaranteeing standards of performance, but ensuring adequate recruitment. Authorisation by society in this way infers that clientele will also accord authority to the professional and allow themselves to be guided.

(6) *Characteristic inter-action with clients*, limited to the specialised activity, affectively neutral, and in which client needs are uppermost.

On the basis of the above criteria, it has been argued that social work is only a semi-profession.

(1) BODY OF KNOWLEDGE

This is said to be insufficient for full professional status: it is not sufficiently specialised, being little more than common knowledge, or is derived from other areas. Evidence for its insufficiency is the short training period required. I would argue, however, that we have specialised knowledge in two areas:

(i) The impact of stress on personal functioning.

(ii) The impact of intervention (relationship and its use) and have begun to feed this specialised knowledge to other professions where it can be of value to them.

What needs to be known for social work practice has generally been worked out by the profession, and it has typically been conveyed by members of it—whether teachers in educational establishments or field supervisors. But this determination and conveying has not been under the complete control of the profession. Earlier, psychiatric and medical social work were under professional control, but child care and probation were under the control of the Home Office (though they employed professionals to manage training), and welfare work under the control of the Council for Training in Social Work—a quasi-independent body, by no means entirely professional (though, again, employing professionals as managers.) The new Central Council for Education and Training in Social Work has been modelled on C.T.S.W. lines, but still does not cover training for all methods of social work: group and community work courses are largely outside their sphere as yet, though they may well be incorporated soon. The British Association of Social Workers does not really include these groups yet, either.

The key issue is the accrediting and supervision of training courses, involving the acceptability of the syllabus, and teaching staff; and the adequacy of resources (from libraries to training placements). Here the C.C.E.T.S.W. has a difficult task involving:

(a) The bringing together of specialised and disparate pre-existing training courses and identifying a common core in the light of current needs.

(b) Identifying, in a time of radical change in social work itself, what training is needed and viable.

(c) Delicate relationships with autonomous bodies such as universities and the Council for National Academic Awards while keeping in mind the needs of employers.

(d) Delicate relations between social work professionals and those academic disciplines on which social work still depends and how these are to be incorporated and taught.

The content of professional courses is still a matter of debate, while the needs for post-professional training and its accrediting are only at the preliminary discussion stage.

(2) ETHICS

At best these are only vaguely formulated (for example the B.A.S.W. discussion document)[1] though an ethical tradition has existed for many years in social work—though it has been said this is no more than 'middle class' ethics, or derived from medicine (plus a nod to reformism). There are no systems of subscription, registration, or punishment; nor are these likely in the near future. It is difficult to see how any systems can be effective without an accompanying exclusive right to practise.

(3) SKILL

The determination and control over skills is in much the same state of confusion and lack of full professional control as the body of knowledge. The C.C.E.T.S.W. have issued no guidelines of their own (though some exist from earlier periods) and seem to be devolving this responsibility more to educational establishments—though retaining a degree of control via accreditation and supervision of courses and approval of external examiners. Evaluation is still confined to the training stage, not professional practice. Employers exercise some control over this, but not the profession.

(4) AUTONOMY

While social work has some autonomy (if only because transactions between client and worker are typically unseen), it is not complete: its specialisation is not fully recognised by the public or other professions, it has a less firmly established right to privileged communication, and it is much more under administrative control. This is bound to happen to a degree when social workers are involved with the distribution of goods as well as their services and these goods are not generally necessary to maintain life, are distributed to particular groups of clients (some of whom may be stigmatised and involve ambivalent feelings on the part of the providers). We therefore, have no right of *prescription*; but our area of prescription is increasing—for example care orders under the Children and Young Persons Act 1969, and administrators, magistrates and other professions may be now rather more diffident in turning down professional social work opinion. Our autonomy is growing.

Four other reasons have been suggested for social work's remaining lack of autonomy:

(a) The majority of social workers are women and there are links between social work and women's social status, roles and socialisation. As 'inferior' beings, they are not accorded the occupational autonomy of men and are subject to more supervision. Other occupations dominated by women (teaching, nursing) remain semi-professions, and even where women have obtained entry to male-dominated full professions they remain small in numbers and influence. This is attributed to women's two roles: work and family, with family predominating. In turn this leads to a reduced identity with the profession, and a lowered inclination for collective action which may be needed for full professional status. With a break in her career for family reasons, a woman does not secure as much promotion or, therefore, influence. Through socialisation, women seem more committed to an individualised caring approach, with satisfaction derived from personal contacts with clients—again inhibiting collective action, especially if this involves say, strike action which might hurt clients' interests. However, now social work is a more attractive career and attracting more men, the force of this argument may diminish in future.

(b) Most social work recruits are drawn from social classes III and IV, for whom social work represents some upward social mobility. No status is likely to accrue to a profession with this recruitment base, and recruits may bring with them an inbuilt deference to those other professional groups whose recruitment base is more typically classes I and II.

Moreover, this recruitment base may influence the social workers' clientele (typically classes III, IV and V). Classes I and II seek their 'social work' help from the established professions of medicine, the law—even perhaps the Marriage Guidance Council with its class II counsellors; or can 'buy' their way out of trouble by sending difficult children to boarding school for example. Again, by a 'halo effect', little status may accrue to a profession with this clientele, and in turn be reflected in the recruitment base.

Now social work has a higher proportion of graduates as recruits, again the force of this argument may be diminishing.

(c) Status, high income, etc. in social work tend to come from promotion into administration, leading to an identity with administration to the detriment of the professional identity. There is a distinct difference here from the older professions where status remains combined with practice (consultants for example). If more Directors with social work qualifications are appointed, however, Social Services Departments might become more akin to professional organisations (though lay control would remain). So this argument may also lose some force.

(d) Social work may also feel guilty about its claim to professionalism and autonomy, knowing this is not justified, but rejecting alternative identifications with white or blue collar workers, feeling a
'cut above' these, so pressing for the only alternative, however unjustified.

(5) EXCLUSIVE RIGHT TO PRACTISE

There is no licensing system for social work, nor is this likely
in the immediate future. It is not yet regarded as sufficiently specialised or 'dangerous'. But even licensing would not immediately give
exclusive right to practise—only distinguish between 'approved' and
unapproved practitioners. In any event, to exclude would be very
difficult; it would mean establishing distinctions between voluntary
and professional work; and distinguishing professional work from
the social work element in other professions (medicine, teaching,
health visiting, etc.). It is the only profession which tries to give
away its expertise to others (including clients).

If we have no exclusive right to practise, we have at least got
to the stage where training is a major pre-occupation, and pressure
for training is producing results. Training has to balance the need
for numbers against educational requirements; but with no lack of
recruits, the bottlenecks are rather more likely to be in employment
and training opportunities rather than recruitment.

(6) CHARACTERISTIC INTER-ACTION

Social workers would concur that inter-action is limited to a specialised activity: problem solving; but not all clients may yet see
it this way—and not all social work writers, even, who suggest that
the activity is now so diffuse it can hardly be regarded as specialised.
The affective neutrality of social work is not quite the same as in
other professions: while we assist whether we like people or not,
we have to establish a relationship (though this remains purposive)
since it is a primary channel of social work help. Client needs are
uppermost, but clients are more likely to have their own ideas about
what is wrong and how it is to be put right than in other professional

spheres, so we are much more dependent for success on establishing mutually agreed goals and engaging clients' co-operation. We are not nearly so able to determine goals and decide on methods as other professionals—and as a consequence have not the same aura of omnipotence or mystique, perhaps. On the other hand, not all our clients can withdraw if they are not satisfied with our services; and even those that do may have more difficulty in getting another social worker than they do another doctor or solicitor.

The particular problems of a profession are said to be:

(i) Conflict between self-interest and the service ideal;

(ii) Maintenance of professional cohesion to avoid sub-groupings.

Both of these are linked to questions of professional identity.

Social workers often find themselves in conflict when they press for good salaries and a career structure to recompense for a tough job and to ensure an adequate flow of able recruits in times of competition from other careers or professions: or for adequate numbers or working conditions to enable them to do their job properly. At the same time they are aware that their clients are suffering from lack of resources and they ought to get priority, especially at times when resources are scarce. They often feel guilty about and separated from their clients' experience, when they are 'all right, Jack'.

It is arguable whether all social workers (especially community workers) see themselves as professionally cohesive anyway. Those community workers particularly, who see themselves or their work as basically to produce radical change, are more identified with politics than social work. Even those identified with the profession of social work are divided about means even if not about ends.

For such reasons it is suggested we are only semi-professionals and that we should settle for this: we will never be full professionals. Given there are social work elements at least, in many others' tasks, which we will never be able to separate out (in theory or practice); that we are experts in the 'ordinary' or 'common sense'; that our concern is for the quality of life rather than vital issues of life and death or liberty; and that we also try to convey our skills to others (particularly our clients) eroding our exclusiveness; we will never be accorded the autonomy of the 'full' professions. It has also been suggested that all the caring professions are inevitably caught up in politics and will never, therefore, be completely autonomous.

Though not yet a fully established profession, social work has come a long way towards it, and the process is continuing. Being 'on the brink' perhaps, raises a number of issues.

(a) Are we ready for full professionalism? It would give us opportunity, but with it would go a frightening responsibility (as individuals and as a professional group) and be accompanied by a critical evaluation (by society and our clients) also on a personal and professional level. In many ways we may not be ready yet.

(b) Are we being pushed into it? There are many social pressures for something to be *done* about social problems. Social workers have claimed they can do something for years: now we may be called upon to try and substantiate our claims. Do we like this, or would we be more comfortable on the sidelines, criticising?

(c) We are still debating what social work is, what its aims should be, what its base of operations should be, the knowledge, ethics and skills involved, its ideological commitment, what specialisms it involves, whether we should strive for a register of social workers, etc. The 'crunch' question becomes, in effect, do we want to be a profession or not?

Many social workers are against full professionalism and think we have gone too far already. Their arguments might be summarised as:

(i) To become professionalised means being acceptable to the establishment, basically supporting it, and developing a stake in perpetuating it. Given that the bulk of social problems are the products of the existing power and resource allocation system, social workers should be encouraging their clients and joining them in their efforts to overthrow the existing structure and establishing a society based on the co-ownership of property and democratic control.

(ii) Professionalism puts distance between worker and client: the existing distance of class is reinforced by a professional training which emphasises psychological factors and individualised therapeutic methods while client needs are primarily practical and the remedies structural.

(iii) Professionalism perpetuates the helper/helped distinction which insults the client, and ensures his continued dependency on, and subservience to the very system which created his problems. The social work aim must be to help the client really cure his problems—mainly through collective action with his fellows.

(iv) Professionalism will almost inevitably lead to a pre-occupation with self-interest.

The protagonists of professionalism would argue:

(i) That it is the best way to safeguard client interests by ensuring standards of practice (including ethics).

(ii) That by no means all clients' ills are structural: even in a perfect society many would need professional help. Where ills are structural, a profession may be in a better position to bring about reform, since it has more influence where it counts.

(iii) That effective reforming involves many of our professional skills anyway (following the client for example) and training may be just as distancing through imposing a sociological answer to problems, equally alien to the client.

(iv) All good practice aims at making the client self-directing—and would not exclude assisting self-help groups.

This argument is confused by existing concepts of professionalism, largely derived from analyses of existing situations in (predominantly) medicine and law. The validity of applying such derived conceptualisation to social work is debatable.

Looking at existing models we often do not like what we see. Professionalism derives from knowledge and its inevitable concomitant specialisation. Specialised knowledge brings power—not only power over individual clients (who cannot challenge the knowledge) but also social power. Society's dependency on the specialists has been used to gain privileges such as exclusive right to practise, which in turn have been manipulated (despite the controls of the service ideal) to enhance status, prestige, remuneration, etc.; i.e. professionalism has got caught up into the class system of society if indeed, it is not a product of it—and there is quite some evidence of this.

Given that professional equals knowledge, access to this via the education system has always had a class bias. Hence recruitment to the professions has been typically social class I and II. Reinforcement of this recruitment base has come partly from ideas of social acceptability to peers (i.e. the social interaction and solidarity which some sociologists mention as one of the prime factors in the development of professional cohesion) and reflected in selection of recruits for training; partly (especially in medicine) from a kind of nepotism; and partly (especially in law) from the need to possess capital to get into and establish oneself in the professional group and practice.

The connotations of professional *style* or manner also have an effect. The image is urbane, courteous, competent—perhaps to the point of being patronising: 'put yourself in my hands; all you need do is co-operate'. This style is often reinforced by a spacious office, and big desk. Already at a disadvantage because he is the one with the needs, the class III, IV and V client is put at a further social disadvantage.

The whole setting is one that smacks to him of power and privilege and makes demands on social skills that he rarely gets the chance to practise. Inevitably he is at a disadvantage. This disadvantage is not felt by the class II client, able to treat as a peer, or the class I client who has the means to pick and choose his advisers and to whom even the professional may become subservient, rather like a tradesman. Style, then, is no more than a manifestation again of class/power relationships and an adoption of the way that typically the upper middle class handles its relations with other classes. In other words, it has little to do with *task* but is a carry over of pre-existing class relations, subsequently rationalised as necessary to the professional relationship.

Given the social work ethos, it is understandable that such overtones of professionalism are rejected. But I do not think it is valid to reject professionalism for this reason. What we need is a new model: a professionalism *which arises from the task*.

As a beginning let us take the existing model and see what is valid in terms of social work task; task being defined as assisting psycho-social functioning.

Task certainly requires knowledge—of what makes individuals, groups, communities and societies 'tick', what resources of all kinds can be brought to bear to remedy ills—including the resource of the self, which implies self knowledge.

Task will also require ethics. If knowledge is power, then society and our clients will need reassurance that this power will be used towards ends of which they approve: that our integrity is guaranteed in some way. If society is not satisfied it will impose safeguards such as lay/political/bureaucratic controls (and we know how cramping these can be at times in terms of task) while our clients will withhold until they are personally reassured about the individual worker and again cramp the task until this reassurance is forthcoming.

Without ethics (and knowledge and skill too) we will have little autonomy and we know from practice, how lack of it distorts our work for our clients.

In terms of skill, we shall achieve little unless we understand what the difficulties are and this implies a skill at receiving (eliciting and decoding) all communication and focussing it in an assessment. Clients will feel frustrated if their messages are not understood; at best we will not be assisting them effectively, at worst they will break off with problems unresolved or even exacerbated. Without assessment we will not be able to make our contribution (to put it no higher) to objectives (goals) nor to working out means (methods) to achieve them. This implies an ability to communicate outwards effectively—to clients, to colleagues involved in multi-faceted situations, or the other people, groups or organisations involved in the problems or the remedies. (And to communicate outward to colleagues and others also implies an ability to hear what they are communicating to us: 'inwards' again.) Without skills of this nature, again task is vitiated.

Exclusive right to practise I would reject, especially if this meant avoiding equipping clients with knowledge, skill, etc. for them to use, since this is an essence of our task. Nor can we deny our knowledge and skill to those others who need them to more effectively carry out their task, or again people will be suffering.

We would also reject the existing concept of characteristic interaction with clients since our type of involvement through the relationship is essential to our task (though it may not be for other sorts of professionals).

I would like to go a stage further and also apply the same test of task validity to the principles and methods by which we operationalise the professional task:

For principles, I go to Biestek[2].

(1) Individualisation is valid. There are common, general elements in situations which psychology and sociology have helped us to identify, but we need to comprehend how these generálisations apply in this particular instance. If clients feel categorised they will feel misunderstood, humiliated or angry and perhaps break off, vitiating the task once more.

(2) Acceptance and non-judgmentalism. Clients are often judged as failures or unacceptable and to repeat these processes merely invites repetition of the process which brought them to us anyway. They will hide, not communicate fully, we will not understand and not be able to assist effectively.

(3) Purposeful expression of feeling is valid. Given that all situations have objective and subjective elements, (with the latter the more crucial sometimes) we will not understand or be able to assist effectively unless these are communicated.

(4) Client self-determination is valid. We play God if we think we always know best; demean and humiliate the client and rob him of motivation—all of which militate against task.

(5) Confidentiality is valid. If people cannot trust our confidence again they will not communicate and the task is negated.

(6) Controlled emotional involvement is valid, though I have left this till last since it raises a number of issues. Controlled has connotations which I do not like. It smacks of the affective neutrality which in certain respects, we have discarded already; and I suspect we use it to justify not getting involved where this raises feelings in us (even though we need to get involved in terms of task). I prefer the term directed—i.e. getting involved in ways which assist and avoiding involvement which will not.

The fear of 'over-involvement' (so warned against by casework teachers) has another association for me, which harks back to what I was saying about style and the model of professionalism which we have taken over from elsewhere. The professional model derives from what is also typically I:I practice, using verbal means of communication a great deal, based on the formal interview, at least as the precursor of any action that might be needed. Casework assimilated this model without difficulty, failing to recognise that it created barriers to the task in many circumstances, and even created barriers between social workers. It has taken us a long time to accept that what group, community and residential workers were doing was also social work, not something different because they did not use the model of professionalism casework had adopted. We have had to learn from groupworkers that we can communicate in and out, assess and contribute to objectives and means through *activity*. We have had to learn from community workers that advocacy, negotiating, communicating with and intervening in *systems* is as much a part of task as communicating in the I:I interview; and we are beginning to learn from residential workers that we can use feeding, toileting, plastering knees, cuddling (touch), bedtimes and washing up times as task opportunities. Interviews do not have to be the formal affairs caseworkers have made them. They can effectively happen in the interstices of other activities, and arise out of activities. In other words, the caseworker's great fear of socialising may on occasions be a defensive myth and that if a client is more able to communicate over a pint at the local pub then it is professionally valid to 'interview' in this way. We have had to learn that you cannot use the traditional ways when dealing with children and inarticulate adults, anyhow. This is not to decry the traditional casework way, which still has its validity, but to recognise that the task may demand that we get out of the straitjacket of saying social work can only be done from the derived professional model. We have things to learn from each other that will enable us all, whatever method we use, to be more effective—i.e. to get rid of the block of style, and focus on task.

I know that Biestek's principles have limitations and qualifications and I am not denying these: I will return to them later, but in another context.

For validating methods, I am using Hollis's[3] categorisation. The fact that these were established for casework will, perhaps, make my point of validity whatever the method, more strongly—even if the categorisation has to be stretched a little to be encompassing. Sustaining techniques are valid. Clients will need nurture, empathy, support, encouragement, at times. We will need to establish ourselves, too, as 'that sort of person' before we can establish a useable relationship or our help become acceptable to others. For us, the *way* we help is as important as the help: what we *are* as vital as what we do.

Direction—by which I mean those elements from giving information via advice to degrees of control (i.e. the use of authority)—is valid since at times clients will need it and look to us for it. Our skill will be involved in knowing what direction to give, when and to what degree.

Ventilation—largely the purposeful expression of feelings of Biestek, which we have already discussed, is valid. Apart from its place in communication and assessment, it can be a relief and clarification to clients as well as the essential precursor of the employment of other methods.

Reflective discussion is valid. Exploration, clarification, getting matters into proportion, weighing up alternatives, are all vital before effective action is undertaken—and may be the only action the worker need take if the client has the capacity for the necessary implementation.

Referral is valid. Many of the problems—or the resources needed to deal with them—are outside the scope of social work or our agencies; but our task demands that we see the aid needed from elsewhere is brought into play.

Material aid is also valid. Many problems are material and psychosocial functioning crippled without material resource.

Environmental manipulation is valid. Many client problems are engendered by the attitudes, feelings of others and the social processes they are caught up in. Even if the problems are not engendered there, to assist the client we may need to call upon these networks or sustain them in the process of meeting client's needs.

What the texts do not usually look at are the professional implications of what they are saying, though this is the crux of so many of the current debates in social work. If we accept that a professional requires knowledge, skill and ethics and that we will not achieve greater autonomy until we have established these, we are still grappling with what knowledge we need; what skills we have and what we still need to develop; while ethics are only now being formulated. We are still grappling with problems of how do we make knowledge and skill transmissible—to new practitioners (with all this implies in terms of student selection, curricula, teaching methods, evaluation and who should control the whole process); and to existing practitioners. Given that social work as well as society is in a constant state of change, how do we update performance or monitor that performance is still adequate in terms of developing criteria? Transmission is not just an internal matter either: we need to convey to others (employers, colleagues, clients) what we do, how we are changing, and find out their responses.

If we accept the Biestek principles are there not also implications here for others too? We would not seek to impose our principles on colleagues from other disciplines, since their task may require others. Other disciplines might require categorisation rather than individualisation; they might not push acceptance, client self-determination or expression of feelings as far as we do for perfectly good reasons. But for a co-operative effort to resolve clients' problems, we need to understand and respect their principles and ask them to do the same with ours. This implies our conveying them formally or informally, since if we do not, no one else will. This may be especially important as regards our employers, since agency and workers are virtually indivisible. Confusion and conflict for all concerned are almost inevitable if while the professional worker is trying to convey individualisation, non-judgmentalism and confidentiality, other agency staff, or the very premises, are by implication conveying categorisation, judgment and scant regard for confidences. In Social Services Departments, now multifunctional and multi-disciplinary, with professional social work becoming a minority activity (however influential it remains) the situation is becoming more complex.

If we accept Hollis's methods, again what are the professional implications? I feel they are enormous, and can sketch only a few.

Sustaining needs time, for example, with all this implies in terms of numbers of staff and caseloads.

Direction asks for many things, from sound, comprehensive and up-to-date reference material, through opportunities for staff refresher courses, to a thorough questioning of our professional scope, role, and the ethics of our responsibilities for statutory intervention.

Ventilation and reflective discussion have implications again for knowledge, skill, time and facilities.

Referral again needs information, time and good means of communication from telephones, typists and records, to opportunities to meet, discuss and plan with others, since referral usually means parting with only part of a situation and thus involving on-going teamwork.

Material aid means information about what is there, where, how we get it and acting as negotiator or advocate if necessary, to see our clients get it. If the aid needed is not there, it means finding ways to ensure that it is. This may mean initially the hard slog of collecting facts and figures of need to convince others (and how bad we are at this).

But it also means, to use the systems analysis approach, identifying the client group (whether this is an individual, a specific group such as the mentally handicapped; or whether the deprivation applies across several groups such as recipients of social security; or even to a certain strata of society); identifying the 'target' group (i.e. the group which has the power to remedy matters, whether this be our own agency, a local or national organisation or institution) and identifying the means by which influence or pressure can be brought to bear (the worker individually, a staff group, a professional association, a pressure group, a political party, etc.) to remedy matters. We will need to determine tactics—from information, through education to pressure or confrontation.

Environmental manipulation has much the same ramifications as material aid and may be closely allied to it in the sense that material allocations are reflections often of the attitudes and value systems which environmental manipulations seeks to change. Altering values and attitudes is possibly even more difficult, though, than obtaining material aid: we are dealing with less tangible or quantifiable yet more personal areas, arousing more threat in various ways. Often we are asking change of people with a considerable stake in maintaining things as they are. Again, after our 'systems analysis' we have to determine targets and tactics.

What I am talking about is, in effect, the reformist tradition in social work. It is a professional necessity in terms of task, but it is the most difficult element to incorporate into the concept of professional for a number of reasons:

(a) Reform activity is by no means the monopoly of social workers. A wide range of far more numerous groups from conservation societies via trade unions to political parties are also concerned, at least with certain aspects. Indeed for too long we have perhaps regarded ourselves as the exclusive 'carers' and have not shared the responsibility with others. We have not only taken all the world's burden on our shoulders and groaned under the weight, but have also speciously claimed a role that was not exclusively ours to the detriment of our relations with others, putting ourselves into the position of a very convenient scapegoat for others when things go wrong..

How we share our responsibilities with others may vary: we may inform, 'ginger', or pressurise from the inside or the outside, or work in collaboration. We may not be the only profession that is facing problems of where reform fits in: medicine, law, teaching, nursing, have all had their problems and still have.

(b) There is no such person as a professional social reformer, nor do I see how there can be. Reform movements need a base, be it populist, political, trade union or what. The range of bases needed for general and/or specific issues seems so disparate that it becomes very hard to see what common ground there can be for a profession of 'reformer' to emerge.

(c) The discharge of the professional responsibilities emerging from our task is probably wider than can be encompassed by our employment situation. The scope and the implications of what I am saying would be too much for any one agency, however large, and while we may have a responsibility to try to extend the scope of the agency's concept of the professional social work task, we will have to accept, I feel, that there is a distinction to be drawn between what is professional and what appertains to employment. Part of our professional responsibilities will have to be discharged outside our employment.

The implications of what I have said for social work knowledge, skills, training, etc. are enormous; nor is this concept of professional a comfortable concept. It is a good deal more tense than current formulations. But it would seem to me that tension is endemic in social work, given its focus. It seems to me that there will be an inevitable tension between the individual and society. It is a fact of human existence that we cannot be really human without society and we are dependent on society for the bulk of our satisfactions; but at the same time the price we pay is that we sacrifice at least some of ourselves for membership of society. The same goes for groups and communities within societies—even between societies. Even if the revolution came tomorrow this would be true—whether the revolution were fascist, communist, anarchist or hippy. No society can exist without some concept of normative behaviour involving some degree of sacrifice of self-expression, or its corollaries—forms of social control, reward/punishment and categorisation. This is not to say that within existing societies there are not balances between the individual and society to be redressed or that balances might not be more just under new structures.

Just implies a value. Social work, as I suggested in Chapter I, has two basic values:

(1) the intrinsic worth of the individual;

(2) the individual's right to develop his potential to the full.

We may all subscribe to these values—the problems are in operationalising them: how do we interpret worth in tangible forms (like wages), but more especially how can we afford full potential to one if this impinges on another's worth or potential? If we look at them, so many values in society, subscribed to as vitally important, if pushed to extremes, collide in themselves; or in specific situations it has to be decided which of the values extant should supervene to determine how that situation should be handled. If this sphere of interaction is ours, then the tension is endemic.

I can only suggest two guide lines for us based on professional criteria:

(a) That if our concern is for the individual (be it person, group, or community) then as social workers I feel the onus is on others to justify what they are doing to our clients rather than the onus on our clients to justify themselves and their claims to others.

(b) That while our caring is primarily for our clients, caring is indivisible: we have to care for all people and while pursuing our clients interest, there comes the point sometimes, when our caring for others has to supervene even our care for our clients, because of the damage our client is doing to them. This is what I was getting at earlier when I suggested Biestek's principles were not absolute. Though admirable as working premises, they are not absolute for this caring reason.

Although some of what I have been saying about a redefinition of professional social work practice might go some way to reconciling the pro- and anti-professionalism argument, I feel the argument is basically about where the appropriate base for social work activity lies. And this is not an argument any redefinition of social work can resolve.

There are many potential bases for social work, but as illustrations I have chosen three: the consensus/establishment base, a political base and the client group base.

Concensus base does give us power, influence and the resources needed, but at the price of further identification with concensus values. The developments under the Children and Young Persons Act, 1969 and the Criminal Justice Act, 1972 have given us much greater professional responsibility, scope and discretion, but at the price of involvement and identification with control mechanisms which in other ways we deplore. There is a glimmer of hope in that I think we have seen an extension of what is permissible reformist activity within consensus. Participation and consultation are 'in' concepts while even the occasional confrontation may not be altogether outside the pale—though 'illegal' and revolutionary activity still are. But the views about what is permissible activity still vary widely, as well as views about the effectiveness of the reformist options available in a consensus context. Consultation, etc. can be little more than a public relations mask.

From a political base we may feel more at ease as regards values and activity, though accompanied by some loss of power and resource and influence (especially over those of another political persuasion). Large parties are still agglomerates though, and may require us to 'go along' and be identified with ideas we do not share. Identification with the Labour Party may be happier but at the cost of being identified with say, a policy of further nationalisation, which may be contentious if it involves larger bureaucracies and even less worker participation. The self-help, individualism of Conservatism may also validly appeal, but perhaps at the price of a policy emphasis

on selective, means tested benefits that many social workers vehemently deplore. If we join a smaller party, we may be more in accord,
but have still less power, influence or resource.

With a client base we may feel complete accord (though given
the very disparate nature of the client groups we currently serve,
I wonder about this) but have even less power, influence or
resource.

Clearly, the choice of base will have a profound effect on the whole
of professionalism: knowledge, skill, ethics, autonomy, and training.
At the moment, we struggle to compass them, but dress the issues
up as arguments about professionalism, course content, etc.

The real problem is that the bases may be mutually exclusive.
A consensus base may rule out a political or a client base, since
if the establishment felt its social work 'servants' were encouraging
unacceptable political or client activity, its power, influence and
resources would be cut and its activity handed over to other more
acceptable institutions.

Similarly an establishment base would be unacceptable to many
of the more radical political groups: and to many client groups too.
If society is the enemy and social workers its agents, then clearly
they are *persona non grata*.

Yet if the whole range of psycho-social functioning is our concern,
then we need these different bases to work from if we are to meet
the needs which are our professional responsibility: we need the pro-
and anti-professional view, in effect. We have to struggle to contain
what seems to be the incompatible in the name of professional task.
Can we acknowledge the validity of what each says: can we acknowledge that if we do shatter the tender unity of social work we shall
all lose? If an ability to cope with tension is a sign of maturity
is such a young emerging profession able to be this mature? I do
not know.

Finally, can I acknowledge that what I have been saying has frightening implications for us as individuals. It is beyond us to discharge
all these aspects of professionalism. It is vital though that we identify
and share the vision (for that is what it is) but then partialise our
problem by asking ourselves which parts of it we can operationalise
given our particular aptitudes, limitations and circumstances—with

perhaps a glance over our shoulders to see what others are doing to avoid overlap or plug a gap.

References

1. *A Code of Ethics for Social Work*, Discussion Paper no. 2, British Association of Social Workers, 1972.
2. F. P. Biestek, *The Casework Relationship* (George Allen & Unwin), 1967.
3. Florence Hollis, *Casework: a Psycho-social Therapy* (Random House), 1972.

Further Reading

The material in this chapter owes much to Amital Etzioni's *The Semi-professions and their Organisation* (Free Press) and Nina Toren's *Social Work: The Case of a Semi-profession* (Sage).

The radical view of Social work is consistently presented in the magazine *Case Con* which I suggest all students read: while among the articles which examine this matter are: 'Casework or reform' by Jeff Smith (*Social Work Today*, June 1970); 'The challenge of primary prevention' by Peter Leonard (*Social Work Today*, 3.6.71); 'Social action' by Anne Lapping (*New Society*, 28.10.69); 'Consensus or conflict' by Carole R. Smith (*Social Work Today*, 13.12.73); 'Social conflict; implications for social work' by Ben H. Knott (*British Journal of Social Work*, Winter 1972); and 'Professionals in the firing line' by Richard Bryant (*British Journal of Social Work*, Summer 1973).

I would also recommend the British Association of Social Worker's publication *Social Work and Social Action* and Ray Lees' book *Politics in Social Work* (Routledge & Kegan Paul).

An article which emphasises the more traditional view of what casework can offer is Ron Baker's 'Challenge for British casework' (*Social Work Today*, 9.8.73). I would also recommend Helen Perlman's contribution 'Social casework: its place and purpose' in *Casework within Social Work* (Dept. of Social Studies, University of Newcastle-upon-Tyne) and Roy Borley's 'Community work in the local authority' (*Social Work Today*, 15.6.72).

Discussion

Any discussion of professionalism is likely to be acrimonious and troubled: acrimonious since a few students are likely to feel strongly either for or against; troubled since perhaps the majority of students will see the validity of both arguments and not know quite where they stand on this issue.

Attempts to re-define professionalism are not always easy to assi-milate, given the strength of the stereotypes which exist; nor is any re-definition likely to make matters easier, given that (as I see it) tension is endemic in the sphere of social work practice and endemic in any re-formulation. To accept that we have to live with tension, even if it happens to be the mature view, is hard and understandably we all look for a clear, secure, unambiguous base at times. The idea of partialisation on the individual level may assist; but I feel it is vital that students form an idea of themselves as professional people. Not only is this necessary for their own peace of mind and confidence in practice, but it will, of course, deeply colour their approach to their work. This is not to suggest that academic study will be the only factor forming their ideas: personality factors and, especially, their work experience involving clients, agencies, other agencies and colleagues, will also have a profound influence—influences that will clearly be brought into the discussion.

But crystallisation of the professional self may be of particular importance for those students who will be returning to Social Service Departments. Given their wide range of functions, multi-disciplinary staff and often bureaucratic structure, a problem of definition seems to exist for these Departments; and I have heard staff comment that they really do not know what they are supposed to be doing these days. While this problem may resolve itself over time, at least in the interim some framework in the form of a professional identity is essential if students are to function after qualification. In the longer term, the professional identity may be highly significant in the way Social Services Departments do eventually define themselves. This identity problem does not seem to trouble probation students nearly so much. In England, the probation service seems to hover between a definition as court officers (if only to stay out of the clutches of Social Services departments) or a definition as Social Workers. Most students (on mixed courses, anyway) seem to be firmly on the side of social work.

CHAPTER XIII

The Professional Worker and the Volunteer

A great deal of voluntary social work takes place within statutory services (councillors, members of Area Health Authority Committees, etc.); in conjunction with statutory services (welfare service, self-help and pressure groups); or as a covert function of a wide range of other individuals and groups (from clergy and trade union officials to young wives' groups and working men's clubs). The roles of such volunteers in relation to professional workers are usually quite clear though this does not preclude occasional clashes between them. It is where the nature of the work undertaken by the volunteer is similar to the professional's (Marriage Guidance Council, Samaritans for example) or a similarity arises from the development of a relationship which goes beyond the bounds of definition of the original contact, that difficulties begin—becoming particularly acute where volunteer and professional though involved with the same situation, owe their allegiance to different organisations and/or different ideologies; or cannot acknowledge the particular contribution of the other.

The typical volunteer is an adult of under 25 or over 40, is as likely to be a man as a woman (i.e. volunteers are drawn roughly 50/50 from each sex), and to have been recruited through a friend or acquaintance already involved in the work. The middle class is over-represented in organised voluntary work, but remember that probably more voluntary work is done spontaneously and outside any organisation, by friends, relatives and neighbours. Voluntary work is not the prerogative of the middle class.

Tensions between professionals and voluntary workers have a number of potential origins. Social work itself is a new profession,

319

still fighting to establish itself, and voluntary work can be seen as a threat—a 'watering down' of the profession. Occasionally, professionals feel guilty when they see the enthusiasm, commitment and selflessness of the volunteer; or jealous when volunteers get tangible, practical results and the appreciation of the client and the community. Professionals may envy the volunteers' freedom of action and of choice, lack of on-going responsibility and freedom from accountability. The threat is reinforced by the voluntary worker who sees little difference between what he does and what the professional does—but feels that he does it better, gets more results and only uses commonsense to achieve them. What the volunteer does may fit in better with the client's expectation of what social work is about—practical help given by a dedicated individual.

Relations between volunteer and professional are bedeviled by the poor stereotype each has of the other. The volunteer thinks of the professional as cold, inflexible, tied in red tape, inaccessible, rather 'toffee-nosed', with little commitment—apathetic and 'doing a job'; hidebound and part of 'them'. The professional view of the volunteer is that they are extremely choosey and highly selective about what they will or will not do; they are unreliable; they expect a lot of gratitude for what they do from the client and the professional; they will work in their own way and not be told. The professional is chary about the volunteer's enthusiasm, questions his motivation, and is very afraid the volunteer will get over-involved in a case, mess it up, leaving the professional to straighten it out and 'carry the can' for the mess. Confidentiality poses a continuing problem. The idea that volunteers can save the professionals time is dismissed: the volunteer's job is seen as something different, and to use them effectively takes as much time (in organisation, consultation and support) as any time that might be saved.

The volunteers see themselves as spontaneous, outgoing, flexible, committed, firmly identified with their clients and decidedly not part of 'them'. They know what they like doing: interesting, practical, purposeful jobs in which they can use their skills and see results; involving people but only a limited commitment. They enjoy working with the elderly, children and sick in hospital (interestingly, the dependent), especially when they are appreciative. They prefer working in groups rather than individually. They know, too, what they do not like: the dull, menial, repetitive jobs where they feel they are exploited as 'slave labour', where they see no results; jobs which are away from people and offer no involvement—or too near people and they 'smell' a degree of involvement they are not prepared to accept. They do not like working with adolescents, the mentally disordered, the physically handicapped, disfigured, or deviants—or the ungrateful. Primarily, in voluntary work they are looking for interest, change, satisfaction, an opportunity for altruism in a non-competitive setting—and occasionally, drama, I suspect.

Clients are often unclear as to who the volunteer is or what his function is—especially in 'friendly visiting'; but they generally like them—though tending to discount the contribution they make other than practical services. The volunteer is not often prepared to be a 'friend' as the clients interpret this (i.e. the volunteer dictates the terms of the relationship). The housebound especially tend to feel 'captive' for the volunteer, but the volunteer does bring in the local gossip and a feeling of the 'outside'. This seems to suggest that it is better to let any relationship grow out of an initial specific task.

But remember that these are stereotypes and specific experiences may be regarded differently or as exceptions to the stereotype even where this stereotype persists.

Volunteers undertake a plethora of activities, but these may be grouped as:

(1) Practical;

(2) Involving particular skills (from first aid to hair-dressing);

(3) Involving relationships.

While (1) and (2) will also involve relationships, it is where the focus is relationship that most wariness occurs between professionals and volunteers. Communication becomes suspicious and inhibited—though often rationalised on both sides as a question of confidentiality.

The use of volunteers is not justified as gap-fillers where resources are short; nor as cheap labour in order to get social services as economically as possible (though occasionally I suspect Government support of voluntary work has a tinge of these reasons about it).

But their use is profoundly justified for several reasons:

(1) As an expression of community care by a caring community. Personally, I would hate to live in a society where all help was given by paid professionals. Such a society would have reached the ultimate in anomie—sloughing off concern for others by hiring people to do it. ('Hiring' professionals to do what lay people cannot is another matter). Both givers and receivers would be robbed of something of profound significance to each: the satisfaction of giving (your offering being acceptable to another), and the feeling of worth (that another cares enough to offer without the 'bribe' of being paid).

(2) As a means of educating the public about what the social services are:

(a) Trying to do—their objectives, methods, and the rationale of them; their limitations; and the difficulties they work under—especially shortages of manpower and resources—with the volunteers, hopefully, becoming part of the pressure of opinion to remedy these.

(b) The people they are trying to help—so, hopefully, changing public attitudes to social problems and minority groups—especially the stigmatised, where such stigma is so much part of the problem of isolation, misunderstanding and disparagement such groups suffer from and which casework can do little about.

(3) As a means of keeping the social services under some public scrutiny and therefore on their toes. The insularity of many of our social services can lead to high-handed ways of dealing with clients—and, occasionally, downright cruelty (for example, the subnormality hospital scandals).

(4) Because volunteers can do what the professionals cannot—which is the main justification for their use. They have:

Time: with 'caseloads' limited to the volunteers' availability, they can do many of the practical things (from lighting fires, mending fuses, getting meals, collecting pensions, doing shopping, baby-sitting, etc.) which professionals cannot, but which are of enormous significance for the clients' well-being.

Skills: decorating, gardening, hairdressing, etc. which the professional may not have.

Continuity: the professionals come and go when their function ends or they change jobs.

Flexibility: they have few rules, agency boundaries, administrative 'red tape' to work within.

Availability: no office hours—indeed their best time for helping may be in the evenings or at weekends.

Local links: be part of a network which not only provides pertinent gossip for the client, but a source of help the volunteer can call upon, or knit the client into.

Above all, they offer a different kind of relationship which meets different needs. Essentially, I see volunteers as friends or good neighbours—and we all need both if we are to feel secure, of worth, to feel as though we belong, or to feel we are contributing. In other words, the relationship between volunteer and 'client' is much more social and much more mutual than that of professional and client; and able, therefore, to meet needs for friendship, belonging and reciprocity, the professional relationship, by its very nature, cannot. The volunteer/'client' relationship will vary, of course: the degree of intimacy/distance and responses will not be the same—but neither are they the same with friends and neighbours ordinarily. Even distanced relationships have their satisfactions.

The degree of intimacy/distance is a matter for the volunteer and 'client' to determine; but always one of the difficulties in introducing the one to the other is the awkwardness of knowing how far this relationship is going to go. This is particularly true of friendly visiting: people are 'expected' to be friendly and intimate long before they have really got to know each other or even decided that they like each other. Breaking off is equally awkward, so friendliness is assumed as a sort of mask initially until it really grows (or doesn't). The social ungainliness of this sort of encounter may be another reason for letting relationships grow out of specific tasks and roles— much more manageable initially.

The fact of an introduction, though, does mean possibly that for all the similarities with friendship and neighbourliness, there remains something a little different about relations between volunteer and 'client'—though over time this difference may become insignificant and only rarely come to the surface: a bit of 'helper/helped' may remain, the mutuality be a little one-sided, between people who would not ordinarily become friends, perhaps. Maybe, too, the volunteer will not be quite spontaneous and have an additional modicum of tolerance, understanding and altruistic helpfulness in this relationship that (because of a slight degree of distance, perhaps) he would not bring to bear in relations with his real intimates. But this could be to the 'client's' advantage.

But given that as professionals we would like to utilise volunteers with people or in situations we are involved with, for the sake of what they can contribute to meeting needs, how might this be done?

Initially, the task is to get the 'jobs and the volunteers. The job may be requested by the client, be a referral, or be something you yourself have seen. If the job you see happens to be in an institution, there may be a long and delicate stage of getting the staff to see it and then helping them to accept it as a job a volunteer might do: but something akin to this process could occur with an individual client. Volunteers may *offer* a specific service, or put a particular skill at your disposal, or be prepared to 'do anything'; or they may be *recruited* by the worker (by public meetings, speaking engagements, advertising, contacting existing specific voluntary organisations, or tapping sources of goodwill—from church groups to Lions and Chambers of Commerce)—again for specific tasks, particular skills or in more general terms.

After getting job and volunteer, comes a stage of assessment. Particularly if the job is a referred one, the professional should explore it (at first hand if at all possible), to get a realistic picture of the situation and the people in it. With volunteers, however they come and whatever they offer, I feel exploration is also needed. Many have only the vaguest idea of what they might be letting themselves in for, and the worker needs to discuss the reality of situations (in general terms) with them. The worker will also need to know the reality of what is being offered (what, when, how often, etc.)—or help volunteers clarify their own ideas—perhaps in the light of what jobs are available if they are offering to 'do anything'. What the volunteers offer may not fit the jobs that need to be done; so there is a 'matching' problem: can volunteers be 'invited' to do a job that needs doing, or can the worker think of ways of utilising what is offered?

Many professionals are apprehensive that they will recruit unsuitable people who could be damaging to clients, but who might themselves be damaged if their offers of help were turned down. A number of organisations (Citizens Advice Bureaux, Samaritans, Cyrenians, etc.) quite properly insist on selecting their volunteers: but the fact that they do is fairly common knowledge and those who volunteer to work for them accept and expect to be screened. But screening is not usual in the statutory and many of the voluntary services— which makes it even more awkward to refuse an offer. It is rare, however, not to be able to find some sort of niche to offer where positives can be used while the negatives are made harmless. It may take a little persuasion to get the person to accept and all the while the worker may feel he is dealing more with a client than a volunteer—but it could be good preventive work, and is not an outright rejection. In this assessment stage quite a few volunteers will drop out, modify their ideas, or go ahead as they wished but more realistically—though retaining their enthusiasm (or developing more). It is important to sustain this enthusiasm, and the best way is to wrap the volunteer into activity (whether task or preparation for it) as quickly as possible. With delay, enthusiasm wanes and delay may be interpreted as not caring or the rejection of the offer—neither of which will reflect credit on social work, social workers or the agency.

After assessment comes the introduction to a specific situation or client, or to staff of the institution in which the volunteer may be working, for example. Clearly this needs to be carefully prepared and handled.

Mrs. Whittingham had an interest in mental health problems and had become involved in fund raising for a local Association of Mental Health. She approached the social worker to see if there was anything more she could do but in a more direct, personalised way. After exploring the situation with her, the social worker made two suggestions: that she assisted the hard-pressed Occupational Therapist at the local psychiatric hospital in social activities with the long stay patients for one or two sessions each week; and that she might befriend a disturbed and phobic girl who lived not far from her and who had become extremely isolated.

The social worker prepared both situations and introduced Mrs. Whittingham. The hospital involvement went extremely well and

Mrs. Whittingham made a real contribution which she thoroughly enjoyed. The patients appreciated the 'breath of the outside world' she brought with her; and valued the fact that she came because she wanted to and was not paid to do so. After many years in hospital they had felt forgotten and rejected by an uncaring society and this tangible proof that at least one person cared meant a lot to them.

The contact with the girl started quite well. She managed to get over to Mrs. Whittingham's for tea, for example, and enjoyed her contact with Mrs. Whittingham's children in particular. But after a while the relationship spluttered and eventually failed leaving a good deal of uneasiness on both sides and a sense of failure. Both however, said that they really did not know 'what to do' or 'what to say'.

Mrs. George approached the social worker after he spoke at a meeting. She said she had been in hospital herself suffering from a puerpural depression and felt she would like to help others who were depressed since she thought she could appreciate what they were going through. The worker was looking for some voluntary help with the psychiatric social club and suggested this to her. She took up the idea and came to the next club meeting. She began by assisting with the practical things such as helping with the refreshments and washing up, but quite quickly got talking to other members, was invited into their activities and became a valuable and well-liked contributor to the club.

Miss James was a middle-aged primary school teacher, rather diffident, and feeling rather isolated in a new post in a new city. She asked the social worker if she could be of use after reading an article in the local paper about mental health problems in the community. The social worker guessed that she had difficulties of her own but after discussion and preparation, introduced her to a family as a baby-sitter. The family were rather isolated; the husband had been in hospital with an anxiety state and there were certain tensions between the parents and between the parents and the children. The social worker had felt that if the parents could get out a little more together and have an occasional break from the children, this would help to ease matters.

Miss James quickly became quite a friend of the family, though her contacts were confined to baby-sitting for them. The parents appreciated their time together, while Miss James's skills as a teacher enabled her to give the children some most constructive informal education in what amounted to play sessions, and the occasional specific help with the older children's homework. She herself gained a considerable amount from being useful and appreciated outside the school situation.

The education of volunteers is clearly a vital issue. (I use 'education' rather than 'training', since to 'train' volunteers may rob them of some of their invaluable spontaneity and make them think of themselves as quasi-professionals—which is risky and fundamentally robs them of their function as volunteers.) Education can be organised before the introduction: this may help volunteers to avoid mistakes, feel less anxious, and fit in with the organisation much better—but at the risk of such education being merely theory and of little use until practical situations have been encountered to make it meaningful. With experience after the introduction, education becomes useable. Education needs to continue after anyway, to deal with the needs and anxieties of volunteers arising from practice—particularised, in effect, in a way which a prior and generalised pre-introduction education can rarely be.

This on-going education is part of the back-up which is needed in all work with volunteers. They need somewhere and someone to turn to for consultation and support. Often a group is useful here where volunteers can meet and discuss matters of common concern, develop an identity in what they are doing, and be a means of communicating with the professional worker involved. But I feel that an individual contact with the worker is also needed—perhaps to discuss a particular case in a way they cannot bring to the group for reasons of confidentiality or a fear of exposing what they feel to be their ineptitude. Since understandably, too, volunteers welcome some appreciation for the work they are doing (if only to sustain their motivation) this might be more effectively expressed in a one-to-one meeting rather than in more generalised group meetings. (But there is a place for the agency to throw the occasional party for volunteers as a mark of their appreciation.)

328   Casework in Context

Back-up requires elements of organisation in that it is needed to provide a flow of recruits (to expand the work, fill gaps when a volunteer cannot manage a particular occasion, and replace those who leave—or find alternative work for those not very happy with what they are doing). Volunteers also develop new abilities which may mean an extension of their sphere in a particular case, or handling situations of more complexity elsewhere. Allowing for and/or encouraging this sort of growth in volunteers will also need the individualised and organisational aspects of the back-up system.

Using volunteers is not going to save the professionals time and will call for considerable patience and other skills. There is a very good case for a larger agency giving a special responsibility for work with volunteers to one of its staff, or even creating a special post: especially where although a number of volunteers are used, they typically work in two's and three's to any one social worker. The recruitment, assessment, education and back-up group meetings for the volunteers can then be rationalised under the one worker with special responsibility even if the consultation and support functions must remain with the professional worker also involved with a particular case.

A 'special responsibility' post will not come, nor will any allowance in caseloads for individual workers involved with volunteers be made until the agency is convinced of the worth of using volunteers as an extension of their function to meet a wider range of human need than their professional staff can. To educate the agency in this matter may initially be the professional worker's task.

Further Reading

Basic reading are *The Voluntary Worker in the Welfare State* by Mary Morris (Routledge & Kegan Paul) and *The Voluntary Worker in the Social Services*—the report of the joint Committee set up by the National Council of Social Service and the National Institute for Social Work Training under the chairmanship of Geraldine Aves (Bedford Square Press: N.C.S.S./Allen & Unwin).

Not a great deal has been written about the specific use of volunteers by professional workers but a very useful contribution is Hugh Barr's *Volunteers in Prison After-care*, published for the National Institute for Social Work Training by Allen & Unwin. May I also commend R. M. Titmuss's *The Gift Relationship* (George Allen & Unwin) as very pertinent.

Discussion

Students in discussion, reflect the range of social work responses to work with volunteers: enthusiasm, apprehension and hostility; reflecting opinions that volunteers can do most things, some things or next to nothing. Not all that number of students will have had direct experience of working with volunteers, so some of the discussion may inevitably be a trading in stereotypes. A few students will have come into full-time social work, or on to training, via being volunteers themselves and their contribution can be very pertinent—though I have noticed that one or two students with this experience tend to compartmentalise it and see it as something very different from what they are doing now. They need some help to establish links between the two.

The predominant reaction, though, is to make students reflect once again on just what it is that they have to offer as professionals; just what it is that makes their contribution different. Examining work with volunteers, then, can be a useful reinforcement of earlier work on the professional relationship and professional identity.

CODA

Issues in Social Work Practice

In this book, I have touched upon many of the tensions in current social work theory and practice. I attempt to summarise them here quite deliberately, since I feel no text should risk leaving behind the impression that it is the final word; that all problems have finally been answered. In effect, the profession (if that is what it is) has to respond to four questions:

(1) What Constitutes Social Work Practice?

Despite unitary theories, one still wonders whether the answer to this does not still rest upon either:

(a) Orientation (whether of ideology or preferred theory for practice) with the cultural and personal influences that underlie it. What brings us as people into social work: to what 'cultural' processes are we subjected once we come into it; and what interactions take place to finally determine at the individual, group or social work 'community' level how we see what social work 'is'?

(b) Position—whether given to us by society at large (or rather, parts of it) which has its own ideas, be they confused or contradictory; by the agency/bureaucracy which employs us; or by some combination of personality and professional culture.

Orientation and position would seem to be very substantial determinants of values, aims, knowledge and skills, and by no means agreed between themselves about what these are. Parts of all of social work are used by others in these days anyway—from politics to big business—which suggests that the most social work can claim is either a particular combination of these attributes or the use of them from a particular position. Neither is a very substantive claim and leave us wide open to a 'carve-up' of our task among others.

We shall only be able to resist this effectively if we can respond to the second question:

(2) Can we Evaluate Practice?

Essentially this means determining what we can *do*. The fundamental problem here is that social work so often deals with the intangible, such as feelings; or the vague, such as wellbeing. Criteria are so difficult to establish. If we could establish them, there are a number of possible approaches.

Perhaps we ought to start with what we actually do. The studies that have been done suggest we spend about a third of our time with clients and the remaining two thirds in meetings, conferences, or committees, being supervised; and keeping the paper work/ administration going. This may be a far cry from what we say we do (and here the problem sounds like fantasy); or think we have been trained to do. Here the problem may be that the training is out of line with the actuality; or that the actuality does not allow us to implement our training, raising all sorts of issues about the deployment of staff, the development of tasks or the nature of social work agencies themselves. But if we claim that we are not doing what we have been trained for, we need to substantiate that the task needs doing and that we can accomplish it. Opinion will vary as to what needs doing, but I feel we can substantiate our view as well as anyone else; it is our accomplishment that is more often questioned or questionable.

It is possible to demonstrate what could be done through theory substantiated by experiment. Experimentation in social work is difficult: quite apart from the ethics involved, there are enormous problems in controlling the variables to establish just what it is that social work has contributed rather than other people, maturation, change of circumstances or just sheer accident or luck. Even substantiated theory often does not get incorporated into practice—sometimes validly, since experimental situations (given the infinite variability of human situations) are rarely completely replicated; sometimes invalidly, since old habits die hard and we reject new knowledge and new ways which appear to denigrate the old to which we have a personal commitment. There is often a discrepancy anyway between theory and practice which makes the theoretical formulations and the professionalism we claim through them, look rather sick.

It is also possible to demonstrate what social work can do by doing it: by good practice, by new and imaginative practices—evaluated and written up. We are not in thrall to theory or theorists: both depend on practice either as their source or their validation.

But determining what we can do is not just a matter of theory or practice: it is also an ethical matter involving what we ought to do or not, and takes its place in the evaluation of practice.

(3) What is the Appropriate Location of Practice?

We have already seen in the chapter on professionalism, some of the issues here; but accepting for the moment that areas of reformist practice require a client or voluntary organisation base and other areas of practice require an institutional base, the question arises of which institutions. One of our principal social work services, the probation service, already has its base in the penal system. The other principal service has virtually created its own institutional system base—the Social Services Department. I sometimes wonder if this is the most effective base. We have seen elsewhere the problems it generates for practice; its complex administrative machinery (if not downright bureaucracy) and its diffuse focus. It has been my experience over the years that students with a local authority background given a probation placement, thoroughly enjoy the professional ethos, the autonomy and the sense of definition in practice in a probation setting. I felt much the same during my own hospital practice. The other thread here is the plea Carol Meyer makes in her book *Social Work Practice: a response to the urban crisis* (Collier Macmillan) for social work to 'get where the action is'—out of its ivory towers and into the institutions which really impinge on people's lives, where the crises occur, where both preventive and effective work can be done. There are a whole range of such institutions and their organisational expression: maternity and child welfare clinics, family planning clinics, nurseries, play groups and nursery

schools, the schools themselves, youth clubs and the Youth Employment Service, in industry, in hospitals and general practice, housing
departments, social security offices, solicitors' practices, C.A.B.'s,
churches, undertakers, etc. There is no aspect of a Social Services
Department's work that could not find an appropriate institutional
or organisational umbrella elsewhere—especially now that Area
Health Authorities have such a broad community based concern.

I realise that in even toying with the idea of dismembering Social
Service Departments I raise other problems. Could the profession,
given such an institutional/organisational scatter, hold together?
Could we as 'aliens' often in such organisations, exert much influence? Would we be back to specialisms which would splinter/
partialise clients' difficulties by symptom or age group? Would we
recreate the multiplicity of workers and co-ordination problems that
the cohesiveness of Social Service Departments was meant to tackle?

But I feel the crucial question to ask is whether, despite the problems, we would be more effective in meeting client need. I am not
utterly convinced that by creating Social Service Departments we
have settled this issue. I know that Departments do have workers
attached to other organisations: hospitals, child guidance clinics, etc.
But the tensions engendered both before and after the incorporation
of hospital social workers will not just go away. The education service, for a start, seems determined to keep its social workers, the
education welfare officers, to itself; while a number of housing departments, at the district level of Local Government, are appointing
social workers of their own—a resurgent housing welfare officer.

Location has a very considerable influence on position, of course;
and earlier we saw the significance of position on the definition of
practice. It could also have a bearing on the final question:

(4) What is the Future of Specialisation?

Social work has now reached the stage of development that medicine and engineering reached in the last century: it is beyond the
compass of one individual to embrace the entirety. We are approaching, or have reached, a cross roads. We have a choice of models:
either we become the equivalent of electrical, mechanical or civil

engineers—almost discrete in themselves; or we choose a medical path—a basic training followed by specialisation. I feel sure that most social workers would prefer the second (though some community workers, at least, might opt for the first). If we adopt the 'basic plus' approach to specialisation, we have to determine what is the 'basic' as well as the range and variety of the 'pluses'. In Chapter II we looked at some of the uncertainty about the latter; in this book I have inferred that the basic is the unitary approach; Whether this is the definitive base remains to be seen: at the moment it is probably the best we have, but it has a newness which needs to be tested—as it will be over time.

At the beginning of this chapter, I suggested that social work needed to respond to four questions: I quite deliberately did not say answer them. Answers also have a finality about them which can become straitjackets, if not coffins. For some aspects of these questions it might not be the right thing to even try for answers. Tensions and uncertainty may be difficult to live with, but at least they are indicators of life, growth and response.

For me, the only finality is that of experience. Experience convinces me that social work is a worthwhile job, which gets results (however immeasurable), which helps people, which for all its agonising and uncertainties, is struggling along the right lines. I am optimistic for its future.

Index

Acceptance
  dilemmas in 82–84
  limiting 84
  nature of 79–80
  reasons for 78–79
Administration
  analysis of
    by goals 276–278
    by process 285–287
    by structure 279–284
  constraints for 275
  functions of 288–290
  tensions with 273–274, 275–276
Administrators
  social workers as 288–290, 292–293
  tensions of the administrative function
    for social workers 290–292
Agency
  frameworks of
    administrative 107
    legal 104–107
    policy 107
    procedural 107
    social 104
  See also Administration, Adminis-
    trators
Authority
  gradations of 112–115
  worker's 108–112
  validity of 310

Bartlett, Harriett 33
Biestek, F. P. 82–83, 85, 89, 307

Casework
  history of 23–27
  process of
    exploration and testing 183–186
    intake and orientation 177–183
    problem-solving 186–188

    termination 188–191
  strengths of 49–50
Clients
  capacity 137, 138, 180
  motivation 137, 138
  needs of
    to be treated as an
    individual 65–67
    to be listened to 71–74
    to be accepted 78–79
    to talk in confidence 85–86
    to be understood 95–103
    to be helped 103–104
  typologies of 72–73
Communication
  verbal 72–73
  non-verbal 73–74
  reasons for limiting 77–78
Community work
  history of 28–30
  strengths of 51
Confidentiality
  breaching 89–92
  guarding 92–94
  passing confidential information to
    clients 94–95
  reasons for 85–86
  sharing confidences 87–89
Contract
  reasons for 115
  re-definition of 100–101
Crises
  aims in 212–213
  categories of 209
  opportunities in 209–210
  process of 211–212
  skills in 214

Data
  fashions in 178
  gathering 127

335

338 *Index*